Red Dragons in Europe

DESERT ISLAND FOOTBALL HISTORIES

Red Dragons in Europe   1-874287-01-5
Coventry City: The Elite Era – A Complete Record   1-874287-03-1
Luton Town: The Modern Era – A Complete Record   1-874287-05-8
Wimbledon: From Wembley to Selhurst   1-874287-20-1
Hereford United: The League Era – A Complete Record   1-874287-18-X
West Ham: From Greenwood to Redknapp – Match by Match 1-874287-19-8
Wimbledon: From Southern League to Premiership   1-874287-09-0
Aberdeen: The European Era – A Complete Record   1-874287-11-2
The Story of the Rangers 1873-1923   1-874287-16-3
The Story of the Celtic 1888-1938   1-874287-15-5
History of the Everton Football Club 1878-1928   1-874287-14-7
The Romance of the Wednesday 1867-1926   1-874287-17-1
The Book of Football: A History to 1905-06   1-874287-13-9
England: The Quest for the World Cup – A Complete Record 1-897850-40-9
Scotland: The Quest for the World Cup – A Complete Record 1-897850-50-6
Ireland: The Quest for the World Cup – A Complete Record 1-897850-80-8

RED DRAGONS IN EUROPE

— A COMPLETE RECORD —

TERRY GRANDIN

Desert Island Books

First Published in 1999

DESERT ISLAND BOOKS
89 Park Street, Westcliff-on-Sea, Essex SS0 7PD
United Kingdom
www.users.globalnet.co.uk/~desert

© 1999 Terry Grandin

British Library Cataloguing-in-Publication Data
A catalogue record for this book is available from the British Library

ISBN 1-874287-01-5

Printed in Great Britain
by
Biddles Ltd, Guildford

The publishers acknowledge with thanks the following
for the provision of photographs for this book:
South West Wales Publications Ltd,
Wrexham Evening Leader, Allan Monument.

CONTENTS

                                    page

Preface by Paul Abbandonato vii
Author's Note viii

1. THE EARLY YEARS

1961   Swansea Town 9
1962   Bangor City 11
1963   Borough United 15
1964   Cardiff City 19
1965   Cardiff City 23
1966   Swansea Town 25

2. THE BLUEBIRDS FLY HIGH

1967   Cardiff City 28
1968   Cardiff City 36
1969   Cardiff City 39
1970   Cardiff City 42
1971   Cardiff City 48

3. ENTER THE ROBINS

1972   Wrexham 51
1973   Cardiff City 54
1974   Cardiff City 56

4. THE ROBINS REACH THE QUARTERS

1975   Wrexham 59
1976   Cardiff City 64
1977   Cardiff City 68
1978   Wrexham 70
1979   Wrexham 72
1980   Newport County 74

5. SWANSEA CITY TO THE FORE

1981   Swansea City 101
1982   Swansea City 103
1983   Swansea City 108

6. THE NORTH WALIANS TAKE A HOLD

1984 Wrexham 111
1985 Bangor City 115
1986 Wrexham 118
1987 Merthyr Tydfil 121
1988 Cardiff City 123
1989 Swansea City 128

7. MAN UNITED AT THE RACECOURSE

1990 Wrexham 131
1992 Cardiff City 136
1993 Cardiff City 138

8. THE LEAGUE OF WALES TAKES OVER

1994 Barry Town 141
1995 Wrexham 143
1996 Llansantffraid 144
1997 Cwmbran Town 146
1998 Bangor City 149

9. THE EUROPEAN CHAMPIONS CUP

1993 Cwmbran Town 151
1997 Barry Town 153
1998 Barry Town 155

10. THE UEFA CUP

1994 Bangor City 157
1994 Inter Cardiff 159
1995 Bangor City 161
1995 Afan Lido 162
1996 Newtown 164
1996 Barry Town 166
1997 Inter Cabletel 172
1998 Newtown 174

11. THE INTER TOTO CUP

1995 Ton Pentre 177
1996 Conwy United 180
1997 Ebbw Vale 184
1998 Ebbw Vale 187

RED DRAGON STATISTICS 190
SUBSCRIBERS 192

Preface

Imagine British teams reaching the last eight of the European Cup-Winners' Cup, stunning crack continental outfits like Real Madrid, Anderlecht, and Sporting Lisbon, and even thumping Serie A clubs such as Napoli, where Diego Maradona once starred. Manchester United, you might be thinking, or Liverpool, Arsenal, Chelsea or any of the other Premiership big guns.

Not in this case. I'm talking about clubs like Cardiff City, Wrexham, Swansea, and even smaller sides like Merthyr Tydfil and Bangor City. Impossible, you might be thinking. Again, not so. The proof of their wonderful deeds, all achieved in the not-too-distant past, has been well documented in the pages of this book. The odd raised eyebrow among some sports followers is understandable, considering the sad state of Welsh football, heading towards the new Millennium. We've seen Cardiff and Swansea stutter in the lower divisions of the Football League, and Wrexham do a bit better, but again only in the lower divisions. And since League of Wales clubs started competing in Europe in the 1990s, we have endured – with the odd notable exception – some hammerings. Understandable perhaps, considering the League is a new concept. But in those not so far off days, Welsh clubs were often a match for anyone in Europe – and how they proved it.

You can take your pick of the best achievements. There was the night in 1976 when Wrexham came within a whisker of beating Anderlecht at the Racecourse. Losing 0-1 from the first leg, Stuart Lee gave the Robins the lead and they were suddenly favourites to reach the semi-finals – until Robbie Rensenbrink pounced fifteen minutes from the end to put Wrexham out by the narrowest of margins – no disgrace considering Anderlecht went on to win the trophy, thrashing West Ham 4-2 in the final.

There was also the night Newport County drew 2-2 with Carl Zeiss Jena. They, too, were within a whisker of the semi-finals. Or how about Merthyr Tydfil, then in the Southern League, beating Atalanta 2-1 at Penydarren Park? Or Bangor City, another non-league outfit, shocking Napoli with a 2-0 triumph at Farrar Road? Or Swansea City's tussles with Panathinaikos, the Greek club who had reached the European Cup final a few years earlier? Brilliant performances, the lot of them.

But all undone, in my opinion, by the March night in 1971 when Real Madrid, yes *the* Real Madrid, went to Ninian Park and were sent packing. Cardiff City sent shock waves throughout football by winning 1-0 against arguably Europe's greatest club. The Bluebirds went down to two second-half goals in the Bernabeu. Three years earlier, City had actually gone one step further, reaching the Cup-Winners' Cup semi-finals where they were beaten by SV Hamburg.

Those were great days for the Bluebirds. Teams with European pedigree like Sporting Lisbon, Nantes and Moscow Torpedo all found the Welsh club too good for them. It's all change these days, with League of Wales minnows taking the European places instead. But amid the thumpings come the fairy tales – like Inter CableTel meeting Celtic, and Ton Pentre making a European bow. Nothing, though, quite captured the imagination as much as little Llansantffraid, the village team from Mid-Wales where there is a population of barely 1,000. They qualified for the Cup-Winners' Cup by beating Barry Town in a rich man-poor man Welsh Cup final.

National newspapers, TV stations up and down Britain, plus radio outlets, all descended on Mid-Wales to write or broadcast features on Llansantffraid's big moment. A sign of the interest in the Welsh club's story was summed up by the fact that more articles appeared in the news than on the sports pages. The Saints didn't disgrace either, drawing 1-1 at home to the Poles of Ruch Chorzow. They lost 0-5 in Poland, but no one can take away the little Welsh club's proudest moment. Nor the exploits of all the sides who have done the Welsh nation proud in years gone by. Yes, there really *was* a time when Welsh football could hold its own against the best.

PAUL ABBANDONATO
Chief Football Writer for *Wales on Sunday*

Author's Acknowledgements

I would like to thank my wife Rita for not continually tidying up after me, my children Sarah and Jason for supporting me right from the beginning of this venture, and my daughter-in-law Bethan for the use of her computer.

Making sure all the information was correctly collated and numbered was an onerous task in which I was ably assisted by my good friend Gregg Jones. Carrying out the research for this book was made so much easier by talking to, and meeting, so many new friends, all with the same love of the game.

I have been very fortunate in my research to have received photographs and/or statistics from the following: Iorys Griffiths (Bangor City), Richard Shepherd (Newport County), Graham Breeze (Llansantffraid), Cec Jones (Conwy United), Gareth Davies (Wrexham), Mike Smith (Bangor City), Don Murray (Cardiff City), Paul Willoughby (Ton Pentre), Ian Garland (Borough United), Chris Aust (Barry Town), Keith Harding (Newtown), and Dave Watkins (Merthyr Tydfil).

I am grateful for the photographs received from Fred Williams (*Wrexham Evening Leader*), Allan Monument (Bangor City) and the *South Wales Evening Post* (Swansea City). Many thanks for all your assistance.

TERRY GRANDIN

1

THE EARLY YEARS

~~~~~~~~~~~~~~~~~~~~~~~~~~~~~~~~~~~~~~~

1961 – SWANSEA TOWN (League Division 2)

~~~~~~~~~~~~~~~~~~~~~~~~~~~~~~~~~~~~~~~

With Wrexham's 1960 Welsh Cup win not rewarded with a place in Europe, Swansea Town became the first Welsh side to take part. They contested the 1961-62 European Cup-Winners' Cup – along with 22 other national cup winners – after defeating Bangor City 3-1 in Cardiff to claim the Welsh Cup.

Their elation soon turned sour when the draw paired them with SC Motor Jena of East Germany. The East German team had beaten Empor Rostock, now known as Hansa Rostock, in their domestic final, but due to a ban on the entry of East German nationals into NATO countries, they were forbidden to travel to Wales. Despite this, the Swansea Town administration were still advertising the first leg at the Vetch Field – and selling tickets – fourteen days before the date originally scheduled for the tie.

The Swans had to find an alternative venue, or risk the fate of Glenavon in the 1960-61 European Cup. The champions of Northern Ireland had also drawn East German opponents, but were expelled from the competition after failing to agree on a 'home' venue, leaving Karl-Marx-Stadt to go through on a walkover

Swansea consulted with Herbert Powell, the secretary of the FA of Wales, and despatched a telegram to Motor Jena inviting them to play in Dublin. The East Germans accepted, but the plan misfired when the FA of Ireland pointed out that no pitches were available in Dublin on the date specified. The Irish Government also refused to issue visas for the Motor Jena party.

A week later UEFA intervened, declaring that the Swans must play their 'home' leg in Sweden, Switzerland, Finland or Austria, and that both ties must be completed by 18 October. The eventual winners already knew their future opponents in Round Two – Alliance Dudelange of Luxembourg.

The Welsh club made arrangements to play in Vienna, but then UEFA sent another telegram, switching the tie from the Austrian capital to the provincial town of Linz. UEFA agreed to reimburse Swansea if receipts from the 'home' leg failed to cover expenses, while SC Motor Jena met the cost of travelling from Austria to Jena for the second leg two days later.

Swansea's squad of fourteen players included Graham Williams, who had scored in Wales' 1-1 draw with England at Ninian Park the day before departure. The squad flew from London to Munich, arriving in Linz a few hours before the scheduled kick-off time, after fog had caused a five-hour travel delay.

16 October 1961   *1st Round, 1st Leg*   *Linzer Stadion*
Linz, Austria   *Attendance: 5,000*

SWANSEA TOWN (1) 2   **SC MOTOR JENA (2) 2**
Reynolds 12, Nurse 69 pen   Lange 10, Ducke R 22

SWANSEA TOWN: Dwyer; Sanders, Griffiths; Johnson, Nurse, Hughes; Davies R, Williams H, Reynolds, Webster, Jones B.
MOTOR JENA: Fritsche; Ahnert, Woltzat; Marx, Stricksner, Egelmeyer; Ducke R, Mueller, Ducke P, Rohrer, Lange.
Referee: F Sepelt (Austria)

The Swans shrugged off their travel headaches to dominate the opening stages. Colin Webster had a clear opening but shot straight at the Jena keeper, Harald Fritsche. Cardiff-born Webster had been in the Manchester United side beaten by AC Milan in the semi-final of the 1958 European Cup, shortly after the Munich air disaster.

In Motor Jena's first attack, Lange exchanged passes with Rohrer, outpaced Mel Nurse, and scored with a low drive that surprised Swansea keeper Noel Dwyer. Undaunted, the Welshmen continued to carry the game to their opponents, and were quickly rewarded when Brayley Reynolds seized upon a Harry Griffiths through-ball to equalise from close range. The East Germans stepped up the pace and it was no surprise when Roland Ducke headed in Lange's cross to restore their lead.

In the second half, Swansea changed tactics and went on the attack. They were denied by stout defending until Egelmeyer fouled Webster in the area and Nurse levelled from the spot. It was just reward for Nurse, who had been forced to postpone his wedding due to the clash of dates.

Disaster struck in the 82nd minute, when Webster was sent off. Having been fouled by Egelmeyer and awarded a free-kick, he decided to exact further retribution and charged into the Jena left-half. The Viennese referee, who had earlier warned Webster, immediately sent him off, leaving the ten-man Swans to see out the remaining minutes.

18 October 1961   *1st Round, 2nd Leg*   *Ernst Abbe Sportsfeld*
Jena, East Germany   *Attendance: 20,000*

SC MOTOR JENA (2) 5   **SWANSEA TOWN (1) 1**
Mueller 15, 44, Lange 62,   Reynolds 8
Ducke P 75, Ducke R 80

MOTOR JENA: Fritsche; Otto, Woltzat; Marx, Stricksner, Egelmeyer; Ducke R, Mueller, Ducke P, Rohrer, Lange.
SWANSEA TOWN: Dwyer; Sanders, Griffiths; Johnson, Nurse, Hughes; Jones B, Davies R, Reynolds, Williams H, Williams G.
Referee: L Horn (Holland)

(MOTOR JENA won 7-3 on aggregate)

The Swansea party were escorted into East Germany through repeated border controls en route to Jena for the second leg. Colin Webster was automatically suspended following his dismissal and, with Peter Davies still unfit, manager Trevor Morris drafted in Graham Williams instead of Webster for the only change. The captains exchanged flowers before kick-off. This – and the playing of the national anthems – put back the start by fifteen minutes.

The Swans opened strongly with Brayley Reynolds scoring early: Reg Davies lobbed into the Jena goalmouth and Reynolds volleyed a brilliant goal. Peter Ducke, a veteran of more than 50 East German internationals, rallied his team and they levelled through Helmut Mueller, who added a second just before half-time. Thereafter, the Swans defended desperately, keeping their technically superior opponents at bay until Ducke outsmarted Griffiths and sent Lange clear for a third and decisive goal. The match had by now drifted away, and the Ducke brothers each netted in the closing minutes.

The East Germans reached the semi-finals, where they were beaten 0-5 on aggregate by the eventual winners, Atletico Madrid.

~~~~~~~~~~~~~~~~~~~~~~~~~~~~~~~~
1962 – BANGOR CITY (Cheshire League)
~~~~~~~~~~~~~~~~~~~~~~~~~~~~~~~~

Having been losing finalists in the 1961 Welsh Cup, Bangor City went one better by defeating Wrexham in 1962 to earn a place in the Cup-Winners' Cup. The South Wales 'Big Three' of Cardiff City, Newport County and Swansea Town were well aware of the huge rewards for winning the Welsh Cup, but none made any impression in the competition, with Cardiff City losing to the eventual winners in an earlier round.

After Swansea's bitter and costly experience of East German opposition, the Cheshire League part-timers were delighted to be paired with Napoli of Italy. It was Napoli's first season in Europe, having beaten Spal Ferrara 2-1 to win the Italian Cup.

5 September 1962   *Preliminary Round, 1st Leg*   *Farrar Road*
Bangor   *Attendance: 12,000*

BANGOR CITY (1) 2   NAPOLI (0) 0
Matthews 41, Birch 82 pen

BANGOR CITY: Davies; Souter, Griffiths; Birch, Murphy, Wilkinson; Matthews, Ellis, Brown, McAllister, Hunter.
NAPOLI: Pontel; Molino, Mistone; Ronzon, Rivellino, Fraschini; Mariani, Rosa, Tomeazzi, Corelli, Tacchi.
Referee: J Martens (Denmark)

The Italians found it hard to come to terms with the close proximity of the crowd and a pitch made greasy from overnight rain. They were also short of match practice, as the Italian League was not due to start until mid-September.

The home side almost snatched the opener in the fifteenth minute, when an Eddie Brown back-header beat the Napoli keeper but rolled wide. Napoli were reduced to breakaways as Bangor's confidence grew, though Fraschini found time to shudder the crossbar and Tomeazzi forced Bangor goalkeeper Len Davies to save with his knees. The goal the Welsh side deserved came just before half-time, when Reg Hunter crossed into the Napoli goalmouth. 19-year-old Roy Matthews reacted quickest, swivelling on the edge of the area and firing in a low shot. Play was held up for several minutes after the goal while police ushered hundreds of spectators from the pitch. The 6ft 7in referee warned that any further disturbance would result in the game being abandoned.

The much-vaunted Napoli side, containing a handful of internationals, were unable to prise any openings in the home defence during the second half, and as Bangor pressed to increase their lead Matthews missed with a header and Brian Ellis struck the crossbar with a point-blank shot.

The second goal arrived when skipper Ken Birch lashed home a penalty awarded after Corelli had impeded Brown. The Italians protested so strongly at the decision that the referee had to snatch the ball away from a Napoli player to allow the spot-kick to be taken. In the dying seconds, Matthews headed straight at the keeper from close range as the North Walians proved their superiority on the day. But no matter: Bangor City had become the first Welsh side to win a match in European competition.

27 September 1962   *Preliminary Round, 2nd Leg*   *Stadio San Paolo*
Naples, Italy   *Attendance: 80,000*

NAPOLI (2) 3   BANGOR CITY (0) 1
Mariani 29, Ronzon 34   McAllister 79
Pornella 84

NAPOLI: Pontel; Molino, Mistone; Girardo, Gatti, Mariani; Fanello, Ronzon, Pornella, Rosa, Tacchi.
BANGOR CITY: Davies; Souter, Griffiths; Birch, Murphy, Wilkinson; Matthews, Ellis, Brown, McAllister, Hunter.
Referee: D Mellet (France)

(3-3 on aggregate)

The Bangor City side contained only three Welshmen but, following their heroics in the first leg, manager Tommy Jones – the former Everton and Wales international – named the same side for the return in Italy.

Disaster was narrowly averted when the plane carrying the Bangor party was struck by lightning and forced to land in Switzerland. The players were allowed to disembark to inspect the damage but were then asked to re-board and continue their journey.

Bangor started with a rush, attacking the home side from the outset. Reg Hunter, the former Wrexham and Manchester United winger, was prominent in the early moves, with Jimmy McAllister and Eddie Brown posing problems for the Napoli defence.

The Italians gradually found their touch and opened the scoring when Mariani – who had played at Wembley against England two seasons previously – collected the ball on the edge of the area and shot past an unsighted Len Davies. Worse was to follow for Bangor. The tie was levelled on aggregate when Davies fumbled a shot and Ronzon was first to the loose ball.

Breakaway attacks in the second period, featuring Brown and Hunter, came to nought as the Napoli defence held firm. With a little over ten minutes left for play, the visitors regained the overall lead following a long throw-in by Birch. The trajectory of the throw deceived the Napoli defence, allowing McAllister time to force the ball in.

That goal sparked uproar among disgruntled Napoli supporters, who had turned up expecting a comfortable victory. They gave vent to their feelings by showering the pitch with thousands of programmes. They were soon appeased. With only a few minutes remaining, Rosa's swift pass to Pornella caught the Bangor defence napping, and the centre-forward beat Davies to force a play-off.

10 October 1962   *Preliminary Round, Play-off*   *Highbury*
London   *Attendance: 21,895*

BANGOR CITY (0) 1   NAPOLI (1) 2
McAllister 66   Rosa 36, 83

BANGOR CITY: Davies; Souter, Griffiths; Birch, Murphy, Wilkinson; Matthews, Ellis, Brown, McAllister, Hunter.
NAPOLI: Pontel; Molino, Taralo; Caroli, Rivellino, Fraschini; Mariani, Rosa, Pornella, Ronzon, Tacchi.
Referee: A Holland (Barnsley)

In the early years of the competition the away-goals rule was not yet in force. As the teams were level on aggregate, a play-off match was required. Had the away-goals rule been employed, then Bangor City would have gone forward in the next round.

Napoli objected to UEFA's decision to hold the play-off in England, refusing to consider Wales as anything but part of England as far as football administration was concerned. Understandably perhaps, they regarded London as much a 'home' venue as Farrar Road. Their objections were, however, over-ruled and the match was scheduled for Highbury.

Coachloads of supporters, and the players' wives, left Bangor for London on the morning of the match. They did some sightseeing before heading for Highbury in time for the 7.30 pm kick-off.

Bangor officials were delighted with the attendance, which brought gate receipts of £4,406, particularly as heavy mist shrouded the stadium at the start of the game.

Napoli were reduced to ten men following an early clash of heads. Rivellino had to leave the field for eight minutes to receive attention. The part-timers failed to capitalise on their numerical superiority and it was the Argentinian, Rosa, who set the tie alight when Len Davies allowed his twenty-yard shot to go in off the far upright. Rosa had played inside-forward with John Charles prior to being transferred to Napoli. The Bangor keeper soon made amends with superb stops to foil Pornella and Fraschini.

Brian Ellis shot tamely when put through, but shortly afterwards nodded down to Jimmy McAllister, and the scorer of Bangor's goal in Naples coolly slotted the ball past the Italian keeper. With seven minutes remaining, Napoli netted the winner when Rosa collected a rebound to net his second goal.

Napoli were taken to a play-off in the second round by Ujpest Dozsa of Hungary, which they won 3-1 in Lausanne. In the third round they were again taken to a play-off, but this time were beaten 1-3 by OFK Belgrade in Marseilles.

1963 – BOROUGH UNITED (Welsh League: North)

The Welsh League (North) champions caused a major upset by defeating Newport County in the two-leg Welsh Cup final. Little known, even in Wales, Borough United went on to make history by becoming the first Welsh club to reach Round Two of a European competition. Such feats were, however, far from the thoughts of the club's fund-raising committee, which was charged with raising £4,500 to cover the anticipated costs of European participation.

Borough broke Welsh records by winning four senior trophies in the 1962-63 season, but lost £73 in doing so. They started the new season with just £4 in the bank. Their achievements were recognised by the local authority, who afforded the team a civic reception once all their trophies had been paraded through Conway and Llandudno Junction on an open-topped bus.

Borough United had been formed in 1954 after an amalgamation between Llandudno Junction and Conway Borough. Colours of maroon shirts and white shorts were agreed upon, and the new name chosen so as not to favour either of the former clubs. It was also decided that the Junction's ground at Nant-y-Coed was preferable to Conway's Morfa Ground. This decision was to prove crucial.

The fund-raising committee organised a lottery, with first prize being a bungalow in Llandudno Junction valued at £2,500. All 92 Football League clubs were invited to sell £5 worth of tickets, and most helped in some way, though eight clubs returned their allocation unsold.

A cheque for £100 was received from Mr John Moores, chairman of League champions Everton, but generally the response was poor. The Mayor of Conway gave the Borough party a civic send-off as they left Llandudno Junction on the first stage of the trip to Malta. The Borough chairman took a doll dressed in Glamorgan flannel and Welsh tweed to present to the president of the Sliema club.

The journey proved to be a nightmare, lasting 31 hours and ending just four hours before kick-off. Such was the sorry state of the players – they had snatched only a couple of hours' sleep after the aircraft carrying them from Liverpool developed engine trouble and was forced to land in Marseilles – that a 24-hour postponement was suggested. It was turned down.

15 September 1963　　*1st Round, 1st Leg*　　*National Stadium*
Gzira, Malta　　　　　　　　　　　　*Attendance: 15,000*

SLIEMA WANDERERS (0) 0　　BOROUGH UNITED (0) 0

SLIEMA WANDERERS: Debono; Falzon, Aquilina J; Spiteri, Bonnici, Buttigieg; Cox, Caschieri, Cini, Aquilina E, Nicholls.
BOROUGH UNITED: Walker, Morris, Harrison; Hodges, Owen, Clowry; Pritchard M, Pritchard K, Duffy, Russell, Bolton.

The first leg was played on a Sunday, provoking indignation from certain quarters in Wales. Given that Borough's average gate receipts amounted to only £30, it was unlikely that the club would be plagued by a boycott of supporters.

Needing to acclimatise to the sandy pitch, Borough adopted a well-executed defensive game, but created one or two chances of their own. The Welsh team received unexpected support from Royal Navy personnel stationed on the island, and the sailors were given plenty to cheer as Mike Pritchard, a 19-year-old insurance clerk – one of three amateurs in the side – did his best to unsettle the Maltese defence. Borough keeper Dave Walker made a point-blank save from Nicholls and at the other end Keith Pritchard, brother of Mike, saw his shot pushed onto a post by Debono.

---

3 October 1963   1st Round, 2nd Leg   Racecourse
Wrexham   Attendance: 17,613

BOROUGH UNITED (1) 2   SLIEMA WANDERERS (0) 0
Duffy 35, Pritchard M 57

BOROUGH UNITED: Walker; Morris, Harrison; Hodges, Owen, Clowry; Pritchard M, Pritchard K, Duffy, Russell, Bebb.
SLIEMA WANDERERS: Debono; Bonnici J, Aquilina J; Spiteri, Bonnici P, Falzon; Cox, Buttigieg, Cini, Caschieri, Nicholls.

(BOROUGH UTD won 2-0 on aggregate)

Borough United were refused permission to use their Nant-y-Coed ground for the second leg. Fortunately, Wrexham allowed them the use of the Racecourse. The Sliema party flew into Ringway Airport, Manchester, where they were welcomed by officials of the Welsh club. The round trip to Wales cost the Maltese £800, but this had been covered by receipts from the first leg.

Joe Bebb appeared on the left wing for the only change in the Borough line-up, while Sliema made three changes, and had the Bonnici brothers playing as twin centre-halves. The Maltese, most of whom had never played on grass before, tossed flowers into the crowd before the kick-off.

With Derek Owen marshalling the defence and 37-year-old Harry Hodges running the midfield, Borough won a historic victory. They went ahead in the first half when left-back Aquilina failed to clear, leaving Gerry Duffy – formerly of Oldham Athletic – to pounce. Early in the second half Keith Pritchard shot straight at Debono, but it was all Borough and they increased their lead when a corner was nodded down to Mike Pritchard, who netted from close range.

Borough's joy at reaching the second round was matched by gate receipts of £2,955, and the news that Wrexham FC had generously waived the fee for staging the tie at the Racecourse.

---

11 December 1963   *2nd Round, 1st Leg*   *Racecourse*
Wrexham   *Attendance: 10,196*

BOROUGH UNITED (0) 0   SLOVAN BRATISLAVA (0) 1
                           Molnar 52

BOROUGH UNITED: Walker; Morris, Harrison; Hodges, Owen, Clowry; Pritchard M, Pritchard K, Duffy, Russell, Bebb.
SLOVAN BRATISLAVA: Huson; Urban, Filo; Venglos, Popluhar, Cral; Moravcik, Obert, Molnar, Jokl, Cvetler.

Borough were matched with Slovan Bratislava of Czechoslovakia in the next round. The Czechs had won their cup with a 9-0 replay victory over Dynamo Prague, after the first match ended goal-less. Slovan were actually drawn to play the home leg first, but following the intervention of FA of Wales Secretary Herbert Powell, they agreed to switch the opening leg to Wales.

Upon their arrival the Czechs were given a civic reception by the Mayor of Conway. It was their second successive season in the Cup-Winners' Cup, having been beaten 2-6 on aggregate in the previous season's quarter-finals by the eventual winners, Tottenham Hotspur. Their side contained five full internationals, including the massive, balding Jan Popluhar at centre-half, who had been picked for the Rest of the World against England at Wembley. Also in the side was Josef Venglos, later to achieve short-lived fame as manager of Aston Villa, and then coach at Celtic.

The match was fiercely contested with no holds barred, and during the interval the referee warned both captains about over-zealous tackling. Borough's defence coped well with Slovan's close-passing game, and Eric Morris and Derek Owen looked solid, but the forwards could not get the better of Popluhar, whose great experience made him a dominant figure.

The Czechs should have scored immediately after the break, when Moravcik raced through and passed to Obert, who completely miskicked. The respite was only temporary, however, as Molnar soon drove a rising shot into the net. Borough fought hard to get on terms and almost equalised when the ball rolled along the Slovan goal-line. Sadly no forwards were on hand to prod it in.

---

15 December 1963   *2nd Round, 2nd Leg*   *Tehelné Pole*
Bratislava, Czechoslovakia   *Attendance: 6,000*

SLOVAN BRATISLAVA (0) 3   BOROUGH UNITED (0) 0
Molnar 52, 85, Moravcik 53

SLOVAN BRATISLAVA: Schrojf; Urban, Filo; Venglos, Popluhar, Cral; Moravcik, Obert, Molnar, Jokl, Cvetler.
BOROUGH UNITED: Walker; Morris, Harrison; Hodges, Owen, Clowry; Pritchard M, Pritchard K, Duffy, Hallett, Bebb.
                    (SLOVAN won 4-0 on aggregate)

Borough were met by interpreters when their 51-seater plane landed at Bratislava International Airport, after leaving Speke, Liverpool. The club had requested interpreters from the Foreign Office after communication problems during the home tie. Some 30 supporters also made the trip. Brian Hallett replaced Billy Russell at inside-forward for the only change in the Borough side.

The icy pitch was covered in powdery snow, making conditions difficult. Close marking and keen tackling – a feature of Borough's play in the first leg – kept the Czech side at bay until half-time. But eventually the dam had to burst, and Molnar laid the explosive with a sizzling shot. A minute later Moravcik added a second, seizing on a rebound after Dave Walker had pushed away Jokl's effort. Slovan had the ball in the net a third time but the 'goal' was ruled out, and they had to wait until the final minutes before Molnar's solo run secured his second goal.

Walker was Borough's hero, making a string of fine saves. They were also well served by skipper Frank Harrison, Brian Clowry, and the three amateurs – Derek Owen and the Pritchard brothers. The home side applauded the Welsh players off the field at the end.

In April 1967, Borough were hit by a bombshell when they were informed by the owners of Nant-y-Coed – a Roman Catholic Order based in Dublin – that they must vacate the ground by August 1968. As the club could not finance a move to Conway's old ground at Morfa, this effectively ended Borough United's short but spectacular existence. At the club's AGM on 15 June 1967, it was decided to withdraw forthwith from the Welsh League (North). They continued for two further seasons in the Vale of Conway League. The club finally folded in May 1969, less than six years after playing in Europe. Several club officials switched allegiance to Llandudno FC, who changed their name to Llandudno Borough, though they soon reverted to the previous name.

Perversely, the religious order failed to make use of the Nant-y-Coed ground, and it remains a large open field. On the other hand, the Morfa Ground in Conway has been upgraded into a well-appointed venue for Conwy United FC.

A reunion of players and officials marked the thirtieth anniversary of Borough's European adventure. It was organised by Steve Houghton, the club's six-year-old mascot at the time.

~~~~~~~~~~~~~~~~~~~~~~~~~~~~~~~~~~~~~~
1964 – CARDIFF CITY (League Division 2)
~~~~~~~~~~~~~~~~~~~~~~~~~~~~~~~~~~

The Bluebirds began their first season in Europe with a new manager. Jimmy Scoular had been appointed on 13 July, replacing George Swindin, who had been relieved of the position on the eve of City's Welsh Cup triumph. Bangor City, playing in their third final in four years, were beaten 0-2 in a play-off in Cardiff.

There were now 30 clubs in the Cup-Winners' Cup competition, an increase of three on the previous year. City were drawn against Esbjerg of Denmark in the first round. The Welsh side had met the Danes on a club tour in 1959, winning 4-0, with Derek Tapscott – the only survivor of that side – netting a hat-trick.

New goalkeeper Bob Wilson was signed from Aston Villa too late to be eligible for the first two rounds, so Dilwyn John remained in goal. Cardiff had made a poor start to the season and were lying second from bottom of Division Two with only three points and no wins from five league games. Scoular and his party flew from a mist-shrouded Cardiff (Rhoose) Airport for the first leg in Denmark.

9 September 1964   *1st Round, 1st Leg*   *Idraetsparken*
Esbjerg, Denmark   *Attendance: 10,000*

ESBJERG (0) 0   **CARDIFF CITY (0) 0**

ESBJERG: Gardhoje; Hansen, Jensen P; Nielsen, Madsen, Petersen J; Petersen K, Christiansen, Bruun, Jensen E, Kikkenborg.
CARDIFF CITY: John; Rodrigues, Peck; Williams, Charles J, Hole; King, Charles M, Halliday, Allchurch, Farrell.

In a dull and uninspiring introduction to European football, Cardiff were continually caught offside as the Danish side, boasting nine internationals, stifled any attempt at attacking play. Peter King was City's liveliest forward, while John Charles was unbeatable in the air at centre-half. The only light relief in a miserable match came when City complained that the ball was too soft. It was pumped up at half-time only for Esbjerg to complain that it was too hard.

---

13 October 1964   *1st Round, 2nd Leg*   *Ninian Park*
Cardiff   *Attendance: 8,784*

CARDIFF CITY (0) 1   **ESBJERG (0) 0**
King 56

CARDIFF CITY: John; Rodrigues, Peck; Williams, Murray, Hole; Farrell, King, Tapscott, Charles M, Lewis.
ESBJERG: Gardhoje; Hansen, Jensen P; Jensen E, Madsen, Petersen J; Petersen K, Christiansen, Theogersen, Neilsen, Kikkenborg.
Referee: V Loraux (Belgium)

(CARDIFF won 1-0 on aggregate)

The injured John Charles was replaced by 18-year-old Don Murray. City suffered a further blow when Ivor Allchurch was hurt during training on the morning of the match and replaced by Mel Charles. Other changes saw Bernard Lewis come in on the wing, and Derek Tapscott take the place of Chick Halliday. Tapscott had played in the Fairs Cup in 1956 when he was selected in a London XI while still at Arsenal. Although now bottom of Division Two, City had won their first league game, defeating Derby County 2-1.

In a much improved performance, City created more chances than the score suggests. Esbjerg keeper Eric Gardhoje pulled out the stops to deny the Bluebirds, but was helpless when Peter King headed in Greg Farrell's cross. It was Cardiff's first European goal.

---

16 December 1964   *2nd Round, 1st Leg*   *Estadio Jose Alvalade*
Lisbon, Portugal   *Attendance: 20,000*

SPORTING LISBON (0) 1   **CARDIFF CITY (1) 2**
Hilario 81   Farrell 32, Tapscott 67

SPORTING LISBON: Carvalho; Gomes, Alfredo; Hilario, Mendes, Carlos; Sitoe, De Silva, Figueredo, Pinto, Morais.
CARDIFF CITY: John; Harrington, Rodrigues; Charles J, Murray, Hole; Farrell, Williams, Tapscott, King, Lewis.
Referee: R Kreitlein (West Germany)

City's opponents in the next round were Sporting Lisbon, who were defending the European Cup-Winners' Cup they had won by defeating MTK Budapest 1-0 in an Antwerp replay, after the sides had drawn 3-3 at the Heysel Stadium, Brussels.

En route to the final, Sporting had beaten Manchester United 5-0 in Lisbon. Though currently third from bottom of the Portuguese League, it came as a surprise to find that Sporting had suspended French coach Jean Luciano.

The tough tackling, inaptly named 'Sporting', bludgeoned their way through the match, with City receiving scant protection from referee Kreitlein – who would achieve lasting notoriety by sending off the Argentine skipper Rattin against England in World Cup '66.

John Charles, playing sweeper with four stitches in a head wound, cleared off the line as City soaked up early pressure. A first-half breakaway brought them the opening goal, Peter King and Derek Tapscott setting up Greg Farrell's low shot.

Halfway through the second half, Farrell swung a diagonal ball out to Tapscott, who sent over a curling 30-yard cross-shot which deceived Carvalho and went in off a post. Portugal's leading scorer the previous season – Ernesto Figueredo – then headed against the bar. Sporting pulled a goal back when Hilario drove in Carlos' pass.

---

23 December 1964   *2nd Round, 2nd Leg*   *Ninian Park*
Cardiff   *Attendance: 25,000*

CARDIFF CITY (0) 0   **SPORTING LISBON (0) 0**

CARDIFF CITY: John; Harrington, Rodrigues; Charles J, Murray, Hole; Farrell, Williams, Tapscott, King, Lewis.
SPORTING LISBON: Carvalho; Gomes, Alfredo; Hilario, Mendes, Carlos; Sitoe, De Silva, Figueredo, Pinto, Morais.
Referee: W Schaut (Belgium)

(CARDIFF won 2-1 on aggregate)

City had performed so well in Lisbon that Jimmy Scoular named the same side for the second leg a week later. Once again John Charles was at his majestic best and Sporting made little impact. In fact, it was the home side who might have opened the scoring: they were denied a penalty after Gomes clearly handled Farrell's shot on the goal-line. Derek Tapscott busied himself up front, despite being covered in blood from a face wound received after a typically robust challenge on keeper Carvalho.

It was a fine City performance against far more experienced opponents, and the home crowd refused to disperse until the players appeared in the directors box at the end of the game.

---

20 January 1965   *Quarter-final, 1st Leg*   *La Romareda*
Zaragoza, Spain   *Attendance: 30,000*

REAL ZARAGOZA (2) 2   **CARDIFF CITY (2) 2**
Lapetra 1, Pais 12   Williams 16, King 41

REAL ZARAGOZA: Yarza; Peppin, Reija; Violeta, Santamaria, Pais; Canario, Santos, Marcelino, Lapetra, Encontra.
CARDIFF CITY: Wilson; Harrington, Rodrigues; Charles J, Murray, Hole; Farrell, Williams, Tapscott, King, Lewis.
Referee: H Ottmar (Switzerland)

The reward for beating the cup holders would present another stern test for Cardiff City. The quarter-final draw paired them with Real Zaragoza, holders of the Inter-Cities Fairs Cup. Having overcome Juventus in the quarter-final, they defeated Valencia 2-1 at the Nou Camp, Barcelona, to take the trophy. Zaragoza were currently second in the Spanish League and unbeaten at home. Their forward line – 'Los Cincos Magnificos' – were mainly responsible for a seven-game winning streak.

Jimmy Scoular made one change, preferring Bob Wilson in place of Dilwyn John in goal, but City made a disastrous start. Seconds after kick-off Gareth Williams fouled Violeta outside the box and Lapetra blasted the free-kick into the top corner. City's keeper made amends with athletic saves from Lapetra and Marcelino, but was powerless to stop the nimble Spaniards doubling their lead when Pais wriggled through to shoot high into the net.

City's fighting spirit was evident when they pulled a goal back with a move fashioned and finished by Williams. Feeding Greg Farrell on the wing he raced into the area to power Farrell's centre past Yarza in the Zaragoza goal. Farrell gave international full-back Reija a torrid time, and just before the break, City's recovery was complete when another Farrell centre brought the equaliser. Peter King climbed high to meet the cross and nod past the keeper.

It was a triumphant return to the Romareda Stadium for John Charles, who had netted twice there for Roma in the Fairs Cup.

---

3 February 1965   *Quarter-final, 2nd Leg*   *Ninian Park*
Cardiff   *Attendance: 38,458*

CARDIFF CITY (0) 0   **REAL ZARAGOZA (0) 1**
                               Canario 73

CARDIFF CITY: Wilson; Harrington, Rodrigues; Charles J, Murray, Hole; Farrell, Williams, Tapscott, King, Lewis.

REAL ZARAGOZA: Yarza; Cortizo, Reija; Isasi, Santamaria, Violeta; Canario, Santos, Marcelino, Lapetra, Encontra.
Referee: A Haeben (Belgium)

(REAL ZARAGOZA won 3-2 on aggregate)

Real Zaragoza's visit to Wales was overshadowed by their intention to field two players suspended by the Spanish FA. Joaquin Cortizo had been banned for 24 games following incidents in a match against Atletico Madrid and was omitted from the first leg. Marcelino was suspended for six games after being sent off against Bilbao. UEFA explained that if a national association chose not to inform them (UEFA) of a suspension, then that player *was* eligible for European matches.

City created enough first-half chances to have put the result beyond doubt, but the second period degenerated into an untidy scrap that silenced the large crowd. Derek Tapscott buffeted the goalkeeper so often that he was earmarked by Spanish defenders for retribution. A linesman had to rush on to drag away furious Zaragoza players after one of Tapscott's muscular challenges.

In a disappointing end, right-winger Canario – a former member of Di Stefano's awe-inspiring Real Madrid – waltzed through to net the winning goal. Defeat meant that Cardiff missed the chance of an all British semi-final against West Ham. The Hammers beat the Spanish side 3-2 on aggregate before becoming the second British club to win a European tournament. A double from Alan Sealey – later to spend a short period on the coaching staff at Ninian Park – gave the Londoners a 2-0 win over TSV Munchen 1860 at Wembley.

~~~~~~~~~~~~~~~~~~~~~~~~~~~~~~~~~
1965 – CARDIFF CITY (League Division 2)
~~~~~~~~~~~~~~~~~~~~~~~~~~~~~~~~~

Having enjoyed their first European adventure, Cardiff City made sure of a second opportunity with a Welsh Cup victory over Wrexham. After beating the North Walians 5-1 in the first leg, City lost the second 0-1. Under FA of Wales rules at the time, a play-off was required. City duly won that game 3-0.

Play-offs no longer featured in the Cup-Winners' Cup, as UEFA had introduced the away-goals rule. City were drawn against the Belgian side Standard Liege, whose all-international line-up usually consisted of nine Belgians, a Yugoslav, and Louis Pilot – the captain of Luxembourg. Standard had made a sluggish start to the new season, without a win from their first six league matches.

Yet again City had to face a player suspended in his own country. Roger Claessen had been banned for throwing mud at the referee during Standard's Belgian Cup final defeat by Anderlecht. But Claessen was cleared to play in Cardiff.

City suffered a blow when Peter King failed a fitness test on an ankle injury. His place was taken by new signing Terry Harkin, a Northern Ireland international signed from Crewe at the start of the season. Derek Tapscott had joined Newport County in July, allowing 18-year-old George Johnston a regular first-team place.

8 September 1965   *1st Round, 1st Leg*   *Ninian Park*
Cardiff   *Attendance: 12,738*

CARDIFF CITY (1) 1   **STANDARD LIEGE (0) 2**
Johnston 31   Claessen 48, Semmeling 68

CARDIFF CITY: Wilson; Harrington, Rodrigues; Williams, Murray, Hole; Farrell, Johnston, Charles J, Harkin, Lewis.
STANDARD LIEGE: Nicolay; Vliers, Marchal; Beurlet, Spronck, Raskin; Semmeling, Paesschen, Claessen, Naumovic, Storme.
Referee: J Aalbrecht (Holland)

The Belgians conceded numerous fouls as they tried to knock City out of their stride. The match became an endless stream of feuding and petty infringements which the referee was powerless to prevent. Pandemonium raged after Peter Rodrigues was chopped down by Jacques Beurlet, who then slumped to the floor as if shot. A free-for-all ensued as Rodrigues was carried off for attention.

John Charles took a few blows from Lucien Spronck as Standard confirmed their intent for a draw. City were more adventurous and took the lead when winger Johnston capitalised upon Greg Farrell's centre, which was poorly cleared, and slipped the ball home.

The Belgians levelled in their first attack of the second half, with the home defence caught napping. Worse was to follow, as Jan Semmeling beat Bob Wilson to a centre and headed into an empty net. City lost their poise as the visitors continued their obstructive ways to the very end. Such was the mood of the crowd at the final whistle that Spronck needed a police escort to get off the field.

---

20 October 1965   *1st Round, 2nd Leg*   *Stade de Sclessin*
Liege, Belgium   *Attendance: 32,000*

STANDARD LIEGE (0) 1   **CARDIFF CITY (0) 0**
Storme 53

STANDARD LIEGE: Nicolay; Vliers, Marchal; Beurlet, Spronck, Pilot; Semmeling, Paesschen, Claessen, Jurkiewics, Storme.

CARDIFF CITY: Wilson; Harrington, Rodrigues; Summerhayes, Murray, Hole; Farrell, Johnston, Charles J, King, Lewis.
Referee: J Guerra (Portugal)

(STANDARD LIEGE won 3-1 on aggregate)

City were plagued by injuries for the second leg, which was played six weeks after the Ninian Park battle. Gareth Williams had fractured a cheekbone in a training accident, and his place was taken by 17-year-old David Summerhayes, Cardiff's first ever playing substitute. Don Murray and Barrie Hole needed late fitness tests, but Peter King was fit and resumed in place of Terry Harkin. City made their headquarters in the nearby town of Spa.

Eschewing their spoiling tactics of the first leg, Standard pressed from the off and Bob Wilson saved splendidly from Claessen and Jurkiewics. City hoped to succeed where Rangers and Hearts had failed in previous seasons, and Johnston, King and Charles all went close to opening City's account.

Early in the second period – following the breakdown of a City attack – Standard took the lead with a simple goal. Semmeling beat Peter Rodrigues out wide and Storme headed in his cross. Contrary to expectations, it proved to be a clean and open match and the large crowd rose to acclaim the City players at the final whistle.

John Charles sustained a knee injury in what was to be his final first-team appearance for City. In the next round Standard were beaten 2-5 on aggregate by Liverpool.

~~~~~~~~~~~~~~~~~~~~~~~~~~~~~~~~~~~~~~~
1966 – SWANSEA TOWN (League Division 3)
~~~~~~~~~~~~~~~~~~~~~~~~~~~~~~~~~~~~~~~

The Swans earned a second tilt at European opposition by defeating Chester in the Welsh Cup final. Though struggling for points in Division Three, Swansea were keen to eradicate memories of Motor Jena. This time they were drawn to face Slavia Sofia, a Bulgarian side containing three players who appeared for Bulgaria in the World Cup in England that summer. Slavia had been League champions on ten occasions, won the cup four times, and were currently top of their domestic League. In their most recent match they had defeated the army side Red Banner in the Bulgarian Cup final in front of 80,000 spectators.

Lack of communication from Bulgaria caused headaches for the Swansea administration. It was not until four days before the first leg that a cable was received giving squad members and travel details. Ivan Davidov, Slavia's brightest star, was unfit and did not travel. After a gruelling trip by plane, coach and train, the party arrived in Swansea four hours late. As none of them could speak English, an interpreter from the Russian Department of Swansea University was recruited to assist.

Swansea permitted Slavia to play in their normal white shirts and white shorts, while the Swans would wear their second strip – tangerine at that time. The gesture would be reciprocated by the Bulgarians for the second leg.

Once again fate had been unkind to the Swans. They had played Bristol City at the Vetch Field in a Football League Cup replay just 48 hours before their European tie. They won 2-1, but had been taken to extra-time before clinching a place in the third round draw. As a result, manager Glyn Davies was pressed into naming reserve full-back Len Beavan as substitute keeper.

21 September 1966   *1st Round, 1st Leg*   *Vetch Field*
Swansea   *Attendance: 12,107*

SWANSEA TOWN (0) 1   SLAVIA SOFIA (0) 1
Todd 58   Tassev 80

SWANSEA TOWN: Heyes; Evans R, Gomersall; Jones A, Purcell, Hughes; Humphries, McLaughlin, Todd, Allchurch, Evans B.
SLAVIA SOFIA: Simeonov; Schalamanov, Kostov; Alexiev, Largov, Petrov; Tassev, Haralambiev, Vassilev, Vrajev, Manolov.
Referee: M Pettersen (Iceland)

The wing play of Willie Humphries and Brian Evans delighted the crowd in this thriller. Wonder saves from Simeonov drew generous applause from the home fans. Swansea pressure finally told in the second half, when Humphries took a return pass from Jimmy McLaughlin and fired in a hard, low centre. Keith Todd was first to the ball and cracked in a fine goal. Swansea keeper George Heyes brilliantly denied Tassev as Slavia probed for a quick equaliser, but as the game moved into the final quarter the Welshmen increasingly showed the effects of Monday night's gruelling cup-tie.

The Bulgarians equalised in fortuitous circumstances. Full-back Schalamanov sped down the right and his cross was met by Tassev, who miscued his shot but saw the ball lob over the stranded Heyes.

---

5 October 1966   *1st Round, 2nd Leg*   *Slavia Stadium*
Sofia, Bulgaria   *Attendance: 30,000*

SLAVIA SOFIA (1) 4   SWANSEA TOWN (0) 0
Tassev 8, 60, 86, Vrajev 48

SLAVIA SOFIA: Simeonov; Schalamanov, Kostov; Alexiev, Petrov, Davidov; Tassev, Haralambiev, Vassilev, Vrajev, Manolov.
SWANSEA TOWN: Heyes; Evans R, Gomersall; Jones A, Purcell, Williams H; Humphries, McLaughlin, Todd, Allchurch, Evans B.
Referee: D Babajan (Turkey)

(SLAVIA SOFIA won 5-1 on aggregate)

Swansea's gate receipts of £2,262 were enough to cover the costs of their trip to Bulgaria. The squad flew from London to Sofia two days before the second leg, but required fourteen hours of travelling before they arrived at their hotel. Cardiff City chairman Fred Dewey sent a good luck telegram that was much appreciated by the Swansea management.

The Swans showed only one change, with Herbie Williams – who had played against SC Motor Jena in 1961 – coming in for Brian Hughes, the only other Jena survivor.

Glyn Davies' attacking intentions came unstuck when Tassev – the scorer in the first leg – netted with a simple tap-in. McLaughlin might have levelled on the half-hour when clean through, but generally the Swans were rarely in the game.

Vrajev increased the home side's lead early in the second half, and despite fine goalkeeping by Heyes – who was doubtful before the match with a bruised elbow – Slavia went 3-0 up through Tassev, who went on to claim his hat-trick in the closing minutes.

Ivor Allchurch, the first Welshman to play in Europe for two different Welsh clubs – having played for Cardiff against Esbjerg in 1964 – made occasional forays into the Slavia half, but there was little power in the Swans' attack and they finished well beaten.

2

THE BLUEBIRDS FLY HIGH

~~~~~~~~~~~~~~~~~~~~~~~~~~~~~~~~~~~

1967 – CARDIFF CITY (League Division 2)

~~~~~~~~~~~~~~~~~~~~~~~~~~~~~~~~~~~

When the Bluebirds beat Wrexham in the Welsh Cup final it began a sequence of five successive cup triumphs. Their League form, however, was dire: in 1965-66 and 1966-67 they avoided relegation to Division Three by just one place.

Jimmy Scoular had rung the changes. Alan Harrington, Barrie Hole, Greg Farrell, George Johnston, John Charles and Bernard Lewis had departed from the last eleven fielded by City in the Cup-Winners' Cup. Included now was Brian Harris, who had won an FA Cup-winners medal for Everton in 1966. Scoular also gave a first European outing to rising young star John Toshack.

A kind draw paired the Bluebirds with Shamrock Rovers from Dublin – part-timers whose weekly wage bill was £125, top payment being £10 per week. What they lacked in quality, Rovers made up for in experience. They had played in Europe for nine consecutive seasons, and were the League of Ireland cup winners for the fourth consecutive year. In 1966 they defeated Spora Luxembourg for their only European victory to date, then drew at home against Bayern Munich 1-1, before losing the away leg 2-3.

20 September 1967   *1st Round, 1st Leg*   *Dalymount Park*
Dublin, Republic of Ireland   *Attendance: 21,883*

SHAMROCK ROVERS (1) 1   **CARDIFF CITY (0) 1**
Gilbert 17   King 47

SHAMROCK ROVERS: Smyth; Courtney, Mulligan; Kearin, Nolan, Fullam; O'Neill, Dixon, Gilbert, Leech, Kinsella.
CARDIFF CITY: Wilson; Coldrick, Ferguson; Williams, Murray, Harris; Jones B, Clarke, Toshack, King, Bird.
Referee: L Van Raevens (Holland)

Cardiff endured a torrid opening and Bob Wilson was called upon time after time to keep the Irish team out. He was beaten when Republic international Bobby Gilbert headed in Tommy Kinsella's cross. Gilbert injured his shoulder soon afterwards and was little more than a passenger thereafter.

Barrie Jones sent Ronnie Bird clear just before the break, but the winger miscued. Two minutes after the resumption City drew level when Peter King half-volleyed in from Jones' corner. Cardiff then took command. King netted a second time, only to be ruled offside.

---

4 October 1967   *1st Round, 2nd Leg*   *Ninian Park*
Cardiff   *Attendance: 14,180*

CARDIFF CITY (1) 2   **SHAMROCK ROVERS (0) 0**
Toshack 30, Brown 74 pen

CARDIFF CITY: Wilson; Coldrick, Carver; Williams, Murray, Harris; Jones B, Brown, Toshack, King, Bird.
SHAMROCK ROVERS: Smyth; Courtney, Kelly; Dixon, Nolan, Kearin; O'Neill, Leech, Richardson, Tuohy, Kinsella.
Referee: V Loraux (Belgium)

(CARDIFF won 3-1 on aggregate)

Liam Tuohy – a former Newcastle club-mate of Jimmy Scoular and currently player-coach of Shamrock Rovers – made five changes for the second leg, including 20-year-old Damian Richardson at centre-forward for the unfit Bobby Gilbert. Cardiff had David Carver at full-back in place of Bobby Ferguson, while Bobby Brown took over from Malcolm Clarke.

City's all-round superiority left the result in no doubt, though it took a second-half penalty to put the game beyond the gallant part-timers. The opening skirmishes lacked any urgency until Peter King carved out a goal for John Toshack. King dispossessed Mick Kearin, and delivered a perfect pass to the unmarked Toshack, who bagged his first goal of the season. Rovers' keeper Mick Smyth made many fine saves, while Bob Wilson was only called upon once, saving from Richardson. A needless handball by Dublin butcher Kearin gave Bobby Brown the chance to double the lead from the spot.

---

15 November 1967   *2nd Round, 1st Leg*   *Philips Stadium*
Eindhoven, Holland   *Attendance: 15,000*

NAC BREDA (1) 1   **CARDIFF CITY (0) 1**
Visschers 8   King 68

BREDA: Van der Merwe; Van Gorp, Van Ierland; Vermeulen, Pelkmans, Rijnders; Snoeck, Bouwmeester, Visschers, Pirard, Nouwens.

CARDIFF CITY: Wilson; Derrett, Ferguson; Clarke, Murray, Harris; Jones B, Brown, King, Toshack, Bird.
Referee: K Sirevaag (Norway)

In the first round proper City were drawn against NAC Breda, who had lost the Dutch Cup final to champions Ajax. Breda were currently tenth out of eighteen in Holland's First Division. In the first round they had defeated Floriana of Malta.

With the away leg first, Malcolm Clarke was recalled as a defensive wing-half. Graham Coldrick was unfit and replaced by 19-year-old Steve Derrett. Bobby Ferguson took over from David Carver.

The home side took a deserved early lead when leading scorer Jak Visschers – having previously struck a post – headed past Bob Wilson. City's first-half efforts amounted to a Peter King effort which hit an upright and a Bobby Brown shot pushed onto the bar by Van der Merwe. It was King who silenced the home crowd midway through the second half when he linked with Brown and darted through to equalise. Cardiff pressed strongly thereafter.

---

29 November 1967   *2nd Round, 2nd Leg*   *Ninian Park*
Cardiff   *Attendance: 16,411*

CARDIFF CITY (2) 4   **NAC BREDA (1) 1**
Brown 3, Jones 19   Nouwens 28
Clarke 66, Toshack 68

CARDIFF CITY: Wilson; Coldrick, Ferguson; Clarke, Murray, Harris; Jones B, Brown, King, Toshack, Bell.
BREDA: Van der Merwe; Van Gorp, Van Ierland; Graaumans, Pelkmans, Rijnders; Vermeulen, Bouwmeester, Visschers, Lauret, Nouwens.
Referee: G Mikkelson (Denmark)

(CARDIFF won 5-2 on aggregate)

Ticket sales for the second leg were brisk, with few ground tickets at 7 shillings and sixpence (38p), or enclosure tickets at 12s 6d (63p), available. Fit again Graham Coldrick took over from Steve Derrett, and Gary Bell – signed from Lower Gornal – was preferred to Ronnie Bird on the left wing. For Breda, Frans Bouwmeister, who played for Holland against England in 1964 and once scored four times in a European tie, refused to travel on account of his fear of flying. He was replaced by his nephew, who shared his name.

Following Cardiff's league victory at Carlisle – which dashed the Cumbrians' unbeaten home record – their boots went missing. They turned up in Bristol, where British Rail forwarded them to Cardiff.

Bobby Brown lost no time in setting the Bluebirds on their way, collecting a Coldrick free-kick to rifle the opener. With less than twenty minutes on the clock Barrie Jones doubled the score. Everyone except Jones had stopped, expecting the referee to blow for a City penalty after Brown had been felled. The ex-Swansea Town player prodded the ball over the line.

Lack of concentration by Bob Wilson gifted Breda a goal when he allowed a harmless 30-yarder from Gerard Nouwens to loop over his head. Wilson made amends minutes later by saving splendidly from Visschers at the second attempt.

City tailed off after their bright start, and it was not until midway through the second half that they made the game safe, when Malcolm Clarke arrowed a shot into the far corner. Clarke had signed for Cardiff from Leicester in August, and had enjoyed an extended run in the side following the October transfer to Bolton of skipper Gareth Williams.

The icing on the cake came when Peter King sent Coldrick racing down the right flank. Toshack met the centre to notch City's fourth goal. By then Breda were down to ten men, Frans Vermeulen having been carried off with a groin injury.

---

6 March 1968 *Quarter-final, 1st Leg* *Ninian Park*
Cardiff *Attendance: 30,567*

CARDIFF CITY (1) 1 **MOSCOW TORPEDO (0) 0**
Barrie Jones 43

CARDIFF CITY: Wilson, Derrett, Ferguson; Clarke, Murray, Harris; Jones Barrie, Jones Bryn, King, Toshack, Bird.
MOSCOW TOR: Kavazashvili; Shumakov, Shustikov; Yenets, Pakhamov, Lenev; Nepomilujev, Shcherbakov, Streltsov, Brednev, Pais.
Referee: R Schaut (Belgium)

Moscow Torpedo were Cardiff's formidable quarter-final opponents. They brought back memories of that famous earlier visit to Wales of Moscow Dynamo, who had thrashed City 10-1 at Ninian Park.

The Torpedo skipper, Valery Voronin, possessed more than 50 Soviet caps, and had been one of his country's outstanding players in the 1966 World Cup finals. Also in the Torpedo team was Eduard Streltsov, who rejoined the club after his release from prison.

Every Torpedo player was an international, but because of the Soviet winter shutdown, they had not played a competitive match since late November. Voronin was unfit, but the Soviets did include Gregori Yenets, whose name was added to the list submitted to

UEFA, though no one knew exactly if and when the player had been registered.

Pre-match ticket sales were at record levels and receipts were expected to exceed £15,000. Enclosure and ground spectators could pay at the turnstiles. Coach Vladimir Zolotov, a former Torpedo player, watched City's league game against Bristol City. However, as the Bluebirds included three new signings – Brian Clark, Fred Davies, and Leslie Lea – none of whom was eligible for the Torpedo match – not much could have been learned.

Bob Wilson returned in goal for his first senior outing of 1968. There was a place at inside-forward for 20-year-old Bryn Jones from Llandrindod Wells, despite his being on the transfer list since October. Cardiff were the only British side left in the competition. The Soviets left two players up front and concentrated on defence. City played a controlled game, with Don Murray and Brian Harris rock-like in defence. Harris, curiously, had been in the Everton team that beat Moscow Torpedo in 1960.

The only goal arrived just before half-time. The move began with Bryn Jones. He sent a short pass out to Ronnie Bird, who curled over a dangerous cross. Peter King glanced the ball towards the far post, where it was met by the head of Barrie Jones.

Harris directed a header inches over the bar, and a John Toshack lob grazed the far post as City looked for a second goal. It was Moscow Torpedo who found the net in the 82nd minute, but the referee disallowed Streltsov's effort for a foul on Murray.

---

19 March 1968   *Quarter-final, 2nd Leg*   *Prakhator Stadium*
Tashkent, Soviet Union   *Attendance: 65,000*

MOSCOW TORPEDO (1) 1   CARDIFF CITY (0) 0
Gershkovitch 33

MOSCOW TOR: Kavazashvili; Shumakov, Pakhamov; Yenets, Lenev, Shustikov; Stanishev, Streltsov, Shcherbakov, Gershkovitch, Pais.
CARDIFF CITY: Wilson; Derrett, Ferguson; Clarke, Murray, Harris; Jones Barrie, Dean, King, Toshack, Bird.
Referee: B Loev (Sweden)

(1-1 on aggregate)

For the second leg, City faced a 3,500-mile trek to Tashkent, 300 miles from the Chinese border. Their journey began on Thursday, 14 March with an eight-hour flight from London to Moscow. From there it was another 2,000 miles to Tashkent, a city that had been wrecked by an earthquake in 1966.

City supporters were stunned to learn that the club had sanctioned John Toshack's £70,000 transfer to Fulham. Fortunately, Toshack turned down the move. The squad trained at the Lenin Stadium in Moscow before travelling on to Tashkent. Norman Dean, who had signed from Southampton, was preferred to Bryn Jones in the only change from the first leg.

City's tactics became apparent immediately, with Brian Harris operating as sweeper and Dean slotting into a defensive wing-half role. Torpedo squared the tie on the half-hour. Streltsov fed Mikhail Gershkovitch, who wriggled clear of Dean and Bobby Ferguson to loop a deflected shot over Bob Wilson. City players were aghast that the referee awarded the goal, claiming a linesman had flagged for an infringement.

Ronnie Bird created a fine opportunity, only to have his goal-bound shot saved by the Torpedo keeper. The tie ended one goal apiece on aggregate, which meant a play-off to determine who went through to the last four. Once again, City lost track of their boots. Fortunately, the Russians located them and forwarded them on to Cardiff by way of a flight to London.

---

3 April 1968   *Quarter-final, Play-off*   *Rosenau Stadium*
Augsberg, West Germany   *Attendance: 35,000*

MOSCOW TORPEDO (0) 0   CARDIFF CITY (1) 1
                                    Dean 42

MOSCOW TOR: Kavazashvili; Nepomilujev, Pakhamov; Yenets, Lenev, Shustikov; Stanishev, Streltsov, Shcherbakov, Gershkovitch, Voronin.
CARDIFF CITY: Wilson; Coldrick, Ferguson; Clarke, Morgan, Harris; Jones Barrie, Dean, King, Toshack, Bird.
Referee: H Fritsche (West Germany)

When the issue was raised at a post-match banquet in Tashkent, the officials of Cardiff City and Moscow Torpedo were unable to agree on the play-off date or venue. UEFA eventually decreed that it would be staged in Augsburg, West Germany.

Jimmy Scoular's plans for Cardiff City's most important match for years were disrupted by injury to Don Murray. He received treatment up to departure day in the hope that he would be fit. The bus taking the party to Glamorgan (Rhoose) Airport stopped off at a surgery in Cardiff so that Murray could receive yet another injection. He would not make it, however, forcing him to miss his first game since September 1966, a total of 84 consecutive first-team games. His place was taken by 21-year-old reserve stopper Richie

Morgan, who had yet to sample League football. The other change was at full-back, where Graham Coldrick replaced Steve Derrett.

The squad were delayed at Rhoose Airport for several hours because of a blizzard, and this was to wreck plans for a training session at the 55,000 capacity Rosenau Stadium in Augsburg.

The game kicked off in wintry conditions but the weather soon cleared. Torpedo included Voronin for his first match against the Bluebirds. The Soviet Footballer of the Year, Eduard Streltsov, gave Morgan a hard time, roughing him up at every opportunity. One kick caught him in the throat.

The priceless goal arrived just before the interval. It was scored by Norman Dean, who volleyed in John Toshack's headed pass. Bob Wilson was kept busy as Moscow Torpedo chased an equaliser, his best save coming in injury-time, when he leapt across goal to deny Gershkovitch. Despite slipping to third from bottom in the League, City had reached the semi-final of the Cup-Winners' Cup.

---

24 April 1968   *Semi-final, 1st Leg*   *Volksparkstadion*
Hamburg, West Germany   *Attendance: 65,000*

SV HAMBURG (0) 1   **CARDIFF CITY (1) 1**
Sandeman 69   Dean 4

SV HAMBURG: Oezcan; Sandeman, Kurbjuhn; Dieckmann, Horst, Hellfitz; Schulz H, Kraemer, Libuda, Hoenig, Doerfel G.
CARDIFF CITY: Wilson; Carver, Ferguson; Dean, Murray, Harris; Jones Barrie, Clarke, King, Toshack, Lea.
Referee: O Mendibel (Spain)

The Bluebirds changed their travel plans for the semi-final first leg in Hamburg, using a scheduled flight from Heathrow. Contrary to previous trips, no fans or pressmen were permitted to travel with the official party. 50 City fans made their own way to Hamburg.

The Germans were without striker Uwe Seeler and Willie Schulz – who had been voted the best sweeper in the 1966 World Cup. Both were injured. A fit Don Murray replaced Richie Morgan at centre-half, Leslie Lea came in for his first European game, in place of Ronnie Bird, and David Carver was selected at full-back.

Cardiff scored in their first attack. Peter King sent Malcolm Clarke away to thread a diagonal ball through to Norman Dean. The scorer of City's play-off winner squeezed a shot between Turkish goalkeeper Ankos Oezcan and a post.

Two minutes later, a slip by Dean let in Franz-Josef Hoenig but Bob Wilson saved. Wilson was also out of his goal quickly to deny

Hans Schulz on the interval. City hung on until midway through the second period, when intense Hamburg pressure finally told. From Gert Doerfel's corner, unmarked right-back Helmut Sandeman thundered in a shot that gave Wilson no chance.

Forced ever more onto the defensive, City relied on breakaways by Dean and Clarke to relieve the pressure. Clarke needed stitches after being bundled onto the running track after one challenge.

---

1 May 1968   *Semi-final, 2nd Leg*   *Ninian Park*
Cardiff   *Attendance: 43,070*

CARDIFF CITY (1) 2   **SV HAMBURG (1) 3**
Dean 10, Harris 78   Hoenig 15, 90, Seeler 56

CARDIFF CITY: Wilson; Carver, Ferguson; Clarke, Murray, Harris; Jones Barrie, Dean, King, Toshack, Lea.
HAMBURG: Oezcan; Sandeman, Kurbjuhn; Hellfitz, Horst, Schulz W; Schulz H, Kraemer, Seeler, Hoenig, Doerfel.
Referee: L van Raevens (Holland)

(HAMBURG won 4-3 on aggregate)

The German side were strengthened for the second leg by the return of Seeler and Schulz. Cardiff City relied on the same eleven that had performed so well in Hamburg.

One of the most important games in City's history began brightly when Dean scored from Clarke's pass. Though Hamburg hit back within five minutes, with a fierce drive from Hoenig, City turned on the style and Oezcan had to save from Barrie Jones, Leslie Lea and Peter King.

Soon after the restart Bob Wilson allowed a speculative Uwe Seeler effort to drift over him and under the bar. The Germans scarcely deserved to be in front, but chants of 'Uwe-Uwe' from the travelling band of German supporters confirmed that Hamburg had seized the initiative.

City were not finished, however, and – after Seeler had struck an upright – they dramatically levelled. Brian Harris headed in Barrie Jones' corner for his first City goal in his 88th appearance.

Exuberant youngsters celebrated by racing onto the pitch, and play was held up while it was cleared. The price of that 'invasion' would become clear in due course.

Dean had a shot cleared off the line as the Bluebirds went for the kill. Under UEFA rules, away goals did not count double in semi-finals. A drawn second leg, whatever the score, would necessitate a play-off to decide which club would contest the final in Rotterdam.

Three minutes into injury-time, Hoenig tried a 25-yarder. It was more of a time-waster than a serious attempt on goal. But Wilson, whose series of top-class performances had been instrumental in City reaching the semi-final, allowed the ball to evade his grasp and nestle in the corner of the net. No sooner did the game restart than the referee blew. Hamburg, though, lost the final 0-2 to AC Milan.

~~~~~~~~~~~~~~~~~~~~~~~~~~~~~~~~~~

1968 – CARDIFF CITY (League Division 2)

~~~~~~~~~~~~~~~~~~~~~~~~~~~~~~~~~~

Skipper Brian Harris and manager Jimmy Scoular – now in his fifth season in charge at Ninian Park – both prophesied improved league fortunes for City after their recent relegation battles. The club undertook a six-week tour of Australia, New Zealand and Tasmania in the close season, playing fourteen matches in all.

In fact, the Bluebirds' league form gave immediate cause for concern. They lost their first three games – two of them at home. The 0-4 home thrashing by Crystal Palace in the opening match prompted Scoular to consider fining players for lack of effort, and even placing senior professionals on the transfer list. Club chairman Fred Dewey went on record to state that too many players were stale after the arduous summer tour.

City stepped up a gear to record four successive victories. This shot the Bluebirds up to sixth in Division Two, though they lost 0-3 at Huddersfield in their last fixture prior to their latest European adventure. Having comfortably dispatched Hereford United in the Welsh Cup final, they were drawn against FC Porto of Portugal.

Bobby Brown was fighting a losing battle to regain fitness after a Boxing Day injury against Aston Villa, and 25-year-old Peter King, who had been at Ninian Park since signing from Worcester City as a 17-year-old, demanded a transfer for the third time in two seasons. His wish was granted, despite King having missed only one senior outing since August 1965. A newcomer to the squad was Mel Sutton, a 23-year-old signed after a two-week trial in November. Sutton had formerly been with Aston Villa. The scoring hero of the previous season's European run, Norman Dean, left the club in September to sign for Barnsley.

A new UEFA ruling had been introduced this season. Five substitutes could be named, with any two to be called upon.

18 September 1968   *1st Round, 1st Leg*   *Ninian Park*
Cardiff   *Attendance: 19,202*

CARDIFF CITY (1) 2   **FC PORTO (0) 2**
Toshack 24, Bird 51 pen   Pinto 57, 60

CARDIFF CITY: Davies; Derrett, Bell; Sutton, Murray, Harris; Jones Barrie, Clark, King, Toshack, Bird.
FC PORTO: Americo; Sucena, Bernardo; Valdemar, Acacio, Rolando; Pavao (Pinto), Chico, Djalma, Gomez, Nobrega.
Referee: G Pintado (Spain)

Brian Clark almost scored in the sixth minute, but his shot came back off the legs of Porto keeper Americo. John Toshack won his aerial duels as City pressed for that important first goal. It came midway through the opening period, when Barrie Jones floated in a centre and Toshack soared to head into the far corner. Clark then hit a post after a dazzling run, but it was not until the second half that City increased their lead. Toshack was fouled in the area, and Ronnie Bird made no mistake from the spot.

The Portuguese, who won few friends with their niggling, obstructive tactics, reduced the arrears with a glancing header from Pinto – a second-half substitute for Pavao. Within minutes, the same player silenced the home crowd by netting a controversial equaliser. The Porto winger Nobrega appeared to allow the ball to run over the goal-line before flighting a centre to the far post, where Pinto headed in. City's protests were ignored.

Following the match, Cardiff City made an official protest to UEFA, via the Football Association of Wales, citing the shirt tugging, obstructive tactics of the Porto players. They also complained about the appointment of a Spanish referee, who – coming from the Iberian Peninsula – was not considered truly impartial.

---

2 October 1968   *1st Round, 2nd Leg*   *Estadio das Antas*
Oporto, Portugal   *Attendance: 60,000*

FC PORTO (1) 2   **CARDIFF CITY (0) 1**
Djalma 8, Pinto 77   Toshack 52

FC PORTO: Americo; Bernardo, Valderma; Antraca, Sucena, Lisbao; Pavao, Pinto, Djalma, Gomes, Nobrega.
CARDIFF CITY: Davies; Coldrick, Bell; Sutton, Murray, Derrett; Jones Barrie, Clark, King, Toshack, Lea (Phillips).
Referee: J Helies (France)

(PORTO won 4-3 on aggregate)

Scoular made a few changes for the second leg, with Steve Derrett moving to half-back for the unfit Brian Harris, and Graham Coldrick slotting in at full-back. Leslie Lea was preferred to Ronnie Bird on the left wing.

The trip began badly when the City party stormed out of their allotted hotel within a few hours of their arrival. Three floors were being renovated, and the City players were greeted by bags of cement and other building materials. The continuous hammering and general noise of the workmen were other factors in the decision to move twenty yards down the road to a hotel being used by the press and the few supporters who had made the trip. The City management claimed that they had enjoyed better accommodation last season – in Russia! In contrast, the Porto players had a three-day get together at a resort twenty miles from the city. Before the game, each Cardiff player received a bottle of Port.

They might as well have contained acid, for the scenes at the end of this match were a disgrace to European football. Portuguese supporters were allowed to run on and attack Cardiff players and officials as they tried to leave the field. Substitute goalkeeper Bob Wilson was beaten about the head and shoulders, finally reaching safety with blood pouring from a scalp wound. Over 100 policeman, many on horseback, were supposed to keep order, but they failed to prevent home supporters invading the pitch at the end. In fact, in Cardiff eyes, the police were among the biggest offenders, lashing out at visiting supporters with their sticks.

As for the match, the home side settled quickly and Djalma met Nobrega's cross to fire a crisp shot past Fred Davies. Don Murray was lectured by the referee after a series of heavy clashes with the elusive Djalma. The referee then made a bewildering decision. He rightly gave a penalty to City after a blatant foul on Brian Clark, but following vociferous protests from the Porto players he consulted a linesman and instead awarded Porto a free-kick.

Americo was kept busy as the Bluebirds fired in crosses from their wingmen, Barrie Jones and Leslie Lea, but City had a mountain to climb after the 38th minute when Graham Coldrick was sent off for a foul on Gomes. City battled away and equalised early in the second half when Steve Derrett's free-kick was headed into the net by John Toshack. Leighton Phillips became City's first European substitute when he replaced the injured Leslie Lea two minutes later, but ten-man Cardiff slipped behind again when Pinto rifled in a Djalma free-kick. The drama was far from over, however. With four minutes remaining, Toshack was fouled by Pinto. Toshack took the penalty himself, but his shot was safely gathered by Americo and City's hopes of saving the game were gone.

City protested to UEFA once again, this time bemoaning the lack of protection given to players and officials, both during and after the match. They also complained about the confusion generated by the ball-boys, who appeared to be wearing Porto replica shirts.

1969 – CARDIFF CITY (League Division 2)

The Bluebirds were buoyant after ending the 1968-69 season fifth in Division Two, and retaining the Welsh Cup by defeating Swansea.

All was not entirely well, however, as injury-prone Brian Harris requested a free transfer, which was rejected. Of greater concern was the news that Liverpool scouts were trailing John Toshack.

In July, the German side Werder Bremen came over for a friendly at Ninian Park. Brian Clark scored both City goals in a 2-2 draw, but Welsh referee Leo Callaghan sent off City winger Ronnie Bird and Bremen full-back Josef Piontek.

City made a great start to the new League season when Toshack netted after only 28 seconds of the match at Carlisle. City went on to win 3-2. City's first home match was watched by a crowd of 27,971 as stay-away supporters responded to Cardiff's positive start. With only one defeat in the opening seven games, Cardiff reached second place in the division, though they had dropped to fifth by the time the new European campaign commenced.

City were paired with the Norwegian amateurs of Mjoendalen, who – despite losing the Norwegian Cup final 0-3 to league champions SOFK Lyn Oslo – were competing in Europe for the first time. The trip to the remote forests of Norway required a seven-hour air and coach journey – the five-hour flight to Oslo included a refuelling stop in Amsterdam. Jimmy Scoular ordered training as soon as the party arrived at their destination.

City were forced to make a late change when Gary Bell complained of stomach trouble just before the match. Barrie Jones was dropped for the first time since signing for the club two and a half years previously. The Norwegians included twins Boye and Brede Skistad, the sons of Mjoendalen president Hans Skistad.

17 September 1969   *1st Round, 1st Leg*   *Neder Eiker Stadium*
Mjoendalen, Norway   *Attendance: 8,000*

MJOENDALEN (1) 1   **CARDIFF CITY (3) 7**
Olsen 44   Clark 3, 36, Toshack 42, 88,
                             Lea 71, Sutton 74, King 79

MJOENDALEN: Nilsen; Broch (Kristian), Jensrud; Loe, Svendsen, Skistad Brede; Kristiansen, Solberg E, Holman (Larsen) Skistad Boye, Olsen.
CARDIFF CITY: Davies; Derrett, Carver; Sutton, Murray, Harris; Phillips (Jones), Clark, Lea, Toshack, King.
Referee: J Hannet (Belgium)

The tie was effectively all over inside the three minutes it took Brian Clark to open the scoring, and he was on target again before half-time, taking advantage of a slip by Torbjoen Loe.

A lethargic-looking John Toshack headed in Dave Carver's cross for the third, and the major surprise of the half came when Steve Derrett was outwitted by shop assistant John Olsen, who pulled a goal back on half-time.

Barrie Jones replaced Leighton Phillips for the second half. Leslie Lea and Peter King controlled the midfield and both were rewarded with goals as City piled on the agony. There was also a first senior goal for Mel Sutton, and Toshack finished off the rout with the final score. In truth, City had not played well, yet had found themselves with little to beat. This led one fan to claim that King Olaf's band had played better at half-time than Mjoendalen did before and after.

---

1 October 1969   *1st Round, 2nd Leg*   *Ninian Park*
Cardiff   *Attendance: 14,730*

CARDIFF CITY (4) 5   **MJOENDALEN (1) 1**
King 16, 62, Allan 36, 39, 43   Solberg 38

CARDIFF CITY: Davies; Carver, Bell; Sutton, Murray, Lewis; Jones Barrie, Clark, Allan, Toshack (Lea), King.
MJOENDALEN: Larsen J-E; Broch, Jensrud; Loe, Svendsen, Skistad Brede; Kristiansen (Larsen S), Solberg E, Holman (Solberg K), Larsen E, Olsen.
Referee: H Manning (East Germany)

(CARDIFF won 12-2 on aggregate)

In the league fixture prior to the return leg, John Toshack netted his first ever hat-trick as City beat Division Two pacesetters QPR 4-2. Terry Venables scored from the spot for one of Rangers' goals.

Sandy Allan – a 22-year-old Scot signed from Cheshire League side Rhyl – was chosen to lead the attack, despite having made only four appearances in two seasons. Brian Harris and Leslie Lea were out through injury, and a second first-team outing awaited 18-year-old Terry Lewis. The City management presented Mjoendalen with miners lamps and tankards as mementoes.

City pushed forward from the start, seeking to overtake Sporting Lisbon's eighteen-goal aggregate record win in the competition. Toshack hit the woodwork twice, but was replaced by Leslie Lea after taking a knock in a collision with builder Jan-Erik Larsen, the Norwegians' second-choice keeper. Regular No 1, plumber Runar Nilsen, was being rested for his team's next match, a Norwegian cup semi-final.

Peter King topped and tailed the scoring, sprinting through unopposed for the first, and back-heeling a shot from Lea for the fifth. Sandy Allan notched City's first European hat-trick in seven breathless minutes, during which the Norwegians also managed to score. Centre-forward Egil Solberg lashed a left-wing corner past Fred Davies. Among the referee's more bizarre decisions in the match was to book Cardiff's keeper for time-wasting!

---

12 November 1969   *2nd Round, 1st Leg*   *Alsancak Stadium*
Izmir, Turkey   *Attendance: 20,000*

GOEZTEPE IZMIR (3) 3   **CARDIFF CITY (0) 0**
Fevzi 14, Ertan 30, Neilson 32

GOEZTEPE IZMIR: Ali; Mehmet I, Caglayan; Ozer, Mehmet A, Ihsan; Mehmet F, Ertan, Neilsen, Fevzi, Gursel.
CARDIFF CITY: Davies; Carver, Bell; Sutton, Murray, Harris; Lea, Clark, King, Toshack, Sharp (Allan).
Referee: V Jakse (Yugoslavia)

City's second-round opponents, Goeztepe Izmir, won the Turkish Cup by defeating Galatasary. The trip to Turkey required a journey surpassed in difficulty only by the marathon trek to Tashkent. It lasted eleven hours, due mainly to delays in London because of a porters' strike. Owing to a shortage of steaks on the flight, several City players had to settle for curry, or salad and bread rolls. Izmir was reached via Paris and Istanbul, and flowers were presented to City chairman Mr Dewey on arrival.

Curiously, both teams stayed at the same hotel, with City being given meal vouchers to the value of 42 shillings (£2.10p). Any surplus had to be paid for by Cardiff City. This was contrary to normal practice on away legs, when City would pay for their own meals and accommodation. This was also the case for clubs visiting Wales. Izmir officials explained that the arrangement was necessary because of the restrictions on Turkish currency exchange.

City were without an away win since August, and faced a side containing eight Turkish internationals, including current caps Ali in goal, and wing-half Mehmet. Barrie Jones was out with a broken leg, so the Bluebirds included Frank Sharp, who had signed from Carlisle in February for £5,000.

The Turks rocked City with three goals in the opening 32 minutes as the Bluebirds struggled to come to terms with the peculiar pitch of grey ash and sand. For No 1, Gary Bell handled on the edge of the area and Fevzi curled the free-kick round the wall. Ertan struck the second after taking Fevzi's pass and slicing through the Cardiff defence. Davies was caught out of position for the third goal, misjudging a cross from Izmir skipper Gursel, and allowing the ball to fall to the Turks' Danish player, Neilsen.

Mel Sutton worked tirelessly in midfield, but generally City were let down by shoddy defending and a lack of punch in attack. Allan was brought on in place of Sharp, but it made little difference.

---

26 November 1969   *2nd Round, 2nd Leg*   *Ninian Park*
Cardiff   *Attendance: 17,866*

CARDIFF CITY (0) 1   **GOEZTEPE IZMIR (0) 0**
Bird 78

CARDIFF CITY: Davies; Carver, Bell; Sutton, Murray, Harris; Allan, Clark, Lea (Bird), Toshack (Coldrick), King.
GOEZTEPE IZMIR: Ali; Mehmet I, Caglayan; Ozer, Mehmet A, Nevzat; Fevzi, Ertan, Neilsen (Dursun), Gursel, Mehmet F.
Referee: G Droz (Switzerland)

(GOEZTEPE won 3-1 on aggregate)

City's new signing, Bobby Woodruff was ineligible for this round, so they began with the eleven that ended the first leg. The Turkish team, who in 1969 had reached the semi-final of the Fairs Cup, presented the Bluebirds with boxes of raisins and figs.

The Bluebirds carved out numerous goal attempts in a frantic first half as they tried to claw their way back into the tie. Sandy Allan might have scored in the fifth minute, but shot into the side-netting. In general, City's pressure was soaked up by a five-man Turkish defence who packed their penalty area.

As time went on it became clear that City were incapable of pulling back the three-goal deficit. Ronnie Bird replaced the injured Leslie Lea after 59 minutes, and Bird's direct running discomfited the Izmir defence. With little time remaining he thundered in one of his specials, helped by a decoy run from Graham Coldrick – a substitute for John Toshack up front.

Turkish fans and City supporters clashed at the end of the game and police were called to break up the disturbance.

~~~~~~~~~~~~~~~~~~~~~~~~~~~~~~~~~~

1970 – CARDIFF CITY (League Division 2)

~~~~~~~~~~~~~~~~~~~~~~~~~~~~~~~~~~

Having ended the season in seventh position, manager Jimmy Scoular bought and sold. Goalkeeping hero Bob Wilson departed for

Exeter City, while his successor, Fred Davies, joined Bournemouth. Graham Coldrick took the well-worn path to Newport County. Into the City squad came Frank Parsons, a keeper from Crystal Palace, and experienced midfielder Ian Gibson from Coventry. The new blood helped Cardiff top Division Two after six games, courtesy of beating Birmingham 2-0 in front of a 22,081 home crowd.

City's fourth successive season of European football saw them drawn against the amateurs of Pezoporikos Larnaca. The Cypriot side had finished league runners-up and were making their European debuts. They were coached by 55-year-old former Hungarian international Guilio Zsengeller, who had played against England at Wembley in 1936 and netted a hat-trick against Sweden in the semi-finals of the World Cup two years later.

Cypriot clubs had been competing in Europe for ten seasons but only once before faced British opposition. Dunfermline had enjoyed a rampant 12-1 aggregate victory over Apoel in 1968. None of the Larnaca players had ever previously played on grass.

16 September 1970   *1st Round, 1st Leg*   *Ninian Park*
Cardiff   *Attendance: 12,984*

CARDIFF CITY (5) 8   **PO LARNACA (0) 0**
Sutton 18, Gibson 23, King 30,
Woodruff 42, Clark 44, 70,
Toshack 55, 79

CARDIFF CITY: Parsons; Carver, Bell; Sutton, Murray, Harris; Gibson, Clark, King, Toshack, Woodruff.
PO LARNACA: Palmiris (Kiriakides); Petrou, Paridis; Constantinou, Stellis, Thinos; Kunnidis, Karapittas, Loizou, Filiastidis, Melis.
Referee: J Colling (Luxembourg)

This was an absurdly one-sided contest, with City having a reputed 50 goalscoring attempts. Frank Parsons, making his European debut in the City goal, took one goal-kick, collected five back-passes, and stooped to pick up one long-range trundler. The outclassed visitors did not even earn a corner-kick.

It took City eighteen minutes to find their range and by half-time Mel Sutton, Ian Gibson, Peter King, Bobby Woodruff and Brian Clark had all got the better of telephone engineer Palmiris in the Larnaca goal. Kiriakides took over between the sticks for the second half and made some good saves before being beaten three times.

The Cypriot party left Wales with gifts of silver tankards after a drubbing that would make the second leg a formality.

30 September 1970   *1st Round, 2nd Leg*   *GSZ Stadium*
Larnaca, Cyprus   *Attendance: 5,000*

PO LARNACA (0) 0   **CARDIFF CITY (0) 0**

PO LARNACA: Palmiris; Petrou, Paridis; Constantinou, Stellis, Thinos; Kunnidis, Karapittas, Loizou, Filiastidis, Stavrinos.
CARDIFF CITY: Parsons; Carver, Bell; Sutton, Murray, Harris; Gibson, Clark, Woodruff, Toshack (Phillips), King.

(CARDIFF won 8-0 on aggregate)

With costs approaching £2,000 for the trip, City were unlikely to break even on the tie, but they flew out to Cyprus on 26 September following a 1-1 draw away to Leyton Orient. The point dropped toppled City off their perch at the top of the division.

The condition of the pitch, which was a couple of feet of earth laid on concrete and rolled, gave the City players cause for concern and their play was tentative throughout. The afternoon kick-off also meant contending with the heat, and the combination of these two factors elicited a limp performance from the Cardiff team.

City suffered a scare when John Toshack crashed to the rock-hard surface and was assisted off. He was replaced by Leighton Phillips. Neither side looked like scoring, though Stavrinos cut through City's rearguard to force Frank Parsons to save. It was an awful game and Cardiff were glad to hear the final whistle.

---

21 October 1970   *2nd Round, 1st Leg*   *Ninian Park*
Cardiff   *Attendance: 17,905*

CARDIFF CITY (3) 5   **FC NANTES (1) 1**
Toshack 8, 38, Gibson 10,   Gondet 2
King 76, Phillips 80

CARDIFF CITY: Eadie; Carver, Bell; Sutton, Murray, Harris; Gibson, Clark (Phillips), Woodruff, Toshack, King.
NANTES: Fouche; Lemerre, de Michele; Osman, Rio, Michaelsen; Blanchet, Michel, Kervarrec, Pech, Audiger.
Referee: E Reidel (East Germany)

City drew FC Nantes of France in the second round. They had beaten Stromsgodset of Norway in the opening stage, and with six internationals in their line-up they were expected to give City a run for their money. Nantes' arrival at Glamorgan (Rhoose) Airport was delayed by two hours due to technical troubles, but on arrival at the Guest Keen Sports Ground, Cardiff, they quickly set about training.

An injury to out-of-form Frank Parsons meant a first European appearance for Scotsman Jim Eadie in goal. City's substitute keeper on the bench was 18-year-old John Williams.

Current French international Philippe Gondet gave Nantes a dream start. Danish star Allan Michaelson passed out to de Michele on the overlap. His pass to the fourteen-cap Gondet was dispatched into the City net with just 90 seconds on the clock.

John Toshack forced the Cardiff equaliser, after Brian Clark had nodded down Gary Bell's free-kick. Two minutes later Fouche, in the Nantes goal, fumbled a Bobby Woodruff shot and Ian Gibson prodded home the loose ball. Gibson found the net again, but this time the effort was disallowed. Playing their best football for some time, City soon scored another. A Mel Sutton cross was intercepted by Claude Osman, but Toshack retrieved the ball and forced his way past two defenders to make the half-time score 3-1.

Henri Michel, one of the best young players in France – later to manage the French national team – worked feverishly in midfield and the visitors had two goal-bound shots cleared off the line.

In the final quarter, Peter King netted with an angled drive and substitute Leighton Phillips, who replaced Clark, finished off a slick move involving Mel Sutton and Gibson.

---

4 November 1970   *2nd Round, 2nd Leg*   *Marcel Saupin Stadium*
Nantes, France   *Attendance: 10,000*

FC NANTES (0) 1   **CARDIFF CITY (1) 2**
Blanchet 85   Toshack 13, Clark 76

NANTES: Fouche; Lemerre, Rio; Gardon, de Michele, Michel; Michaelsen, Blanchet, Kervarrec, Pech, Audiger.
CARDIFF CITY: Eadie; Carver, Bell; Sutton, Murray, Harris; Gibson, Phillips (Clark), Woodruff, Toshack, King.
Referee: T Latsios (Greece)

(CARDIFF won 7-2 on aggregate)

The visit to Nantes, Cardiff's twin City since 1955, was the shortest of the Bluebirds' European excursions. Brian Harris made the trip only after a late replacement passport was delivered. His original documents had been stolen from his car, along with other personal effects. Nantes bolstered their defence by introducing 18-year-old Bernard Gardon for the injured Claude Osman, but they would be without Philippe Gondet.

Jim Eadie pulled off a couple of magnificent saves as the hosts tried valiantly to reduce the deficit. Henri Michel shot wide from a good position, but in general the Cardiff rearguard coped comfortably with the Nantes raids.

John Toshack reached a career milestone when he was first to react to Peter King's shot, which came back off the crossbar. It was Toshack's 100th league and cup goal for the club.

The referee denied Nantes an equaliser when he blew for a foul by Kervarrec, just as Pech beat Eadie with a shot that went in off an upright. City went further ahead when Brian Clark headed in Gary Bell's cross. Blanchet netted near the end with a chip over Eadie.

---

10 March 1971   *Quarter-final, 1st Leg*   *Ninian Park*
Cardiff   *Attendance: 47,500*

CARDIFF CITY (1) 1   **REAL MADRID (0) 0**
Clark 31

CARDIFF CITY: Eadie; Carver, Bell; Sutton, Murray, Phillips; King, Gibson, Clark, Woodruff, Rees.
REAL MADRID: Borja; Zunzunegui, Sanchis (De Felipe); Grande, Benito, Zoco; Amancio, Pirri, Grosso (Fleitas), Velasquez, Perez.
Referee: V Loraux (Belgium)

Ever since their first appearance in the Cup-Winners' Cup, Cardiff City had aspired to draw one of the giants. At last their wish came true. Teams came no bigger than mighty Real Madrid.

Real were one point off the top of the Spanish First Division, thanks to successive victories over Atletico Madrid, Barcelona, and Athletic Bilbao. None of their three recent victims had so much as scored. As for City, they climbed back to the top of Division Two after beating Carlisle 4-0. Alan Warboys netted all four in the first half, including an eight-minute hat-trick.

Warboys had been signed to replace John Toshack, who departed for Anfield shortly after the win in Nantes. Unfortunately, Warboys signed too late to be eligible for the Real Madrid tie. 17-year-old winger Nigel Rees defied FA of Wales rules by opting to play for his club, rather than for Wales against Scotland in a Youth International match in Wrexham. Trevor Morris, secretary of the FA of Wales warned that Rees might face a charge of misconduct. Rees, incidentally, was also a fine rugby player, having gained two Welsh schoolboy caps as an outside half.

The flight carrying the Real party to Wales was delayed owing to a freak blizzard. This necessitated a change to their normal training routine. Included in the party was Senor Santiago Bernabeu, in his 28th year as president of the club. Real were coached by Miguel

Munoz, right-half in their European Cup winning sides of 1956 and 1957. Such was the phenomenal local interest in the game that it was made all-ticket, earning receipts in the region of £25,000.

Real rarely threatened the City goal, pulling men back as they sought to take a draw back to Madrid. The referee blew for anything and everything, denying the game any opportunity to flow. On the half-hour Bobby Woodruff started the move that climaxed with one of Cardiff City's most famous goals. He played the ball down the line to Rees, who wriggled past two defenders before sending a pinpoint cross into the middle. It was met by Brian Clark, who headed the ball wide to Borja's left.

Mel Sutton should have doubled the lead in the second half, but shot straight at Borja. The only other chance fell to Don Murray, who found himself in the clear after a Gary Bell free-kick, but sliced his shot wide. Peter King incurred the wrath of the referee and earned his first booking in six years. The Belgian official whistled so often that he was likened to a guard on Brussels railway station.

---

24 March 1971   *Quarter-final, 2nd Leg*   *Santiago Bernabeu*
Madrid, Spain   *Attendance: 65,000*

REAL MADRID (0) 2   **CARDIFF CITY (0) 0**
Velasquez 50, Fleitas 52

REAL MADRID: Junquera; Zunzunegui, Sanchis; Grande, Benito, Zoco; Amancio (Manuel Perez), Pirri, Grosso, Velasquez, Maranon (Fleitas).
CARDIFF CITY: Eadie; Carver, Bell; Sutton, Murray, Phillips; King, Gibson, Clark, Woodruff, Rees (Harris).
Referee: K Suska (Czechoslovakia)

                              (REAL MADRID won 2-1 on aggregate)

Nigel Rees suffered from a throat infection and needed a penicillin injection on the eve of the second leg. City players were not over-awed at the task in hand, being psychologically lifted by Real's 0-1 home defeat by Wacker Innsbruck in the previous round – even though that was only Real's third ever home European defeat. Once Rees was passed fit, Scoular plumped for the same line-up.

Real's expected onslaught never materialised and City reached the interval largely untroubled. The Real fans in the half-empty stadium tossed bottles and cans onto the pitch in their frustration at the way the quarter-final was going.

Nigel Rees wasted a headed chance straight after the restart, and that appeared to sting the home side into action. Within two minutes Real had found the net twice, changing the whole course of the tie. Jim Eadie and Don Murray both went for the same cross. Eadie punched the ball to Velasquez, who volleyed in from fifteen yards. Before City could recover from that blow, they gave away a second goal. Dave Carver allowed a pass from Pirri to reach Manuel Fleitas, who flicked the ball beyond Eadie.

City responded by attacking in waves, searching for the away goal that would put them into the semi-final, but Real's time-wasting tactics disrupted the Bluebirds' momentum. In one incident, City trainer Lew Clayton tangled with home keeper Junquera, who tried to prevent him from returning the ball into play.

The referee afforded City little protection and added no time on, even though – after a Pirri shot flew into the stand – the crowd behind the City goal refused to return the ball. It beggared belief to learn that the free-kick count ended 35-6 in Real Madrid's favour, leaving Jimmy Scoular to bemoan the worst refereeing he had ever witnessed. Hard as they tried, Cardiff were unable to score the one goal needed to bring Real to their knees.

Real Madrid defeated PSV Eindhoven in the semi-final, but lost to Chelsea in the final. Staged in Piraeus, the first match was drawn 1-1, but Chelsea triumphed 2-1 in the replay.

~~~~~~~~~~~~~~~~~~~~~~~~~~~~~~~~~

1971 – CARDIFF CITY (League Division 2)
~~~~~~~~~~~~~~~~~~~~~~~~~~~~~~~~~

City made a miserable start to the new season, not registering their first win until the eighth game – four days before their first meeting with Dynamo Berlin. That opening victory was against bottom club Sheffield Wednesday, whose team included former Bluebird Peter Rodrigues at full-back.

Cardiff boasted the worst defensive record in Division Two, and were only two points off the bottom. Their squad for Berlin comprised sixteen players, among them Alan Warboys, who was undergoing intensive treatment for a shoulder injury. New signing Roger Hoy from Luton Town was ineligible, so did not travel. City's two other new buys – Alan Foggon and Ken Jones – had both previously played in the Inter-Cities Fairs Cup. Foggon had even scored for Newcastle United in the away leg of the 1969 final against Ujpest Dosza in Budapest.

The match in Berlin against East Germany's losing cup finalists marked the seventh anniversary of City's European debut, since when they had netted 51 goals. It was also City's 30th game in the Cup-Winners' Cup, a figure unsurpassed by any other European club. Dynamo Berlin had started the season with two losses, but returned to form with a 3-0 win over Lokomotiv Leipzig.

The Welsh contingent crossed through the Berlin Wall in darkness, changing buses in no man's land.

15 September 1971   1st Round, 1st Leg   Friedrich Ludwig Jahn Stadion
Berlin, East Germany   *Attendance: 15,000*

DYNAMO BERLIN (0) 1   **CARDIFF CITY (0) 1**
Schutze 90   Gibson 78

DYNAMO BERLIN: Lihsa; Stumpf, Brillat, Fifohn, Halle, Rohde, Terletzki, Becker, Schutze, Labes, Johanssen.
CARDIFF CITY: Eadie; Jones, Bell, Sutton, Murray, Phillips, King, Clark, Woodruff, Warboys, Gibson.
Referee: R Nyhus (Norway)

Because of the counter attraction of live TV coverage of Dynamo Dresden's European Cup-tie against Ajax, the crowd in Berlin was far smaller than anticipated. Jimmy Scoular switched his formation to 4-4-2 in an attempt to shore up City's defence. Peter King was included in Scoular's starting eleven, his first appearance of the season.

Cardiff were superior all round, and the only surprise was that the interval arrived without a goal to their name. It was Ian Gibson who broke the deadlock when he ran onto a lofted clearance from Gary Bell and swept the ball beyond Dynamo keeper Werner Lihsa.

In the second minute of injury-time, just when it seemed City had claimed another notable away scalp in Europe, Harald Schutze equalised. Schutze, playing with a bandaged head, following an earlier collision, threw City's defenders off balance and lashed a left-foot shot from twenty yards past Jim Eadie. It proved to be a bitter pill to swallow.

On arrival at Heathrow, following their flight from Frankfurt, the Cardiff squad flew directly on to Teeside Airport to prepare for a League match against Middlesbrough. The East Germans – a police team competing in Europe for the first time – had only a friendly fixture to distract them from preparations for the second leg.

---

29 September 1971   1st Round, 2nd Leg   Ninian Park
Cardiff   *Attendance: 12,676*

CARDIFF CITY (0) 1   **DYNAMO BERLIN (0) 1**
Clark 58   Labes 62

CARDIFF CITY: Eadie; Jones, Bell, Sutton, Murray, Harris, Gibson, Clark, Woodruff, Warboys (Foggon), King.

DYNAMO BERLIN: Lihsa; Stumpf, Carow, Trumpier, Halle, Rohde, Terletzki, Becker, Schutze (Schullenberg), Labes, Johanssen.
Referee: F Geluck (Belgium)

(DYNAMO BERLIN won on penalties)

Normal time was disappointing, although City squandered enough chances to have won. Peter King struck the post with Lihsa beaten, but Gibson blasted the rebound over the bar. City created yet more chances during the extra half-hour – when Alan Foggon was introduced. Brian Clark's header bounced off the woodwork and Halle cleared off the line.

It was Clark who had put City ahead from close range after Gibson's astute pass sliced through the defence. Three minutes later King was denied a clear penalty when the referee waved play on, despite being 45 yards from the incident. It was immediately after this let-off that Dynamo equalised. Deiter Stumpf's cross-shot was fumbled by Jim Eadie, and Dietmar Labes knocked home the loose ball.

With the scores level after extra-time, the winners had to be decided by a penalty shoot-out – the first time a Welsh club had endured such drama in Europe. The shoot-out took place at the Grangetown end, with Ian Gibson opening the account for Cardiff. Dynamo made it 1-1 on kicks, and all eyes turned to Don Murray. Sadly, he sent his kick high into the stand and although King, Gary Bell and Bobby Woodruff all scored, the East Germans converted all their kicks to win the shoot-out 5-4.

Prior to the start of the season's competition, UEFA had issued a directive to referees to stamp out foul play. City's disciplinary record in their seven years in the competition comprised one booking (King against Real Madrid) and one dismissal (Coldrick against FC Porto). Gary Bell added to the list by being booked in Berlin.

The East Germans reached the semi-final of the Cup-Winners' Cup, where they were beaten on penalties by Moscow Dynamo.

3

ENTER THE ROBINS

~~~~~~~~~~~~~~~~~~~~~~~~~~~~~

1972 – WREXHAM (League Division 3)

~~~~~~~~~~~~~~~~~~~~~~~~~~~~~

The Robins' first taste of European football ought to have come in 1960. Instead they had to wait eleven years from when the Welsh Cup winners first received automatic entry. This delay was surprising, since Wrexham had lifted the Welsh Cup more than any other club, and did so again in 1972 by defeating Cardiff City.

Their involvement was to prove costly, as they needed to spend heavily to bring the Racecourse's facilities up to UEFA standard. The club also budgeted to lose £2,000 on the first leg in Zurich, and for a Third Division club with average gates of 6,000, that might prove a huge financial burden to bear.

During the summer Wrexham manager John Neal had secured the services of seasoned European campaigner Mel Sutton. He was signed from Cardiff at a cost of £15,000 – at that time Wrexham's record signing. The team had made a promising start to the season, lying in fifth place, only one point behind leaders Port Vale.

13 September 1972   *1st Round, 1st Leg*   *Letzigrund*
Zurich, Switzerland   *Attendance: 6,500*

FC ZURICH (0) 1   **WREXHAM (0) 1**
Kunzli 47   Kinsey 48

ZURICH: Grob; Bionda, Heer, Munch, Zigerlig, Martinelli (Stierli), Kuhn, Kunzli, Brunnenmeier, Schweitzer (Konietzka), Jeandupeux.
WREXHAM: Lloyd; Mason, Fogg, Davies G, May, Evans, Tinnion, Sutton, Ashcroft, Thomas, Kinsey.
Referee: P Kostovski (Yugoslavia)

The visitors could have sailed to a comfortable win but for a lack of sharpness up front. Sutton was in sparkling form, and supported by 18-year-old Mickey Thomas and a solid back four, Wrexham posed the Swiss cup-holders many problems. A break involving Brian Tinnion and Bill Ashcroft culminated with Sutton firing into the side-netting. Mickey Evans was cautioned in the first half, along with Kuhn, who, in a fit of pique, blasted the ball straight at the Wrexham player.

Zurich brought on their player-coach, Timo Konietzka, for the second half, and the former German international quickly made the first goal. His dangerously flighted cross fell to the unmarked Swiss international centre-forward Fritz Kunzli, who netted with a smart header.

A minute later Wrexham were level. Sutton's header was cleared by Munch straight to Albert Kinsey, who cracked the ball home from 25 yards. In a frantic finale, the Swiss threw everything into attack, but the towering Eddie May – later to manage Cardiff City in Europe – and his fellow defenders were in uncompromising mood.

---

27 September 1972   *1st Round, 2nd Leg*   *Racecourse*
Wrexham   *Attendance: 18,189*

WREXHAM (0) 2   **FC ZURICH (0) 1**
Ashcroft 63, Sutton 73   Martinelli 56

WREXHAM: Lloyd; Mason, Fogg, Davies G, May, Evans, Tinnion, Sutton, Ashcroft, Kinsey (Mostyn), Thomas.
ZURICH: Grob: Bionda, Heer, Zigerlig, Stierli, Martinelli, Konietzka, Brunnenmeier, Schweitzer, Kunzli, Jeandupeux.
Referee: J Kristensen (Norway)

(WREXHAM won 3-2 on aggregate)

Bill Ashcroft needed a fitness test prior to the second leg, having been taken off in Wrexham's 0-1 defeat at Rochdale. John Neal included 18-year-old Roger Mostyn in the squad as a precaution.

Wrexham required a rocket header by Mel Sutton to proceed through to the next round. It was the first occasion that a player had scored goals in Europe for two different Welsh clubs, and it capped a great fight-back by the Robins. When Martinelli directed a diving header beyond Brian Lloyd early in the second half it looked bleak for the Division Three side, particularly as Kinsey was forced off by injury. He was replaced by Mostyn. Mickey Thomas carved out the equaliser when retrieving a ball seemingly going out of play. His cross was headed in by Ashcroft.

In an ugly melee, a Swiss defender was flattened and substitute Mostyn booked. Eddie May was also cautioned near the end.

---

25 October 1972   *2nd Round, 1st Leg*   *Racecourse*
Wrexham   *Attendance: 19,013*

WREXHAM (3) 3   **HAJDUK SPLIT (0) 1**
Tinnion 14, Smallman 15,   Jovanic 84
Musinic 40 (og)

WREXHAM: Lloyd; Mason, Fogg, Sutton, Davies G, Evans, Tinnion, Smallman, Ashcroft, Griffiths, Thomas.
HAJDUK SPLIT: Vukcevic; Djoni, Boljan, Musinic, Holcer, Boskovic, Bluic, Jerkovic, Nadovesa (Hlevniak), Jovanic, Suriac.
Referee: P Bonnet (Malta)

Wrexham were beset with injury worries as they prepared for their second round ties against Hajduk Split. Eddie May had twisted an ankle against Notts County and was rated doubtful, along with Arfon Griffiths and Mike Evans.

Mel Sutton once again posed the main threat as Wrexham took control of midfield. The Yugoslavs, with five internationals, were often back-pedalling. Brian Tinnion opened the scoring when Split keeper Vukcevic fumbled Dave Smallman's cross. Tinnion was first to the ball and prodded it into an empty net. Wrexham doubled their tally straight from the kick-off when Arfon Griffiths collected a ball on the by-line. He cut it back to Smallman, who hooked it in. The visitors protested that the ball had gone out of play, but the referee consulted a linesman and confirmed a goal. Sutton hit a post midway through the first half, and the Robins went further ahead when Tinnion's shot was deflected into the net off Musinic.

Hajduk replaced top scorer Nadovesa for the second half, and it was substitute Hlevniek who set up their vital away goal. His free-kick found Jovanic, who crashed a shot past Brian Lloyd.

Wrexham were on League duty two days after the European tie. They played Tranmere in a Division Three game, losing 0-4 to a side containing ex-Liverpool stars Tommy Lawrence and Ian St John.

---

8 November 1972   *2nd Round, 2nd Leg*   *Stadion Plinara*
Split, Yugoslavia   *Attendance: 25,000*

HAJDUK SPLIT (2) 2   **WREXHAM (0) 0**
Nadovesa 13, 26 pen

HAJDUK SPLIT: Vukcevic; Djoni, Boljan, Musinic, Holcer, Boskovic, Hlevniak, Jerkovic, Nadovesa, Jovanic, Suriac.
WREXHAM: Lloyd; Mason, Fogg, Davies G, May, Evans, Tinnion, Kinsey (Smallman), Ashcroft (McBurney), Sutton, Thomas.
Referee: S Eksztajn (Poland)

(HAJDUK SPLIT won on away-goals rule)

The Wrexham squad flew to Split from Manchester Airport, training the same evening. They took only one goalkeeper along, Welsh Under-23 cap Brian Lloyd. Usual reserve keeper David Gaskell was sidelined with a long-term injury and John Neal decided that the club's apprentice professional keeper was too raw. A fit Eddie May reclaimed the captaincy from Gareth Davies.

The Yugoslavs looked sharper and much improved on their first-leg showing. Mel Sutton took time to settle, with the result that the Robins never touched the heights. Both Bill Ashcroft and Mickey Thomas had opportunities to open the scoring before the home side went ahead – Nadovesa drove past Lloyd after latching onto a Djoni free-kick. The same player increased the lead from the penalty-spot after being brought down by Davies.

The match now degenerated into a brawl, and when Wrexham claimed a penalty after May's shirt was tugged the linesman's flag was over-ruled by the referee. Thomas, Davies and Mike McBurney were all booked as tempers frayed, and at the final whistle Evans jostled with a linesman, as a consequence of which the referee officially sent him off. To be beaten by the away-goals rule was a sad end to Wrexham's first European sortie.

~~~~~~~~~~~~~~~~~~~~~~~~~~~~~~~~~

1973 – CARDIFF CITY (League Division 2)

~~~~~~~~~~~~~~~~~~~~~~~~~~~~~~~~~

The Treaty of Rome, to which Britain had just signed, was put to the test at the start of this season, and had repercussions for British football. Cardiff City found that the free movement of labour from one Common Market country to another was not all that free.

City needed goalkeeping cover, as Frank Parsons had cancelled his contract by mutual consent. He planned to give up the game and go into business in London. Chris Wind – a 21-year-old Dutch goalkeeper, and the first footballer from within the European Economic Community to settle in South Wales – was forbidden to turn professional with the Bluebirds until he had served a two-year residential qualification. This was a ruling by the Football Association in London. The position was being closely monitored by the European Football Union. All nine Common Market countries attended a summer conference in Zurich in an attempt to thrash out how the Treaty's clauses affected the free movement of professional footballers.

Cardiff had beaten Bangor City to qualify for Europe, where their first opponents were Sporting Lisbon. The Portuguese party arrived in Cardiff after a complicated journey via Paris and Bournemouth. The team trained in the grounds of Cardiff Castle. They included four internationals, among them Dinis, who at 6ft 4in was one of the tallest wingers in Europe.

Sporting declined the opportunity of watching Newport County play Crewe in a Division Four fixture. Mario Lino, the former Sporting defender, who had assumed coaching duties from ex-West Bromwich Albion and England star Ronnie Allen, explained that he did not want his players distracted in any way.

19 September 1973   *1st Round, 1st Leg*   *Ninian Park*
Cardiff   *Attendance: 13,300*

CARDIFF CITY (0) 0   SPORTING LISBON (0) 0

CARDIFF CITY: Irwin; Dwyer, Bell, Smith, Murray, Phillips, Villars (King), Woodruff, McCulloch, Vincent, Anderson.
SPORTING LISBON: Damas; Manaca, Alhinho, Jose Carlos, Pereira, Nelson, Wagner, Peres, Tome, Yazalde, Dinis.
Referee: A Briguglio (Malta)

Vitor Damas in the Sporting goal did more than anyone to send his side home in confident mood, having made three excellent saves from City's former QPR striker, Andy McCulloch.

Only four players remained from the last City side to play in Europe, but the changes had little effect as the Bluebirds put on one of their drabbest performances. Their play was in stark contrast to their stirring display against the same opponents in 1964, which also finished scoreless. This time, the wing trickery of Dinis almost brought a Sporting goal. He crossed to Hector Yazalde, whose close-range header was parried by City keeper Bill Irwin. Yazalde would go on to win the Golden Boot award for top goalscorer in Europe, finishing the season with 46 goals, ten more than second-placed Hans Krankl of Rapid Vienna.

---

3 October 1973   *1st Round, 2nd Leg*   *Estadio Jose Alvalade*
Lisbon, Portugal   *Attendance: 50,000*

SPORTING LISBON (1) 2   CARDIFF CITY (1) 1
Yazalde 24, Fraguito 51   Villars 40

SPORTING LISBON: Damas; Manaca, Laranjeira, Alhinho, Pereira, Fraguito, Nelson, Marinho, Tome (Chico), Yazalde, Dinis.
CARDIFF CITY: Irwin; Dwyer, Bell, King, Murray, Phillips, Villars (Reece), Woodruff, McCulloch, Showers, Vincent.
Referee: J Colling (Luxembourg)

(SPORTING won 2-1 on aggregate)

Four days before the second leg, the Bluebirds had Don Murray sent off during a 1-3 defeat at Hull. Cardiff's goal was scored by Gary Bell, who headed in a rebound after his penalty was saved by Jeff Wealands. It was Cardiff's first defeat in eight matches.

Against Sporting, George Smith failed a late fitness test, so Cardiff included Peter King, veteran of many European campaigns. Such was the growing importance of European football that even the Bluebirds were reputed to be on a £200 win bonus. The second leg was scheduled to kick-off at 9.45 pm local time, which caused Cardiff City to ask UEFA for a standard start-time for all matches.

Sporting edged ahead midway through the first half when the Argentinian ace, Yazalde, met Fraguito's centre and shot hard and low to Bill Irwin's right. In a rare Cardiff attack, Derek Showers broke through but was hauled down by Alhinho. The resulting free-kick came to nothing. Tony Villars equalised just before the interval when he clipped the ball past the advancing Damas after a left-wing cross by Gary Bell.

City fell behind in the second half in unfortunate fashion. Yazalde's cross bobbled about in the goalmouth before the ball reached the unmarked Fraguito. Dinis was then summarily dismissed for throwing a punch at Phil Dwyer, but with only fifteen minutes left to play City were unable to capitalise on their numerical advantage. In the closing moments Villars received a facial injury and was helped from the field. Gil Reece came off the bench as a late substitute.

It was to be the last European match for City manager Jimmy Scoular. He left the club in November to be replaced by Frank O'Farrell, whose appointment was short-lived. Jimmy Andrews, O'Farrell's assistant, completed the season in charge.

~~~~~~~~~~~~~~~~~~~~~~~~~~~~~~~~~~~~~~
1974 – CARDIFF CITY (League Division 2)
~~~~~~~~~~~~~~~~~~~~~~~~~~~~~~~~~~~~

Cardiff City had finished in seventeenth place in Division Two, and even their Welsh Cup victory over non-league Stourbridge left much to be desired, as the Bluebirds scraped home 1-0 in both legs. They made a miserable start to the new campaign, too, and were quickly marooned at the bottom of the division. Money was scarce, and chairman David Goldstone stayed clear of the transfer market until funds were raised from sales. His policy had borne fruit with the sale of Andy McCulloch to Oxford during the close season. The cash received was used to meet losses on the financial year.

Leighton Phillips was unexpectedly withdrawn from the party that flew to Budapest. An offer had been accepted from Aston Villa for the player who had joined City as a 15-year-old. His impending move, plus injury to Gil Reece and suspensions for George Smith and Phil Dwyer, severely depleted the City squad. David Powell and Richie Morgan, neither of whom had made the first-team squad so far this season, were called up as replacements. Powell's late inclusion necessitated a delay on landing at Budapest while the necessary visa was obtained.

18 September 1974   *1st Round, 1st Leg*   *Ulloi Stadium*
Budapest, Hungary   *Attendance: 20,000*

FERENCVAROS (1) 2   **CARDIFF CITY (0) 0**
Nyilasi 15, Szabo 80

FERENCVAROS: Geczi; Viczko, Balint, Mucha, Megyesi, Takacs, Nyilasi, Szabo, Pusztai, Kelemen, Mate.
CARDIFF CITY: Healey; Larmour (Impey), Murray, Powell, Pethard, Charles, Villars, McInch, Farrington, Showers, Anderson.

City battled throughout, but Ferencvaros – whose technical director was Florian Albert, holder of 75 Hungarian caps – were superior and might have won by a bigger margin. They attacked non-stop in the first half, but only had a goal from Ferenc Nyilasi to show for their efforts.

John Farrington should have equalised after a Willie Anderson centre rebounded off the crossbar, but he miskicked from close range and the chance was lost. With Don Murray marshalling the City rearguard, Ferencvaros were kept at bay until 18-year-old Ferenc Szabo doubled the lead with a hotly-disputed goal. Mucha had swung over a cross to dangerman Nyilasi, who nodded down to Szabo. The youngster scored from what Cardiff players insisted was a blatantly offside position.

City fought back and went close with shots from Derek Showers and Jimmy McInch, while Tony Villars forced Hungarian keeper Geczi into a spectacular save.

---

2 October 1974   *1st Round, 2nd Leg*   *Ninian Park*
Cardiff   *Attendance: 4,228*

CARDIFF CITY (0) 1   **FERENCVAROS (0) 4**
Dwyer 81   Takacs 53, Szabo 60, Pusztai 64,
                            Mate 89

CARDIFF CITY: Healey; Dwyer, Murray, Powell, Pethard, Smith, Villars (Impey), Vincent, Reece (Farrington), Showers, Anderson.

FERENCVAROS: Geczi; Eipel, Balint, Megyesi, Takacs, Mucha, Pusztai, Szabo, Kelemen, Ebedli (Onhaus), Mate.

(FERENCVAROS won 6-1 on aggregate)

Leighton Phillips' transfer to Aston Villa was confirmed, the fee a
massive £100,000. City did not halt transfer activity there, for they
offered Gary Bell and Don Murray to Newport County in exchange
for Steve Aizlewood. County rejected the deal.

Skipper Clive Charles missed the return leg through injury, as
did Peter Sayer. Don Murray was selected ahead of Richie Morgan,
despite having been offered to Newport County.

City performed manfully in the opening period without ever
looking likely to score. The outcome hinged on Jimmy Andrews'
half-time decision to push Phil Dwyer up front. While this tactical
shift pepped up City's front line, it cruelly exposed the back four
and allowed Ferencvaros to over-run the midfield.

Johnny Vincent had a good first half, but was totally overshadowed in the second by Laszlo Takacs, a 19-year-old clerk with the
Hungarian Meat Marketing Board. Takacs, playing only because of
the suspension of Juhasz, scored the opening goal and had a hand
in two of the others.

Dwyer headed in a Willie Anderson centre, but missed several
other opportunities. John Farrington, City's record £63,000 signing
from Leicester, came on for Gil Reece, but Ferencvaros were far too
good and deserved the victory sealed by Mate in the final minute.

It was City's worst defeat in ten years of European football, and
although it was inflicted by a side with European pedigree – Ferencvaros had won the Fairs Cup in 1965 – it proved that the Bluebirds' squad required urgent replenishments. The crowd was
Ninian Park's lowest for any first-team game, apart from Welsh
Cup-ties, since the War. This resulted in meagre receipts of £2,210,
peanuts for a club in desperate need of a major cash injection. But
come the end of the season, Cardiff City would be relegated.

In Round Two Ferencvaros knocked Liverpool out of the Cup-
Winners' Cup and marched all the way to the final, where they
were beaten 0-3 by Dynamo Kiev.

4

The Robins reach the Quarters

~~~~~~~~~~~~~~~~~~~~~~~~~~~~~~~
1975 – WREXHAM (League Division 3)
~~~~~~~~~~~~~~~~~~~~~~~~~~~~~~~

The Robins' second season in European competition began with victories in their first six home League games, but defeats in seven consecutive away matches. With home gates averaging just 3,000, money was scarce and there was little change in personnel from the 1972-73 season, when the Robins had reached the second round of the Cup-Winners' Cup. Graham Whittle and Mickey Thomas were injured for the visit of Djurgardens, though Thomas was also suspended for one game having been booked in both legs against Hajduk Split. Wrexham's reserve keeper was named as 16-year-old Eddie Niedzwiecki. In the home game four days before the first leg, an all-time low crowd of 2,654 saw the Reds defeat Gillingham 2-0.

Djurgardens had been Swedish champions four times and were currently second in the league. Strangely, they had never won the Swedish Cup, losing out to double winners Malmo to qualify for the Cup-Winners' Cup. Wrexham's opponents boasted five Swedish internationals in their squad.

17 September 1975   *1st Round, 1st Leg*   *Racecourse*
Wrexham   *Attendance: 9,009*

WREXHAM (1) 2   **DJURGARDENS (0) 1**
Griffiths 34, Davies 90   Krantz 52

WREXHAM: Lloyd; Hill, May, Davies G, Fogg (Lyons), Evans, Tinnion, Sutton, Griffiths, Ashcroft, Dwyer.
DJURGARDENS: Alkeby; Anderssen, Davidssen, Jacobssen, Berggren, Lindman, Samuelssen, Svenssen, Stenback, Karlsen, Krantz.
Referee: B Neilsen (Denmark)

Arfon Griffiths had Welsh hopes soaring when, in only his second first team appearance of the season, he drove in a rebound from fifteen yards. At 34, Griffiths was the oldest player on the field, and he almost made it two with a dipping volley which left Swedish Under-23 international goalkeeper Bjorn Alkeby helpless.

The Swedes equalised in the second half when Anderssen floated over a centre from the right and Sven Krantz headed in unmarked. John Neal sent on striker John Lyons in place of full-back David Fogg, as Wrexham fought to reclaim the advantage.

Svenssen went close for the visitors with one of their rare shots on goal, but then came Gareth Davies – glancing in a header from a Mel Sutton cross – to grab a last-minute winner.

---

1 October 1975   *1st Round, 2nd Leg*   *Olympic Stadium*
Stockholm, Sweden   *Attendance: 1,769*

DJURGARDENS (0) 1   **WREXHAM (1) 1**
Lovfors 70   Whittle 21

DJURGARDENS: Alkeby; Ericson, Berggren, Davidssen, Jacobssen, Lovfors, Lindman, Samuelssen, Karlssenn (Olsberg), Svenssen, Krantz (Stenback).
WREXHAM: Lloyd; Hill, May, Davies Gareth, Evans, Sutton, Tinnion, Thomas, Griffiths, Davies Geoff, Whittle.
Referee: W Reidel (East Germany)

                    (WREXHAM won 3-2 on aggregate)

The Robins made several changes for the away leg, some tactical, others enforced by injury. They now found themselves in the lower half of Division Three, still without an away point to their name.

Wrexham dominated the Swedes from the first whistle in the 65-year-old stadium. Arfon Griffiths and Mickey Thomas were outstanding in midfield on a pitch greasy from the afternoon rain. Mel Sutton found the net in the twelfth minute, but Geoff Davies had strayed offside. Midway through the first half Graham Whittle scored with his first shot in his first game back following a summer cartilage operation: goalkeeper Alkeby foolishly tossed a throw-out straight to Whittle, who volleyed the ball high to the right of the embarrassed keeper.

The Swedes rarely looked like getting back into contention, but a defensive lapse let in Per Lovfors, who steered in a goal from close range. In a rousing finale, Eddie May and Whittle were booked.

---

22 October 1975   *2nd Round, 1st Leg*   *Racecourse*
Wrexham   *Attendance: 9,613*

WREXHAM (2) 2   **STAL RZESZOW (0) 0**
Ashcroft 10, 34

WREXHAM: Lloyd; Hill, May, Davies G, Evans, Sutton, Griffiths, Thomas (Dwyer), Tinnion, Ashcroft, Whittle.
STAL RZESZOW: Jalocha; Sienrauski, Kowalec, Biel, Gawlik, Michaly-iszyn, Kozierski, Curylo (Janiszewski), Krawczyk, Napieracz, Miler.
Referee: Axelryd (Sweden)

The Poles of Stal Rzeszow were Wrexham's opponents in the next round. Stal were unique in being the only side to qualify for a major European competition by defeating a reserve team. In the previous season's Polish Cup they knocked out Row Rybnik, then beat their reserves in the final. It was no walkover – Rybnik Reserves had accounted for no fewer than four Division One sides en route to the final, including Gornik.

Stal, who beat Skied Oslo of Norway 8-1 on aggregate in Round One, had also gained promotion, following three seasons in Division Two. They were, however, having a tough time in the higher league, lying bottom with only one win from ten outings.

The Poles evidently knew little about Wrexham. One of their sports journalists identified 'Horace Blew' as the Welsh dangerman. Though Blew did indeed play for Wrexham, and Wales, that had been more than 50 years earlier. He had been dead for some time.

Wrexham outplayed the Poles and were full value for their two-goal lead. Arfon Griffiths, Mickey Thomas and Mel Sutton controlled midfield and had the Stal defence in all sorts of trouble.

The Robins scored in the tenth minute, when Thomas returned a Brian Tinnion centre and Bill Ashcroft stabbed the ball in from ten yards. Wrexham kept surging forward and Graham Whittle, Sutton and Gareth Davies all missed chances to increase the lead. The bearded Ashcroft claimed his second when Gawlik failed to control a Sutton centre. Ashcroft robbed the Polish defender and forced the ball in. But for good saves by Jalocha and Eddie May's header coming back off a post, Wrexham would have taken a bigger advantage to Poland.

Mickey Thomas had received a penicillin injection to counter an attack of boils. Late in the game he was substituted by Alan Dwyer.

---

5 November 1975   *2nd Round, 2nd Leg*   *Stal Rzeszow Stadium*
Rzeszow, Poland   *Attendance: 20,000*

STAL RZESZOW (0) 1   **WREXHAM (0) 1**
Kozierski 60   Sutton 84

STAL RZESZOW: Jalocha; Blaga, Besoi, Biel, Gawlik (Janiszewski), Dzlama, Kozierski, Curylo, Krawczyk, Napieracz, Kryzinakic.

WREXHAM: Lloyd; Hill, May, Davies G, Dwyer, Sutton, Thomas, Griffiths, Evans, Tinnion, Ashcroft.
Referee: A Kedewil (Luxembourg)

(WREXHAM won 3-1 on aggregate)

Wrexham aimed to become the first Division Three side to reach the quarter-final stage of a European competition, but suffered a setback when Graham Whittle was forced out of the second leg through injury. A squad of sixteen players, together with club officials, pressmen and some 60 fans flew from Manchester Airport to East Poland, 50 miles from the Soviet border. Within an hour of landing, the players were training on the Rzeszow pitch.

The Poles pulled out the stops but Wrexham defended stoutly. Brian Lloyd pulled off a string of fine saves, no doubt celebrating his call-up to the full Welsh squad to play Austria in the European championships. Polish international Marian Kozierski finally broke through on the hour, but the Robins stayed calm and counter-attacked with menace. Arfon Griffiths, Mickey Thomas and Bill Ashcroft went close before Mel Sutton tied the scores on the night.

---

3 March 1976   *Quarter-final, 1st Leg*   *Parc Astrid*
Brussels, Belgium   *Attendance: 35,000*

ANDERLECHT (1) 1   **WREXHAM (0) 0**
Van Binst 11

ANDERLECHT: Ruiter; Lomme, Broos, Vandendaele (Anderson), Dockx, Van der Elst, Haan, Coek (De Groote), Ressel, Van Binst, Rensenbrink.
WREXHAM: Lloyd; Evans, May, Davies G, Fogg, Sutton, Whittle, Griffiths, Thomas, Lee, Ashcroft.
Referee: M Raus (Yugoslavia)

Wrexham's quarter-final opponents were Anderlecht of Belgium, who warmed up for the first leg with a 7-1 win in a Belgian Cup-tie. Robins' players and officials flew from Liverpool, along with six jets chartered to carry more than a thousand fans to Brussels. Many others made the trip by road and cross-channel ferry.

A leading sports outfitters supplied Wrexham FC with two full sets of kit, including boots, and the new all-red kit was worn for the first time against Anderlecht.

Stuart Lee, a £13,000 signing from Bolton in November was rated doubtful, so Geoff Davies was added to the party. Both played, as did new Welsh Under-23 international Mickey Thomas, despite missing the last few games with hamstring trouble.

Included in the Belgian side were Arie Haan and Robbie Rensenbrink, stars of the Holland side beaten by West Germany in the 1974 World Cup final. The Belgium club were playing their 72nd European match and boasted nine internationals on their books.

Wrexham pushed forward at every opportunity against a team greatly experienced in Europe since appearing in the first European Cup back in 1955. Anderlecht became frustrated by the quick-tackling Welsh side and Eddie May, David Fogg and Gareth Davies won the aerial battle. Bill Ashcroft and Stuart Lee raided eagerly, but Lee was guilty of a bad miss in the first half.

When Fogg fouled Rensenbrink, Francois Van der Elst rolled the free-kick to Haan. He, in turn, found Gilbert Van Binst, and the burly front runner netted the game's only goal. Rensenbrink powered into the penalty area and cracked a fierce shot inches wide, but Wrexham continued to harry and chase, with Mickey Thomas and Arfon Griffiths in the thick of the action.

The Belgian side's finishing was erratic, though Haan did shoot narrowly wide just before the close. Upon the final whistle, the dejected home supporters booed their team off the field.

---

17 March 1976   *Quarter-final, 2nd Leg*   *Racecourse*
Wrexham   *Attendance: 19,648*

WREXHAM (0) 1   **ANDERLECHT (0) 1**
Lee 62   Rensenbrink 75

WREXHAM: Lloyd; Evans, May, Davies G, Fogg, Sutton, Tinnion, Whittle, Griffiths, Lee, Ashcroft.
ANDERLECHT: Ruiter; Van der Elst, Broos, Vandendaele, Dockx, Haan, Lomme, Ressel, Van Binst, Coek, Rensenbrink.
Referee: F Biwers (West Germany)

(ANDERLECHT won 2-1 on aggregate)

Following such a spirited performance, Wrexham were looking for bumper receipts from the second leg. They aimed to double their highest league gate of the season – the derby match against Chester – which drew a crowd of 10,486 – and almost did so.

Mickey Thomas missed the game due to an infected left shin, and Brian Tinnion was called up in his stead.

When Wrexham took the lead in the second half, with a Stuart Lee goal, the odds favoured the Welshmen going on to record an historic victory. Ashcroft, Tinnion and Sutton had combined to set up the score, with Sutton's drive across the face of the goal being turned in by Lee, lurking with intent at the far post.

Anderlecht's stylish strike-force of Van Binst, Rensenbrink and Ressel imposed themselves more in the second period, though at times they did not relish the keen tackling of Eddie May and Gareth Davies. In the 75th minute Wrexham were rocked by the goal that was to decide the tie. Rensenbrink cut inside the box and fired into the net off the post. In the final seconds, Ruiter made a spectacular save to keep out a Graham Whittle pile-driver. All Wrexham were left with was a standing ovation, after battling magnificently.

With the aid of playing in their own city, Anderlecht went on to defeat West Ham 4-2 in the final, staged at the Heysel Stadium. Robbie Rensenbrink, scorer of two goals in the final, finished as the competition's leading scorer with eight goals.

~~~~~~~~~~~~~~~~~~~~~~~~~~~~~~~~~~~~~~~

1976 – CARDIFF CITY (League Division 2)

~~~~~~~~~~~~~~~~~~~~~~~~~~~~~~~~~~~~~~~

The Bluebirds' fortunes took a turn for the better when a long unbeaten run earned promotion to Division Two. Cardiff also won the Welsh Cup, with victory over Hereford United.

Manager Jimmy Andrews strengthened his squad with the purchases of Doug Livermore, Tony Evans and Adrian Alston. John Farrington was swapped for John Buchanan of Northampton Town. Johnny Vincent and John Impey, both of whom played in the Ferencvaros ties of 1974, had left the club.

City were drawn to meet Servette of Geneva in the preliminary round. Youth-team coach Alan Sealey spied on their victory over Nantes, which enabled Servette to reach the final of the Alps Cup. The Swiss contingent were met at Heathrow by City representatives and accompanied to their hotel in Barry. Included in Servette's squad was Martin Chivers, who had signed from Tottenham in the summer.

Cardiff had problems to overcome, as several players had been injured in pre-season games, and the early start to the European campaign meant that the League season had not yet commenced. City's only competitive matches had been friendlies against Bangor City and Pwllheli. Willie Anderson faced a late fitness test, but Phil Dwyer was out, having dropped furniture on his foot at home and broken an ankle. He was replaced by Richie Morgan.

4 August 1976   *Preliminary Round, 1st Leg*   *Ninian Park*
Cardiff   *Attendance: 10,226*

CARDIFF CITY (0) 1   **SERVETTE (0) 0**
Evans 88

CARDIFF CITY: Healey; Charles, Morgan, Larmour, Pethard, Buchanan, Livermore, Campbell (Giles), Evans, Alston, Showers.
SERVETTE: Engl; Schnyder, Guyot, Bizzini, Valentini, Barberis, Hussner, Marchi, Pfister, Chivers, Muller (Thouvenel).
Referee: A Ponnet (Belgium)

City began tentatively, befitting a side short of match practice. Once into their stride, however, they showed glimpses of the form that earned them promotion. Transfer-listed Derek Showers presented the biggest threat to the well-organised Swiss defence. Only superb saves from Karl Engl in the Servette goal prevented Showers from getting on the scoresheet. Engl also thwarted Buchanan and Clive Charles. At the other end, Pfister and Muller provided most of the worrying moments for the City, and Ron Healey had to be at his best to save Pfister's flighted free-kick just before the interval.

City's only goal came from a Charles free-kick. Richie Morgan beat Chivers in the air and turned the ball across for Tony Evans to net with a low shot. As for Chivers, he made little impact until the final quarter, when his chipped shot was deflected over the bar.

---

11 August 1976   *Preliminary Round, 2nd Leg*   *Parc des Sports*
Geneva, Switzerland   *Attendance: 21,000*

SERVETTE (0) 2   **CARDIFF CITY (1) 1**
Bizzini 63, Pfister 86   Showers 34

SERVETTE: Engl; Schnyder (Barriquand), Guyot, Bizzini, Valentini, Barberis, Hussner (Thouvenel), Marchi, Pfister, Chivers, Muller.
CARDIFF CITY: Healey; Charles, Morgan (Pontin), Larmour, Pethard, Campbell, Sayer, Livermore, Alston, Evans, Showers (Anderson).
Referee: K Aldinger (West Germany)

(CARDIFF won on away-goals rule)

In a surprising development, chairman Stefan Terlezki confirmed that City would play no competitive match between the first and second legs. City checked into their £35 per night hotel, after an hour's delay, and headed straight to the Parc des Sports Charmilles.

Until they were reminded of UEFA regulations, Servette officials tried to refuse permission for Cardiff to train at the stadium. There was one report of the Servette groundsman being set to turn water hoses on the players if they did not leave the pitch. The Bluebirds were also indignant at comments from Martin Chivers that they would employ brute force to ensure victory. His words also upset Jimmy Andrews, a coach at Spurs during Chivers' time there.

The conditions suited City, as steady rain had been falling for 24 hours. Derek Showers, continuing his fine form from the first leg, scored a priceless away goal when the keeper failed to hold Peter Sayer's cross and Showers beat team-mate Tony Evans to the loose ball. It was Showers' first European goal and it repaid his selection – on account of his pace – ahead of John Buchanan.

Servette now needed to score three, and they attacked strongly in the second half. Just after the hour Ron Healey was beaten by full-back Bizzini, who turned in Schnyder's cross. By then, Richie Morgan's rib injury, sustained in the first half, was slowing him considerably and he was replaced by teenager Keith Pontin.

The tie turned on Healey's dramatic penalty save from danger-man Hans Pfister. The keeper blocked the kick and Bizzini lashed the rebound into the side netting, much to the delight of the travelling Cardiff fans.

Pfister, Servette's outstanding player, surged through to net a fine solo goal, but it was too late to save his team. City held out to win on the away-goals rule, the first time that Cardiff had taken advantage of the rule to progress in the competition.

---

15 September 1976   *1st Round, 1st Leg*   *Ninian Park*
Cardiff   *Attendance: 11,181*

CARDIFF CITY (0) 1   **DYNAMO TBILISI (0) 0**
Alston 74

CARDIFF CITY: Irwin; Charles, Morgan, Larmour, Pethard, Livermore, Alston (Sayer), Buchanan, Campbell (Showers), Evans, Anderson.
DYNAMO TBILISI: Gogiya; Khizavishvili, Kanteladze, Khinchagash-vili, Ebralidze, Chivadze, Machaldze, Chelebadze, Gutsaev, Kipiani, Kopaleyshvili.

City would be without Republic of Ireland international keeper Ron Healey for the ties against Dynamo Tbilisi, as he was undergoing ankle surgery. His place would be taken by able deputy Bill Irwin.

The Cardiff management warned supporters not to encroach on the pitch as that could result in serious consequences. The club had been reported for fans invading the field following Tony Evans' late goal against Servette. Work was done to fence off the enclosure and Canton Stand to prevent a repetition. The Bluebirds needed a gate in excess of 15,000 to break even, as the trip to the Soviet Union for the second leg would entail costs of about £8,000.

Adrian Alston, City's Australian striker, missed an easy chance when he miskicked with the goal at his mercy, but made amends in the second half when he chested down John Buchanan's cross and planted the ball past Tbilisi keeper David Gogiya. Two minutes later, suffering from cramp, he was replaced by Peter Sayer. Derek Showers also came on for Alan Campbell.

The introduction of City's substitutes forced Tbilisi to retreat, and they abandoned their adventurous play of the first half, based around their gifted players, David Kipiani and Vladimir Gutsaev.

---

29 September 1976   *1st Round, 2nd Leg*   *Dynamo Stadium*
Tbilisi, Soviet Union   *Attendance: 80,000*

DYNAMO TBILISI (1) 3   **CARDIFF CITY (0) 0**
Gutsaev 22, Kipiani 73,
Kanteladze 81 pen

DYNAMO TBILISI: Gogiya; Khizavishvili, Kanteladze, Khinchagashvili, Ebralidze, Chivadze, Machaldze, Chelebadze, Gutsaev (Tsereteli), Kipiani, Kopaleyshvili.
CARDIFF CITY: Irwin; Attley, Dwyer, Charles, Pethard, Larmour, Alston (Sayer), Livermore, Buchanan, Showers (Anderson), Evans.
Referee: B Spiegel (Austria)

                                   (DYNAMO TBILISI won 3-1 on aggregate)

Richie Morgan was ruled out of the second leg with a rib injury. Willie Anderson, Doug Livermore, Clive Charles and Derek Showers were also doubtful when the City party set off on the 2,500 mile trip to Tbilisi. They travelled via Moscow, where they checked into a hotel close to Red Square. A meal awaited them, though some players ate only the dessert, along with bread brought from Cardiff.

Assistant trainer Harry Parsons found himself in the hotel kitchen at 8.00 the next morning, helping the chef rustle up bacon and eggs for breakfast. All the ingredients had been brought along with them in hampers.

Although a guided tour of Moscow had been arranged, some players preferred to rest before the 1,000-mile onward flight to Tbilisi. It took two hours for the party to clear passport and visa controls. Most of the players were clad only in summer clothing and suffered badly, not being prepared for a sharp drop in temperature. Items of kit apparently went missing, and Bill Irwin's leather hold-all was damaged beyond repair. There was a further hold-up while he filled out a claim form.

On arrival, City trained for two hours at the Tbilisi stadium, observed by more than 1,000 curious local onlookers. Match tickets cost around 75 pence, with the dearest seats priced at £1.60.

The decision by Jimmy Andrews to change the formation at the last moment backfired. To overcome the loss of Richie Morgan, he brought in Brian Attley and employed Freddie Pethard as sweeper. Buchanan and Livermore were booked as Cardiff manned the barricades, but the referee angered City even more when he turned his back after Anderson had been brought down in the area.

Tbilisi were coached by Slava Metreveli, cousin of the famous tennis player, Alex Metreveli. The home side squared the aggregate scores midway through the first half, when Gutsaev evaded a tackle from Charles and rifled a shot in off the near post.

In the 72nd minute the linesman flagged for handball by Phil Dwyer out by the touchline. The City players ceased playing – insisting afterwards they had heard the referee blow – but substitute Tsereteli carried on and crossed to Kipiani, who beat Irwin from close range. The goal stood.

Nine minutes later Tbilisi were awarded a spot-kick, which was converted by left-back Kanteladze. But for a number of fine saves from Irwin, City would have suffered an even heavier defeat.

~~~~~~~~~~~~~~~~~~~~~~~~~~~~~~~~~~~~

1977 – CARDIFF CITY (League Division 2)

~~~~~~~~~~~~~~~~~~~~~~~~~~~~~~~~~~~~

Another helping of European football awaited Bluebirds fans, even though City had been beaten in the Welsh Cup final by Shrewsbury Town. As an English club, the Shrews were ineligible, so City's place was assured merely by getting to the final.

League form had deserted Cardiff, however. They were without a win in Division Two, lying one point from the bottom. Having narrowly avoided relegation at the end of the previous term, it looked like City had a long hard season ahead of them. Added to which, the Safety of Grounds Act had effectively reduced the capacity at Ninian Park to just 10,000.

Adrian Alston and Derek Showers had departed from the club, but City had recruited Paul Went from Portsmouth. Keith Robson, a new signing from West Ham United, was ineligible for the Cup-Winners' Cup, and Robin Friday was unwell, so did not train. City would also be without John Buchanan, who was serving a one-match suspension for two bookings received in the previous Cup-Winners' Cup campaign.

Austria Memphis, a Viennese side, had made a useful start to the season and were lying second on goal-difference behind Innsbruck. The unusual kick-off time of 5.00 was agreed after consultation between the club and South Glamorgan County Council, who were concerned about the lack of emergency lighting at the ground.

14 September 1977   *1st Round, 1st Leg*   *Ninian Park*
Cardiff   *Attendance: 3,631*

CARDIFF CITY (0) 0   FK AUSTRIA MEMPHIS (0) 0

CARDIFF CITY: Irwin; Dwyer, Went, Pontin, Attley, Byrne, Campbell, Livermore, Sayer, Evans, Giles (Grapes).
AUSTRIA MEMPHIS: Weninger; Sara R, Obermeier, Baumeister, Paritz, Daxbacher, Sara J, Gasselich, Zach, Pirchner, Morales (Drazan).

The combination of early kick-off time, together with City's poor start to the season, enticed the lowest crowd ever for a European fixture at Ninian Park. Those fans who made the effort to attend were treated to a dismal game, with Cardiff never able to impose any superiority over their opponents.

Both sides created and wasted scoring chances and Robert Sara, the Memphis full-back, twice cleared off the line from Peter Sayer. Tony Evans had a blistering shot tipped over the bar by Memphis' second-string keeper Weninger. Phil Dwyer played up front as a makeshift centre-forward but lacked support. The Austrians showed flashes of pace and penetration, and Irwin was called into action several times, particularly in the closing stages.

The result did little to alleviate the Bluebirds' desperate financial straits, and they were forced to go cap in hand to local businesses to help them out. In an attempt to increase numbers through the turnstiles, the club reduced entrance fees from £1.00 to 50 pence for OAPs and children. Elsewhere, the Football League did an about-turn, overturning their earlier ban to permit advertising on shirts during league games. The downside was that the BBC refused to cover matches where shirt advertising was involved.

City recorded their first win of the season on 24 September, when a Fulham side, including George Best, were beaten 3-1.

---

28 September 1977   *1st Round, 2nd Leg*   *Weststadion*
Vienna, Austria   *Attendance: 15,000*

FK AUSTRIA MEMPHIS (0) 1   CARDIFF CITY (0) 0
Baumeister 52

AUSTRIA MEMPHIS: Baumgartner; Sara R, Obermeier, Baumeister, Daxbacher, Sara J, Martinez, Zach, Pirchner, Gasselich, Morales.
CARDIFF CITY: Irwin; Attley, Went, Pontin, Pethard, Byrne, Campbell, Sayer, Buchanan, Dwyer (Bishop), Evans.
Referee: M Kustyn (Poland)

                    (AUSTRIA MEMPHIS won 1-0 on aggregate)

After a power struggle at the club, chairman Stefan Terlezki had been ousted, and replaced by Newcastle businessman Bob Grogan.

Club doctor Leslie Hamilton and physiotherapist Tudor Jones were important members of the Cardiff party which flew out from London for the second leg with Austria Memphis. Tony Evans and Peter Sayer were both struggling to shrug off injuries, and Steve Grapes was ruled out from even making the trip.

The Bluebirds had not won an away tie in Europe since beating Nantes 2-1 in November 1970. They now turned in another feeble performance, though they received little impartiality from the referee. He penalised Phil Dwyer almost every time he challenged for the ball and disallowed what looked to be a legitimate Dwyer goal just after the interval by blowing for handball.

Midway through the second half Jimmy Andrews pulled off Dwyer, who already had a yellow card and was in danger of getting a red. Andrews sent on Ray Bishop in his place. Brian Attley squandered Cardiff's best chance with a weak shot easily gathered by Baumgartner in the Memphis goal. The Austrians went through, thanks to Baumeister's deflected shot, and reached the final at the Parc des Princes, where they were beaten by Anderlecht. It was the Belgian club's second Cup-Winners' Cup success in three seasons.

1978 – WREXHAM (League Division 2)

Arfon Griffiths was now in his second season in charge at the Racecourse, having successfully claimed the Division Three title in his first year. He also became the first person to both play and manage a Welsh side in European competition.

In what had been one of the best seasons in Wrexham's history, the Robins also lifted the Welsh Cup after defeating Bangor City. Bill Ashcroft had left to join former manager John Neal at Middlesbrough, but shrewd purchases by Griffiths – who brought in Dixie McNeil and Les Cartwright – strengthened the squad.

In a surprise move, Griffiths also swooped for Everton's keeper, Dai Davies. He replaced Brian Lloyd, who had played almost 250 consecutive games for City. The Robins warmed up for their tie against NK Rijeka – eighth in the Yugoslav First Division – with an unbeaten start to their first ever season in Division Two. Though the defence looked solid, with one goal conceded in five opening games, the attack gave rise to concern by scoring just three goals.

13 September 1978   *1st Round, 1st Leg*   *Kantrida Stadium*
Rijeka, Yugoslavia   *Attendance: 12,000*

NK RIJEKA (2) 3 **WREXHAM (0) 0**
Tomic 35, Durkalic 45, Cukrov 73

NK RIJEKA: Avramovic (Ravnic); Makin, Hrstic, Cukrov, Radin, Juricic, Durkalic, Fegic (Bursac), Tomic, Ruzic, Desnica.
WREXHAM: Davies D; Hill, Davies G, Roberts, Whittle, Sutton, Thomas, Cartwright, Shinton, McNeil (Williams P), Lyons.

The Kantrida Stadium on the Adriatic coast is one of the most picturesque grounds in Europe – overshadowed by 300-feet-high cliffs rising dramatically above the arena – but the Wrexham players were far too busy to enjoy the view. The Robins gave the Yugoslavs too much scope and were punished by some adventurous attacking play. Rijeka were fast, fluent, and impressive going forward, which they did for much of the match, to the background accompaniment of an enthusiastic brass band.

For half an hour the Robins matched their hosts, and though the Rijeka forwards gave Dai Davies a testing time, Bobby Shinton, John Lyons and Dixie McNeil all screwed shots wide when they might have done better.

Wrexham's wayward finishing was made to pay when Edmond Tomic hammered a shot from 25 yards inside the near post. McNeil almost responded at once when his glancing header from Mel Sutton's cross struck an upright, but the home side stepped up the pace and capitalised upon a mistake by Davies to extend their lead. The keeper fumbled a cross and Sali Durkalic headed into an empty net. Nikki Cukrov lashed in the third goal after his first attempt struck Graham Whittle and rebounded kindly for him.

Wrexham sent on 18-year-old Peter Williams in place of Dixie McNeil, but the Robins' cause was not helped when John Roberts was sent off two minutes from time for a crude tackle on Cukrov.

---

27 September 1978 *1st Round, 2nd Leg* *Racecourse*
Wrexham *Attendance: 10,469*

WREXHAM (0) 2 **NK RIJEKA (0) 0**
McNeil 54, Cartwright 65

WREXHAM: Davies D, Hill, Cegeilski, Davies G, Whittle, Thomas, Shinton, Sutton (Lyons), Cartwright, Williams (Griffiths), McNeil.
NK RIJEKA: Avramovic; Makin, Hrstic, Cukrov, Radin, Juricic, Durkalic (Car), Fegic (Bursac), Tomic, Ruzic, Desnica.
Referee: N Rolles (Luxembourg)

(NK RIJEKA won 3-2 on aggregate)

Wrexham's hopes of staying alive in the competition looked slim, particularly with Roberts suspended and Alan Dwyer still unfit. Graham Whittle continued as an emergency left-back, and Peter Williams started a match for the Robins for the first time. He had not played since his brief appearance as a substitute in the first leg, after suffering a reaction to a smallpox injection.

Wrexham suddenly found the form that lifted them out of Division Three last term. They laid siege to the Yugoslav goal, and the rattled visitors were forced to bring on two defensive substitutes in an attempt to keep the rampant Reds at bay. Even so, they were indebted to Avramovic for preventing Wrexham turning the tie on its head. Twice he saved from McNeil, and then used his body to block a goal-bound shot from Williams.

It was McNeil who finally opened the scoring, taking a pass from Mel Sutton and driving in low from ten yards. Les Cartwright then exchanged passes with John Lyons to net a second goal. Lyons had replaced Mel Sutton in an attempt to provide more firepower.

Forced to go for broke, and score again to level the tie, Wrexham left themselves exposed and Dai Davies had to stay alert to thwart Rijeka's breakouts. Fortunately, they never showed the attacking flair which had earned them a commanding first-leg lead. Griffiths brought himself on for Williams in the closing quarter, but – even with Mickey Thomas playing a blinder – the Reds were denied.

~~~~~~~~~~~~~~~~~~~~~~~~~~~~~~~~~

1979 – WREXHAM (League Division 2)

~~~~~~~~~~~~~~~~~~~~~~~~~~~~~~~

Though beaten by Shrewsbury in the Welsh Cup final, Wrexham took their place in Europe because of UEFA's ruling that banned English winners of the competition. New Robins striker Mick Vinter – a close-season signing from Notts County – was keen to make his European debut, but needed intensive treatment on a strained thigh in an effort to be fit for the first leg against FC Magdeburg of East Germany. Definitely out was Mickey Evans, but he was put to good use, providing Wrexham with a dossier on their first-round opponents. Joey Jones had returned to the club from Liverpool, and reverted to full-back in place of the ineligible Terry Darracott. Assistant manager Mel Sutton had recovered from injury to take his place in the starting line-up.

FC Magdeburg had an impressive record in the Oberliga. Since 1964 they had been East German champions three times and cup winners on five occasions. They were also past holders of the Cup-Winners' Cup itself, having defeated AC Milan 2-0 in the 1974 final at the Feyenoord Stadium, Rotterdam. All eleven of Magdeburg's current starting line-up were East German internationals. Their leading scorer was Joachim Streich, holder of 64 East German caps. As for Wrexham, they started their second season in Division Two in fine form, with four wins from their first six matches.

19 September 1979   *1st Round, 1st Leg*   *Racecourse*
Wrexham   *Attendance: 9,802*

WREXHAM (1) 3   **FC MAGDEBURG (2) 2**
McNeil 2, Fox 61, Buxton 72   Streich 13, Hoffman 41

WREXHAM: Davies D; Jones, Davies G, Roberts, Dwyer, Giles D, Fox, Sutton, Hill, McNeil, Whittle (Buxton).
MAGDEBURG: Heine; Raugust, Dobbelin, Sequin, Delker, Mewes, Pommerenke, Steinbach (Tyll), Streich, Thomas, Hoffman.
Referee: T Manssen (Denmark)

Wrexham began in astonishing fashion with a 73-second goal. Keeper Dirke Heine tipped away a shot, David Giles crossed the ball back in, and Dixie McNeil's glancing header looped into the net. Giles, incidentally, joined the growing band of players to have appeared in European competitions for two different Welsh clubs, having previously made two appearances for Cardiff City.

Despite the goal, the East Germans wrested the initiative, and when Steinbach hurdled a couple of lightweight tackles, Streich was on hand to drill home from twelve yards. Just before the interval Magdeburg took the lead – a mix-up between Gareth Davies and John Roberts let in Martin Hoffman for an easy score.

Early in the second period Graham Whittle made way for Steve Buxton, and within four minutes Wrexham had levelled. The giant Heine punched out a cross under challenge from Buxton, and Steve Fox ran in to drive the ball into the unguarded net.

Wrexham regained the lead with the best goal of the game. Fox – a £90,000 buy from Birmingham – swapped passes with McNeil. The ball was laid back for Buxton to curl a magnificent goal.

---

3 October 1979   *1st Round, 2nd Leg*   *Heinrich Gerner Stadion*
Magdeburg, East Germany   *Attendance: 22,000*

FC MAGDEBURG (1) 5   **WREXHAM (2) 2 (aet)**
Hoffman 28, 55 pen, Mewes 89   Vinter 24, Hill 30
Steinbach 92 pen, Streich 119

MAGDEBURG: Heine; Raugust, Dobbelin (Tyll), Sequin, Delker, Mewes, Pommerenke, Steinbach, Streich, Thomas, Hoffman.

WREXHAM: Davies D; Jones, Davies G, Roberts, Dwyer, Giles D (Buxton), Sutton, Fox, Hill, Vinter, McNeil (Whittle).
Referee: S Thine (Norway)

(MAGDEBURG won 7-5 on aggregate)

The fit again Mick Vinter was recalled in place of Graham Whittle. This was the only change in the Wrexham team for the second leg. The squad flew out from Speke Airport, Liverpool, and landed in West Berlin. From there they were escorted into East Berlin via Checkpoint Charlie.

The magnitude of the task confronting the Robins could be gauged from the fact that their East German opponents had lost only two of 24 European home ties. Yet Wrexham were within 90 seconds of a place in the second round when they fell victim to a calamitous error. Wrexham were leading 5-4 on aggregate when Alan Dwyer under-hit a back-pass to Dai Davies. The ball was seized upon by Martin Hoffman, who set up a goal for Siegmund Mewes which took the tie into extra-time. It was a blow from which the Robins never recovered.

Yet everything had started so well, with Mick Vinter raising Welsh hopes with the first goal, only for the East Germans to rally and level the score through Hoffman.

A fine goal by Alan Hill two minutes later restored the Robins' advantage, which they held to half-time. They were pegged back by the first of two doubtful penalties. Vinter was alleged to have fouled Streich and Hoffman netted from the spot. Dixie McNeil had a goal disallowed for offside as Wrexham resumed control.

Mewes' goal made it 5-5 overall, and with both sides having scored two away goals the tie went into extra-time. After just two minutes, Wrexham conceded a second penalty, this time for Jones' sliding tackle on Streich. Steinbach scored the spot-kick.

The influential Streich rubbed salt into Wrexham's wounds by completing the scoring a minute from time. Davies found himself with little cover, most of his team-mates being camped upfield.

~~~~~~

1980 – NEWPORT COUNTY (League Division 3)

~~~~~~

County had reached the Welsh Cup final for the first time since they were humbled by Borough United in 1963. They were assured of entry into Europe no matter the outcome, as Shrewsbury Town were their opponents. An emphatic 5-1 aggregate victory over the two legs left little doubt that the Gwent side had earned their place on merit.

But with just one home win, Newport had started poorly in Division Three and were near the foot of the table. Notwithstanding, Steve Lowndes and Nigel Vaughan had been selected in Mike England's World Cup squad to play Turkey and Czechoslovakia. Lowndes had scored in Wales Under-21s' 2-0 victory over their Dutch counterparts in Dordrecht, accepting a scoring chance created by former County player Mark Aizlewood. The other Welsh goal had come from Liverpool reserve Ian Rush.

County were drawn against the part-timers of Crusaders from Northern Ireland, who arrived in Wales with two days to spare before the first leg. Manager Ian Russell, a Belfast schoolteacher, had increased training from two to three nights a week in an attempt to improve fitness levels. Crusaders were no strangers to European football, having played eight ties in all, but they were still searching for their first win and had only five goals to their name.

County's first choice keeper, Gary Plumley, had fractured a finger and his place was taken by Mike Dowler.

16 September 1980   *1st Round, 1st Leg*   *Somerton Park*
Newport   *Attendance: 6,285*

NEWPORT COUNTY (2) 4   CRUSADERS (0) 0
Gwyther 7, Moore 8,
Aldridge 56, Bruton 58

NEWPORT COUNTY: Dowler; Walden, Bruton, Oakes, Relish, Vaughan, Tynan, Lowndes, Moore, Gwyther, Aldridge (Elsey).
CRUSADERS: McDonald; Thompson, Gorman, Mulhall, Gillespie, Whiteside, Jess, Fellowes, Byrne (King), Currie, Rice (Cromie).
Referee: G Smith (Scotland)

The anticipated high attendance was much reduced because of the heavy rain, which also made the playing conditions difficult.

The tie was effectively settled in the opening minutes, when County raced into a two-goal lead. David Gwyther opened the scoring with a looping header from Richard Walden's free-kick. Gwyther also contributed to the second goal a minute later, when he carved out a chance for Kevin Moore.

Despite almost continuous Newport pressure on the Crusaders' goal, the Irishmen still found time to make isolated breakaways and Dowler was called upon to make several fine stops. John Aldridge made the game safe before being replaced by Karl Elsey, and Dave Bruton rounded off the scoring to give County an almost insurmountable first-leg lead to take to Belfast.

1 October 1980   1st Round, 2nd Leg   Seaview Ground
Belfast, Northern Ireland   Attendance: 1,300

CRUSADERS (0) 0   NEWPORT COUNTY (0) 0

CRUSADERS: McDonald; Currie, Gorman, Mulhall, Gillespie, Thompson, Jess (Byrne), Fellowes, King, McPolin (Whiteside), Rice.
NEWPORT COUNTY: Plumley; Walden, Oakes, Bruton (Davies), Relish (Elsey), Tynan, Vaughan, Lowndes, Moore, Gwyther, Aldridge.

(NEWPORT won 4-0 on aggregate)

According to manager Len Ashurst, the cost of the away leg was estimated at £3,000, roughly equal to the revenue lost due to the reduced attendance at Somerton Park. Fortunately, funds were generated for the club to break even over the two ties.

Confidence was low after four successive league defeats, and the situation was exacerbated when the Newport directors gave Ashurst permission to talk to Bristol City with a view to taking over as manager at Ashton Gate. On a brighter note, Plumley was fit and resumed in place of Dowler. That was the only team change.

The uneven bounce and strong wind suited Crusaders' long-ball tactics, and their undoubted enthusiasm caused Newport problems. It was a low-key performance by Ashurst's side, with their finishing far from impressive. David Gwyther headed straight at the keeper in the opening minute, and John Aldridge missed a simple chance during the second half. The final whistle marked only the second time in ten European ties that the Irishmen had avoided defeat.

---

22 October 1980   2nd Round, 1st Leg   Haugarsund
Haugar, Norway   Attendance: 4,522

HAUGAR (0) 0   NEWPORT COUNTY (0) 0

HAUGAR: Schiefloe; Vikanes, Hestvik (Undahl), Sorensen, Solberg, Burnett, Christopherson, Helmdahl, Nilsen, Osborne, Foleide.
NEWPORT COUNTY: Plumley; Walden, Bruton, Oakes, Bailey, Vaughan, Lowndes, Tynan, Moore, Gwyther, Aldridge.
Referee: H Harryson (Sweden)

The next round saw County drawn against the Norwegian amateurs of Haugar, who had defeated FC Sion of Switzerland to reach this stage. Haugar were only promoted from Division Three one season earlier, but were now involved in a play-off with Mjoendalen for promotion to Division One. They had been beaten in the final of the Norwegian Cup by league champions Viking Stavanger.

The County squad, with Neil Bailey and Karl Elsey on stand-by for the injured John Relish and Tommy Tynan, flew from Cardiff Wales Airport along with supporters and assorted pressmen. New keeper Mark Kendall was ineligible, so Gary Plumley resumed.

The waterlogged pitch gave cause for concern and the hosts were required to lay down tons of sand and sawdust to make the pitch half-playable.

County had few problems in keeping a third clean sheet, but once again their attack was off colour. John Aldridge had a scoring chance in the 36th minute but the goalkeeper blocked his effort. The same player had a second-half goal-attempt cleared off the line, but that was all County had to show as an attacking force.

The Norwegian Second Division side seldom looked like losing the tie, and might even have snatched victory in the closing stages. Dennis Burnett, Haugar's ex-Millwall player-manager, urged his side on for one final effort and Peter Osborne – an English striker signed from non-league Gravesend – headed wide when well placed.

---

4 November 1980   *2nd Round, 2nd Leg*   *Somerton Park*
Newport   *Attendance: 8,855*

NEWPORT COUNTY (2) 6   HAUGAR (0) 0
Gwyther 13, Lowndes 44, Aldridge 57,
Tynan 60, 79, Moore 76

NEWPORT COUNTY: Plumley; Walden, Bruton, Oakes, Vaughan, Lowndes, Tynan, Bailey, Moore, Gwyther, Aldridge.
HAUGAR: Schiefloe; Vikanes, Larsen, Sorensen, Solberg , Burnett, Christopherson (Undahl), Helmdahl, Nilsen, Osborne, Foleide (Straume).
Referee: C McGrath (Ireland)

(NEWPORT won 6-0 on aggregate)

The Newport directors hoped for a bumper crowd at Somerton Park for the second leg to offset their travelling costs for the first. Entry to Round Three could also mean an expensive away trip, and that had to be accounted for.

The Norwegians used Bristol as their base. They were bubbling with confidence after their 3-0 play-off victory against Mjoendalen, which earned them a Division One place for the first time in their history. Their players were on £50 per man to beat Newport, a sum that – if they were successful – would be paid in gift vouchers.

County had run into form with three successive league wins, and once again the only change from the league side would be Gary Plumley in goal in place of the ineligible Mark Kendall.

The large crowd – which once again meant that the club broke even over the two legs – were quickly rewarded when Dave Gwyther headed in Steve Lowndes' cross.

County's midfield trio of Lowndes, Neil Bailey and Tommy Tynan never gave the visitors time to settle, and Bailey – a free transfer from Burnley – sent over a perfect cross for Lowndes to net the second on half-time. John Aldridge put his name on the scoresheet when diving to head home Kevin Moore's free-kick, and Tynan made it 4-0 minutes later when he finished off a stunning move with keen precision. The shell-shocked Norwegians conceded further goals from Moore and Tynan as County registered their best European victory. Haugar had gone six games without conceding a goal, while the last time Newport had hit six goals in a match was against Llanelli in a 1967 Welsh Cup-tie.

---

4 March 1981   *Quarter-final, 1st Leg*   *Ernst Abbe Sportsfeld*
Jena, East Germany   *Attendance: 25,000*

CARL ZEISS JENA (1) 2   **NEWPORT COUNTY (1) 2**
Raab 22, 85   Tynan 39, 89

CARL ZEISS: Grapenthin; Brauer, Schnuphase, Krause, Lindemann, Trocha, Schilling, Sengewald (Hoppe), Kurbjuweit, Raab, Vogel (Beilau).
NEWPORT COUNTY: Plumley; Walden, Oakes, Davies, Relish, Lowndes, Elsey, Vaughan, Moore, Tynan, Gwyther.
Referee: R Bjornstad (Norway)

County's quarter-final opponents were Carl Zeiss Jena who – as SC Motor Jena – had defeated Swansea Town in the 1961 competition. They were a side brimming with international players and would provide a severe test for County's Third Division outfit.

The East Germans had defeated FC Rot-Weiss Erfurt 3-1 to win their domestic cup, and in the previous season's UEFA Cup had disposed of First Division West Bromwich Albion by winning both legs. They had progressed to the quarter-finals in the European Cup (1970-71), Fairs Cup (1969-70) and the UEFA Cup (1977-78), and so were a team with obvious pedigree.

Newport were in fine form, however, and had lost only one of their previous ten League and cup games. Fearing a huge financial loss from their endeavours, County opted to make a thirteen-hour journey by plane and coach instead of booking a more expensive direct flight. They were held up on the border for two hours before being allowed to enter East Germany. About 100 supporters travelled to the match independently, but the club could only obtain 30 match tickets, leaving the remaining fans to watch the game on television in Jena.

The gulf in class was apparent from the opening minutes, as County were forced to soak up tremendous pressure. But in a courageous performance they twice came from behind to register one of the finest results ever achieved by a Newport side.

The East Germans scored first when John Relish failed to clear, leaving 22-year-old physical education teacher Jurgen Raab to put away Lothar Kurbjuweit's cross.

Tommy Tynan hit back before half-time, when he latched onto a Grant Davies free-kick to strike an angled drive into the net. Transfer-listed goalkeeper Gary Plumley gave a flawless display, but was powerless to prevent Raab netting his second following a corner-kick with just five minutes remaining.

Once more County fought back, and in an amazing finish David Gwyther set up a second equaliser for Tynan.

---

18 March 1981   *Quarter-final, 2nd Leg*   *Somerton Park*
Newport   *Attendance: 18,000*

NEWPORT COUNTY (0) 0   CARL ZEISS JENA (1) 1
Kurbjuweit 27

NEWPORT COUNTY: Plumley; Walden, Davies, Oakes, Relish, Lowndes, Elsey, Vaughan, Tynan, Gwyther, Moore.
CARL ZEISS: Grapenthin; Brauer, Schilling, Burow (Krause), Kurbjuweit, Schnuphase, Overmann, Sengewald, Beilau, Raab, Vogel.
Referee: H Lund-Sorensen (Denmark)
                    (CARL ZEISS JENA won 3-2 on aggregate)

On arrival, the Carl Zeiss Jena party were given a welcoming civic reception by Newport Borough Council. The East Germans were without Lindemann and Krause, both of whom had received a second caution in Jena. John Aldridge was still unfit, so County relied on the same eleven as had started the first leg.

County attacked from the whistle and Hans-Ulrich Grapenthin, in the Jena goal, was the busiest man on the field. Keith Oakes and David Gwyther both saw goal-bound shots cleared off the line, and Tommy Tynan struck the bar.

The East Germans, lying fourth in their league, were forced into a ten-man defence as Newport attacked at every opportunity. Yet the tie was settled, against the run of play, when Gary Plumley – who had played so defiantly in both legs – allowed a 25-yard free-kick from Jena skipper Kurbjuweit to squeeze under his body.

John Relish was booked by the referee, along with three Jena players, as play became ever more desperate. A 1-1 draw would have taken County through on away goals, but for all their pressure they could not score. Their final chance fell to Oakes, but his header was saved by Grapenthin. The only consolation for the Gwent side was the revenue from record gate receipts.

The East Germans went on to defeat Benfica 2-1 on aggregate in the semi-final. Despite scoring first, through Hoppe, they lost the final 1-2 to Dynamo Tbilisi in Dusseldorf. Only 9,000 spectators bothered to turn up at the Rheinstadion to watch it.

Brayley Reynolds in action for Swansea Town

Colin Webster, Swansea Town's centre-forward

Owen Griffiths (right) with Bangor City players and the Welsh Cup (1962)

Bangor City players talk tactics with manager Tommy Jones (left)

Bangor City, winners of the Welsh Cup (1962)

Bangor City players in the San Paolo Stadium, Naples (September 1962)

Borough United, winners of the Welsh Cup (1963)

Cardiff manager Jimmy Scoular and players before flying to Lisbon (December 1964)

Cardiff City's King, Toshack, Clarke and Murray training in Tashkent (March 1967)

Newport's Tynan and Aldridge attack the Crusaders' goal (September 1980)

Haugar's groundsman inspects pitch with Newport players (October 1980)

Carl Zeiss Jena's keeper clears against Newport (March 1981)

Jeremy Charles scores for Swansea against Braga (August 1982)

Barry Horne scores in the last minute against Porto (October 1984)

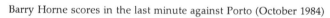

Barry Horne wheels away after scoring against Porto (October 1984)

Wrexham's Andy Edwards goes close against Roma (November 1984)

Goalkeeper Dai Davies came out of retirement to play for Bangor City v Fredrikstad

Atalanta's Stromberg is closely watched by Merthyr's Roger Mullen (September 1987)

Merthyr Tydfil players celebrate victory over Atalanta (September 1987)

Merthyr Tydfil players sightseeing in Bergamo, Italy (September 1987)

Merthyr's Gary Wager in action against Atalanta (September 1987)

Cardiff City (1988-89)

Swansea's Andy Legg beats Jean-Luc Ettori of Monaco (September 1991)

The first match for a Welsh club in the European Cup

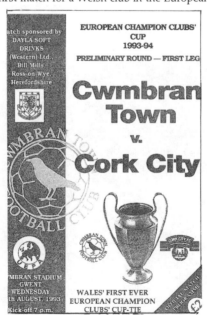

Bangor's Lee Noble races down the flank against Akranes (August 1994)

The Icelanders of Akranes repulse another Bangor attack (August 1994)

Ton Pentre programme cover v Uniao Leira (July 1995)

Bangor's Kevin Langley sets up an attack against Widzew Lodz (August 1995)

Afan Lido's debut in the UEFA Cup (August 1995)

Conwy United programme cover (June 1996)

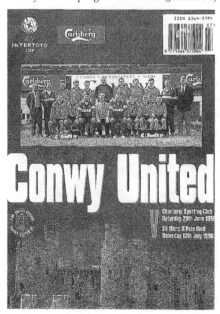

Skonto Riga attack the Newtown defence (July 1996)

Barry Town's Tony Bird tussles with a Dinaburg defender (July 1996)

Llansantffraid take the field against Ruch Chorzow in Poland (August 1996)

Ruch Chorzow's keeper foils a Llansantffraid attack in Poland (August 1996)

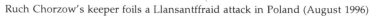

Barry's Dave O'Gorman is blocked by a Vasutas defender (August 1996)

Ebbw Vale programme cover (June 1997)

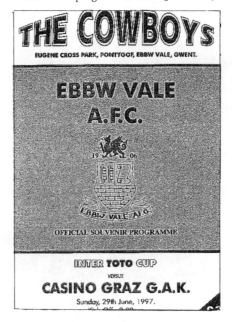

Inter CableTel's historic meeting with Celtic (July 1997)

Eifion Williams in League of Wales action for Barry Town (1997-98)

Kongsvinger v Ebbw Vale programme cover (June 1998)

Bangor's Chris Sharratt takes on two Haka players at Farrar Road (August 1998)

5

SWANSEA CITY TO THE FORE

~~~~~~

1981 – SWANSEA CITY (League Division 1)

~~~~~~

In 1970 Swansea Town had become Swansea City. In the 1981 Welsh Cup final they faced Hereford, winning 2-1 on aggregate, though a European place would still have beckoned had they lost.

Surprisingly, this was the first occasion a Welsh entry had come from the top English division – a consequence of John Toshack's inspired reign at the Vetch Field, which had hoisted the Swans from the depths of Division Four. In fact, following a 3-2 win over Notts County, Swansea occupied the giddy heights of second place. They would, however, have to take on their opponents without recent signings Colin Irwin and Max Thompson, who were ineligible. Jeremy Charles was also an absentee, through injury.

Lokomotiv Leipzig had drawn the short straw and had to contest the competition's only preliminary round tie. They lost the first leg, too – 0-2 in Romania to Politechnica Timisoara – before scoring five goals without reply on their own ground.

16 September 1981   *1st Round, 1st Leg*   *Vetch Field*
Swansea   *Attendance: 10,295*

SWANSEA CITY (0) 0   **LOKOMOTIV LEIPZIG (0) 1**
Kinne 70

SWANSEA C: Davies; Robinson, Hadziabdic, Stevenson, Attley (Evans W), Rajkovic, Curtis, James L (Giles), James R, Latchford, Mahoney.
LOKOMOTIV LEIPZIG: Muller; Joachim, Baum, Dennstedt, Zotzche, Kinne, Moldt, Liebers, Altmann, Schoene, Kuhne.

Lokomotiv immediately funnelled back into defence, blotting out Swansea's attack through weight of numbers. Two early Leighton James crosses promised some reward, but generally Swansea were unable to breach the close-marking Leipzig defence. James was hurt in the 24th minute in a heavy tackle and was replaced by David Giles. The former Cardiff City and Wrexham star thereby became the first player to appear for *three* Welsh sides in Europe.

Lokomotiv rarely threatened in the first half, and it was Alan Curtis who came closest to breaking the stalemate when his shot on the turn whistled past the German post.

Despite further Swansea pressure early in the second period, Leipzig spurned a golden chance when Peter Schoene shot wide from in front of the posts. Wyndham Evans came on for Brian Attley, but apart from a Robbie James effort that also flew wide, the East Germans continued to stifle Swansea's attacks at birth.

The only goal stemmed from an error by Welsh international keeper Dai Davies. The former Wrexham custodian spilled a shot from Lutz Moldt, and Jurgen Kinne poked the ball over the line. The goal was no more than the visitors deserved. Having shut-up shop in the first half, they attacked for long periods in the second.

---

30 September 1981   *1st Round, 2nd Leg*   *Sports Forum*
Leipzig, East Germany   *Attendance: 22,000*

LOKOMOTIV LEIPZIG (2) 2   SWANSEA CITY (0) 1
Kinne 13, Moldt 22   Charles 78

LOKOMOTIV L'ZIG: Muller; Baum, Fritzsche, Dennstedt, Zotzche, Kinne, Moldt, Liebers, Altmann, Bornschein (Schoene), Kuhne (Frossmann).
SWANSEA C: Davies; Robinson, Hadziabdic, Stevenson (Evans W), Mahoney, Rajkovic, Curtis, Charles, James L, James R, Latchford (Giles).
Referee: M Ciulli (Italy)

(LOKOMOTIV LEIPZIG won 3-1 on aggregate)

The Swansea club was in subdued mood for the return leg following news of the death of former Liverpool boss Bill Shankly. Swansea had a strong Merseyside contingent in their team, and the managerial trio of John Toshack, Phil Boersma and Doug Livermore were all ex-Liverpool players. By chance, the Swans next Division One match after the European tie would be at an emotional Anfield.

Swansea's task in Leipzig was formidable. Toshack had never yet been on a winning side in East Germany, having played there three times for Liverpool and once for Wales.

Leipzig attacked from the start and Kuhne shot into the side-netting. Andreas Bornschein was injured crossing the ball, and was substituted by Peter Schoene with just one minute on the clock.

Disaster struck the Swans when Jurgen Kinne stole in on the blind side of John Mahoney to head in Schoene's cross. The enterprising Dieter Kuhne set up the East Germans' second goal, fending off Nigel Stevenson and Ante Rajkovic. Dai Davies fumbled his cross and Lutz Moldt had an easy tap-in from point-blank range.

Swansea's hopes of salvaging the tie were struck a severe blow in the 41st minute, when Alan Curtis was sent off. Having been involved in an ugly scuffle with Stefan Fritzsche, Curtis was seen to elbow, and then slap, his opponent in retaliation.

Stevenson had been given a torrid time and was replaced at the interval by Wyndham Evans. A further unsavoury incident ensued when Davies and Kinne collided, and the referee had to swiftly break up the ensuing scuffle. Swansea's goal came from a ghastly error by the Lokomotiv keeper, Rene Muller, who dropped a Leighton James corner at Jeremy Charles' feet.

In view of the ill-tempered game, it was little surprise to find the teams dispensing with the customary handshakes at the end.

1982 – SWANSEA CITY (League Division 1)

The Swans celebrated their successful debut season in Division One with a Welsh Cup victory over old rivals Cardiff City. Manager John Toshack had assembled an experienced team packed with international players. Only record signing from Liverpool, Colin Irwin, was uncapped in the team selected for the first leg at the Vetch against Portuguese opponents. Confidence was high, even though Alan Curtis was suspended.

17 August 1982 *Preliminary Round, 1st Leg* *Vetch Field*
Swansea   *Attendance: 10,614*

SWANSEA CITY (1) 3   **SPORTING BRAGA (0) 0**
Charles 42, 87, Cordoso 65 (og)

SWANSEA CITY: Davies; Marustik, Hadziabdic, Irwin, Rajkovic, Stevenson (Thompson), Kennedy, James L, James R, Charles, Latchford (Walsh).
SPORTING BRAGA: Helder; Artur, Cordoso, Nelito, Guedes, Serra, Oliviera, Paris, Gomes (Malheiro), Manoel, Santos.

Jeremy Charles, the Welsh international utility player, had been in fine form during the pre-season games, scoring seven times in four appearances. Charles opened the scoring towards half-time when he stabbed the ball home after Colin Irwin's mis-kick came back off a post. It was a triumphant return for Charles, who had missed most of the previous season on account of two cartilage operations.

The Portuguese side never exerted pressure on the Welshmen, even though they lost Nigel Stevenson through injury in the 25th minute. He was replaced by Max Thompson.

Braga keeper Helder was kept busy in the second half as the Swans pressed home their advantage. Helder conceded a corner, pushing a header from new skipper Ray Kennedy over the bar. From the resultant Leighton James corner, the visitors' defence got into a tangle and Braga skipper Cordoso turned the ball into his own net.

The Swans were not finished, and after Braga had failed to clear a Robbie James shot, Charles was on hand to net his second goal. The driving rain failed to dampen the spirits of the Swansea fans who at long last had seen their favourites win a European tie.

---

25 August 1982   *Preliminary Round, 2nd Leg*   *Primeiro de Maio*
Braga, Portugal   *Attendance: 18,000*

SPORTING BRAGA (0) 1   SWANSEA CITY (0) 0
Marustik 88 (og)

SPORTING BRAGA: Helder; Artur, Cordoso, Paris, Guedes, Serra, Oliviera, Spencer (Fontes), Manoel (Malheiro), Gomes, Santos.
SWANSEA CITY: Davies; Marustik, Hadziabdic, Irwin, Rajkovic, Mahoney, James L, James R, Charles, Stanley, Latchford.
Referee: J Baumann (Switzerland)

(SWANSEA won 3-1 on aggregate)

John Toshack flew out to Portugal to make a form check on Braga, who were playing in a pre-season competition. Ray Kennedy and Max Thompson were injured and therefore omitted from Swansea's squad for the second leg. Kick-off time was put back to 9.30 pm, local time, by which hour the heat would not pose such a problem.

Swansea soaked up pressure, leaving Leighton James as the lone striker for most of the game. Even so, Bob Latchford almost netted in the thirteenth minute when his shot scraped the bar after a rare breakaway. The Portuguese were unable to prise open the packed Swansea rearguard, despite forcing ten corners in the first half.

The only goal of an uninspiring game came in the final minutes. Swans defender Chris Marustik attempted a goalmouth clearance but only succeeded in turning the ball past his own keeper.

Swansea were through, but their wider situation was less rosy. Chairman Malcolm Struel was critical of local apathy. Swansea had shown good form in Division One and had some class players, yet support was low. Lack of income meant no further players could be signed, at least not until the balance of the £150,000 fee agreed with Everton for the sale of Gary Stanley in 1981 had been paid off.

---

15 September 1982   1st Round, 1st Leg   *Vetch Field*
Swansea   *Attendance: 5,130*

SWANSEA CITY (4) 12   **SLIEMA WANDERERS (0) 0**
Charles 16, 77, Loveridge 18, 65,
Irwin 22, Latchford 42,
Hadziabdic 62, Walsh 75, 79, 86,
Stevenson 87, Rajkovic 88

Swansea City: Davies; Marustik, Hadziabdic, Rajkovic, Stevenson, Irwin,
Loveridge (James L), James R, Charles, Latchford (Walsh), Kennedy.
Sliema Wanderers: Zammitt; Losco, Camilleri, Tortell, Schembri.
Portelli, Caruana, Fabri, Tabone, Buttigieg, Aquilina.

The first-round draw gave the Welsh side a meeting with Sliema
Wanderers of Malta, who had been beaten by Borough United in
1963. The Maltese, who were not used to playing under floodlights,
never mind on grass, had only twice made the second round after
twenty years of European endeavour. On those famous occasions
they had capitalised upon even weaker opposition from Iceland and
Luxembourg. In 1980, however, they only lost 0-2 at home to
Barcelona, and 0-1 in the away leg – and that goal was a penalty.

The current Sliema side showed six survivors from the Barcelona
tie. They were coached by Edgar Izzo, general manager of an office
equipment company. Swansea were still without the suspended
Alan Curtis, sitting out the last game of his three-match ban.

The low-turn out for a European tie against weak opposition was
put down to increased ticket prices, though it was claimed by the
Swansea management that cheaper tickets would have made no
difference to the gate.

Sliema were put under the hammer immediately. Jeremy Charles
began the rout, and not long after came a first European goal for
Jimmy Loveridge, who hooked the ball over his shoulder for a spectacular score. Colin Irwin quickly made it 3-0, and when Bob Latchford rounded off the first half with the fourth goal, scribes began
poring through the record books.

Midway through the second half Latchford was replaced by Ian
Walsh and the substitute duly helped himself to an eleven-minute
hat-trick as the Swans attacked at will. The Swans' Yugoslavs –
Dzemal Hadziabdic and Ante Rajkovic – added their names to the
scoresheet, as did Nigel Stevenson, and there were second goals for
Loveridge and Charles.

The final scoreline stood as the biggest victory by a Welsh side in
any European competition. It even surpassed Swansea's own record
score of 8-0 against Hartlepool United in 1978. Understandably, the

result injected confidence into the team as they prepared for the visit of Liverpool to the Vetch on the following Saturday.

---

29 September 1982　　　　1st Round, 2nd Leg　　　　*Ta'Qali*
Valletta, Malta　　　　　　　　　　　*Attendance: 2,000*

SLIEMA WANDERERS (0) 0　　**SWANSEA CITY (3) 5**
　　　　　　　　　　　　　　　Curtis 19, 45, Gale 38, 74,
　　　　　　　　　　　　　　　Toshack 90

SLIEMA WANDERERS: Zammitt; Theuma, Camilleri, Losco, Schembri, Portelli, Buttigieg, Fabri, Tortell, Aquilina, Oherno.
SWANSEA CITY: Sander; Lewis, Stevenson, Hadziabdic, Marustik, Charles, Curtis (Toshack), Gale, Stanley, Loveridge, Kennedy.
　　　　　　　　　　　　(SWANSEA CITY won 17-0 on aggregate)

The Sliema party drowned their sorrows by sightseeing for three days in London before flying home to Malta. As for Swansea, they had tumbled down the table as a result of four consecutive losses and were in need of a big win – or any win, come to that – to restore morale.

Toshack rested Dai Davies, John Mahoney, Robbie James and Bob Latchford, and named himself as a substitute. Colin Irwin was also missing after incurring serious knee-ligament damage.

Sliema's goalkeeper was Alan Zammitt, a hotel receptionist, and he was likely to be the busiest player on the field. He happened to be the Maltese record holder over the 100 metre sprint. Their forward line was led by Simon Tortell, who had relinquished the chance of a career with Manchester United to study law.

Sliema's only goal attempt came in the opening minute, when Chris Sander spilled Aquilina's free-kick and 17-year-old Dudley Lewis headed the loose ball behind for a corner. Swansea appeared to take pity on their outclassed opponents, being content to treat the spectators to an exhibition, though that was difficult on a baked pitch scorched by the sun.

Alan Curtis struck twice in the first half, either side of a Darren Gale goal, and the 18-year-old Gale notched his second after the resumption. Toshack took over from Curtis on the hour for his first competitive match in twenty months, and drove in the final nail in Sliema's coffin by scoring in the last seconds. The 17-0 aggregate score was four short of the Cup-Winners' Cup record, registered by Chelsea against Jeunnesse Hautcharage in 1971, but eclipsed Cardiff City's Welsh record aggregate of 12-2 against Mjoendalen in 1969.

---

20 October 1982   *2nd Round, 1st Leg*   *Vetch Field*
Swansea   *Attendance: 9,505*

SWANSEA CITY (0) 0   **PARIS ST GERMAIN (0) 1**
                                    Toko 71

SWANSEA CITY: Davies; Marustik (James L), Hadziabdic, Evans, Lewis, Mahoney, Kennedy, Curtis, Stanley, Latchford (Walsh), James R.
PARIS ST GERMAIN: Baratelli; Fernandez, Pilorget, Bathenay, Guillochon, Lemoult, Zaremba, Ardiles, Dahleb, Toko, Kist.

The second-round draw brought an exciting pairing with French side Paris St Germain. The home leg was billed as the most prestigious European match staged in Wales for years, yet it still failed to draw a capacity crowd, despite the lure of Ossie Ardiles – the former Tottenham and Argentina World Cup star – in the Paris St Germain ranks.

The Swans were minus four centre backs, with Max Thompson, Colin Irwin, Ante Rajkovic and Nigel Stevenson all injured. John Toshack named 31-year-old Wyndham Evans in his starting eleven. Evans had been with the Swans since the dark days in Division Four, and was brought in after Jeremy Charles failed a fitness test.

Ossie Ardiles and Kees Kist were left marginalised as the Swans' defenders sought to nullify their classy opponents. Ray Kennedy let fly with a 30-yarder that forced Baratelli into a spectacular airborne save, and Robbie James saw a header blocked on the line, but for the most part the French defence was tightly organised around sweeper and captain Dominic Barthenay.

The only goal came when the home defence was split asunder by an astute pass from Pascal Zaremba, leaving Nambatingue Toko – who hailed from Chad – to shoot under Dai Davies' body.

Although the Swans enjoyed their share of possession, they were unable to get behind the visitors' defence. But with Leighton James on for Chris Marustik, they might still have saved the game. James crossed to the far post, Ian Walsh headed back into the middle, and Alan Curtis ballooned the chance high over the bar.

---

3 November 1982   *2nd Round, 2nd Leg*   *Parc des Princes*
Paris, France   *Attendance: 49,700*

PARIS ST GERMAIN (1) 2   **SWANSEA CITY (0) 0**
Kist 5, Fernandez 75

PARIS ST GERMAIN: Baratelli; Col, Pilorget, Bathenay, Guillochon, Lemoult, Zaremba, Fernandez, Dahleb, Toko, Kist (N'Gom).

SWANSEA CITY: Davies; Hadziabdic (Lewis), Stanley, Rajkovic, Stevenson, Mahoney, James L, Charles, Curtis, Latchford, James R.

(PARIS ST GERMAIN won 3-0 on aggregate)

After proving his fitness in two reserve outings, Neil Robinson was included in the squad for the second leg. He had not played a first-team game so far this season. Also included in the seventeen-man party was 18-year-old Gary Richards, a defender who had made his debut the previous season.

The second leg was expected to lure a full house to the Parc des Princes, with receipts grossing a staggering £380,000. This could be compared to Swansea's first-leg receipts of just £25,000.

Swansea's hopes were raised by the news that Ardiles was unfit, and with Bob Latchford now the Division One leading scorer they were optimistic about overturning the French side's advantage. John Toshack named himself as substitute in order to circumvent an FA of Wales touchline ban which was in force until March 1983.

Swansea's hopes were dashed as early as the fifth minute, when Dutch international Kees Kist slammed the ball home after Dai Davies had fumbled a shot from Toko, scorer of the only goal at the Vetch. Kist was a former Golden Boot winner, having scored 34 goals for AZ 67 Alkmaar in 1978-79. For good measure he had also been Golden Boot runner-up in 1980-81.

The Swans plugged away gallantly on a foggy Paris evening, and Jeremy Charles had a header saved by Baratelli, who also thwarted John Mahoney. Nigel Stevenson then struck a post to add to the Welsh side's misery.

In the second half, Charles elicited further fine saves from the French keeper, but the outcome was settled in the final quarter, when Luis Fernandez scored from inside the box after being put through by substitute Michel M'Gom.

~~~~~~

1983 – SWANSEA CITY (League Division 2)

~~~~~~

The Swans had been relegated from Division One, and, following the first games of the new season, found themselves bottom of Division Two. Their only ray of light had been their third successive Welsh Cup victory, when they beat Wrexham over two legs. Swansea had seen a big turnaround of personnel during the close season, with Robbie James, the two Yugoslavs, and others all leaving. Jimmy Rimmer had replaced Dai Davies in goal. Rimmer had been Aston Villa's keeper in their European Cup winning side of 1982, before an injury saw him replaced by Nigel Spink in the first minutes.

The dismay at being drawn yet again against East German opposition was tempered by the news that the winners would face Barcelona at the next hurdle. FC Magdeburg had won the East German cup with a 4-0 victory over FC Karl-Marx-Stadt.

24 August 1983   *Preliminary Round, 1st Leg*   *Vetch Field*
Swansea   *Attendance: 7,000*

SWANSEA CITY (0) 1   **FC MAGDEBURG (0) 1**
Walsh 80   Streich 89

SWANSEA CITY: Rimmer; Marustik, Lewis, Robinson, Stevenson, Stanley, Lake, Curtis, Kennedy, Charles, Latchford (Walsh).
MAGDEBURG: Heine; Raugust (Schossler), Stahmann, Wittke, Kraemer, Mewes, Pommerenke, Steinbach, Streich, Halata, Cebulla.

Highly rated Magdeburg could consider themselves lucky to escape with a draw after the Swans had created most of the chances. Magdeburg's defence held out until the closing minutes, when substitute Ian Walsh – having replaced Latchford – was on hand to prod in a rebound from a Ray Kennedy shot. It was Walsh's first kick of the game.

Swansea held the whip hand until the final minute, when Chris Marustik's blunder presented the visitors with the equaliser. He passed back to Rimmer from fully 35 yards out. Tragically, Rimmer was caught flatfooted on the line and the renowned Joachim Streich – now holder of 93 caps for East Germany and scorer in both legs against Wrexham – intercepted and ran in to score.

---

31 August 1983   *Preliminary Round, 2nd Leg*   *Ernst Gruber Stadion*
Magdeburg, East Germany   *Attendance: 25,000*

FC MAGDEBURG (1) 1   **SWANSEA CITY (0) 0**
Pommerenke 34

MAGDEBURG: Heine; Raugust, Stahmann, Wittke, Kraemer, Mewes, Pommerenke, Steinbach, Streich, Halata, Windelband.
SWANSEA CITY: Rimmer; Robinson, Marustik, Charles, Stevenson, Lewis, Curtis, Stanley, Kennedy, Walsh, Latchford (Gale).
                    (MAGDEBURG won 2-1 on aggregate)

Magdeburg had made a blistering start to their domestic season and topped the East German First Division. Two survivors of their 1974 Cup-Winners' Cup winning side remained in their squad – Jurgen Pommerenke and Martin Hoffman. The Swansea party endured a ten-hour journey from Wales before training on a pitch adjacent to the Ernst Gruber Stadion.

First-leg scorer Ian Walsh started the match in place of Darren Lake, but was unable to make any impression on the strong East German defence. The late goal conceded at the Vetch looked likely to prove costly. It meant that Swansea had to score to stay alive, and their task became doubly difficult once Pommerenke was allowed time and space to net on the half hour.

Although they frequently threw caution to the wind, the Swans were unable to trouble the Magdeburg defence, and not even the introduction of young Darren Gale for the tiring Bob Latchford had any effect. It was an anticlimactic end to three seasons of European football, and it would be another six years before Swansea would dig out their passports again.

6

THE NORTH WALIANS TAKE A HOLD

~~~~~~~~~~~~~~~~~~~~~~~~~~~~~~~

1984 – WREXHAM (League Division 4)

~~~~~~~~~~~~~~~~~~~~~~~~~~~~~~~

Wrexham's start to their second season in the football basement was plagued by so many injuries that the board had to confront the issue of raising funds for new players. Unfortunately, crowds were low, and the 1,849 present for the opening game against Port Vale would be bettered only six times during the season.

Although they had finished twentieth, the Robins had reached the final of the Welsh Cup, where they were beaten by Shrewsbury Town, thus gaining their entry into Europe by default.

Porto were last season's beaten finalists in the Cup-Winners' Cup, 1-2 victims of Juventus. Porto's 'spies' keenly observed Wrexham's 1-3 defeat by Peterborough, as a result of which they were understandably bullish that Porto – with eight current Portuguese internationals on their books, not to mention former Everton and Republic of Ireland striker Mick Walsh – would be too strong for the lowly Welsh outfit.

Wrexham could call upon only fifteen fit players, including two YTS lads, so they dashed to sign Chris Sander as goalkeeping cover from Swansea on a month's loan. He was, however, ineligible for the Porto match. Included in the home line-up was Barry Horne, a 22-year-old chemistry graduate from Liverpool University. Horne had been signed from Rhyl during the summer and was giving full-time football a try before deciding upon his future career.

19 September 1984   *1st Round, 1st Leg*   *Racecourse*
Wrexham   *Attendance: 4,935*

WREXHAM (0) 1   **FC PORTO (0) 0**
Steel 77

WREXHAM: Parker; King, Cunnington, Salathiel, Keay, Wright, Williams (Muldoon), Horne, Gregory, Steel, Rogers.
PORTO: Borota; Pinto, Inacio, Eduardo Luis, Enrico, Quim, Frasco, Magalhaes (Ademar), Gomes, Futre (Walsh), Vermelhinho.
Referee: J-F Crucke (Belgium)

Jim Steel was a constant thorn in the Portuguese defence as Wrexham's tactics of pumping high balls into the visiting penalty area paid dividends. During the second half, manager Bobby Roberts replaced Mike Williams with John Muldoon, and it was he who set up the only goal. Steel sent Muldoon away down the right flank, sprinted into the centre to meet his cross and glided a header past former Chelsea keeper Petr Borota.

Wrexham's towering man of the match was central defender Steve Wright, an inspiration to his team.

---

3 October 1984   *1st Round, 2nd Leg*   *Estadio das Antas*
Oporto, Portugal   *Attendance: 25,000*

FC PORTO (3) 4   **WREXHAM (2) 3**
Gomes 6, 27, Magalhaes 10,   King 39, 43, Horne 88
Futre 61

PORTO: Borota; Pinto (Walsh), Inacio, Lima Pereira, Enrico, Quim, Frasco, Magalhaes, Gomes, Futre, Vermelhinho (Quinito).
WREXHAM: Parker; King, Salathiel, Keay, Wright, Cunnington, Horne, Williams (Gregory), Steel, Edwards (Muldoon), Rogers.

(WREXHAM won on away-goals rule)

Lack of funds overshadowed Wrexham's performance in the first leg, a situation which was expected to be aggravated by a loss of £5,000 from the away trip. Wrexham's directors put on a brave face: they were so keen that the players enjoy their European adventure that they opened the champagne on the flight *to* Oporto, not on the way back. The man to watch in the Porto side would again be the Brazilian Fernando Gomes, who had won the previous season's Golden Boot award.

When Porto stormed into a 3-0 lead in swirling wind and torrential rain, all looked lost for the Robins. Gomes lost no time in setting the Portuguese cup holders on their way, scoring an early goal which was quickly followed by another from Jorge Magalhaes. Wrexham found it hard on the heavy pitch and Gomes was on hand to net his second goal with less than 30 minutes gone.

Skipper Jake King was the unlikely Robins saviour with two goals in four minutes just before the interval. Wrexham dominated much of the second period, but fell victim to a breakaway goal by Futre, which gave Porto a 4-2 advantage. As the Portuguese slackened towards the end, Barry Horne burst through for the vital away goal that put Wrexham through for an immortal triumph.

---

24 October 1984   *2nd Round, 1st Leg*   *Olympic Stadium*
Rome, Italy   *Attendance: 36,793*

AS ROMA (1) 2   WREXHAM (0) 0
Pruzzo 38 pen, Cerezo 49

ROMA: Tancredi; Oddi, Bonetti (Giannini), Ancelotti, Righetti, Maldera (Chierico), Conti, Cerezo, Pruzzo, Buriani, Iorio.
WREXHAM: Parker; King, Cunnington, Salathiel, Keay, Wright, Edwards, Horne, Steel, Gregory (Muldoon), Rogers.
Referee: L Padar (Hungary)

Wrexham were plucked out of the hat with AS Roma in Round Two. As all the Italian teams involved in European competitions had been drawn at home in the first leg, Roma officials suggested switching the first leg to the Racecourse. This suited the Robins – who would expect a better crowd for the first leg – but UEFA vetoed the proposal, there being no pressing reason for the change.

AS Roma were an experienced side which had suffered defeat on penalties by Liverpool in the 1984 European Cup final, played at their own Olympic Stadium. Their all-star line-up included Bruno Conti, Carlo Ancelotti, and the Brazilians Tonhino Cerezo and Paolo Falcao, who had been voted best player in the 1982 World Cup. Roma's league record showed five draws and a defeat in their first six matches, but significantly they had only conceded three goals.

By contrast, Wrexham lay sixth from bottom of Division Four, with three wins from eleven outings. Manager Bobby Roberts pinned back his ears when England stars Mark Hateley, Ray Wilkins and Graeme Souness – each of whom was currently playing in Serie A in Italy – volunteered tips on Roma's strengths.

In sweltering conditions, Wrexham held Roma at bay until the referee awarded the hosts a penalty. Pruzzo had headed on Conti's corner when, to the surprise of both sides, the referee was seen pointing to the spot. A Wrexham player had apparently handled. Pruzzo took the kick, sending Stuart Parker the wrong way. Wrexham chairman, Pryce Griffiths, was so angered by the decision that he stormed after the UEFA observer to protest.

The Robins might have equalised when Jim Steel nodded down a Jake King cross, but Kevin Rogers hurried his shot. The miss proved expensive: early in the second half Cerezo increased the Roma lead.

Wrexham tightened up at the back, and Steel's robust challenges resulted in both Bonetti and Maldera limping off to be substituted. Instead of concentrating on football, the Italians countered with fierce tackling of their own, one challenge on Barry Horne bringing a booking for Oddi. David Gregory missed a chance from a Rogers centre, but mainly it was the Italians who looked the more likely, as when Parker had to pull off fine saves to deny Conti and Ancelotti.

---

7 November 1984   *2nd Round, 2nd Leg*   *Racecourse*
Wrexham   *Attendance: 14,007*

WREXHAM (0) 0   **AS ROMA (0) 1**
                                     Graziani 68

WREXHAM: Parker; King, Cunnington, Salathiel, Muldoon, Wright, Edwards, Horne, Steel, Gregory, Rogers.
ROMA: Tancredi; Nela, Bonetti, Righetti, Falcao, Maldera, Conti, Buriani, Graziani (Iorio), Giannini, Chierico (Di Carlo).
Referee: A Martinez (Spain)

(ROMA won 3-0 on aggregate)

Roma were refused permission to train on the Racecourse, as the pitch was too heavy to allow a session under floodlights. They were instead given use of the all-weather surface in the Queensway Sports Complex, a big come-down compared to the facilities their superstar players were used to at the Olympic Stadium in the Italian capital.

Wrexham suffered a blow when Jack Keay dropped out through injury, but the Italian side were equally disadvantaged when finding themselves having to do without their influential Brazilian, Cerezo, for the same reason.

Paulo Falcao masterminded Roma's victory, controlling midfield yet venturing regularly into both goalmouths. The Robins contained the Italian aristocrats for over an hour, without really looking like wresting control from them. Parker saved brilliantly from Falcao in the eleventh minute, then foiled Buriani, who looked likely to score with a vicious drive.

Chances at the other end were few, though Gregory did have a goal-bound shot cleared off the line by none other than man-of-the-match Falcao.

Wrexham's dreams were finally extinguished when Conti broke away down the left flank. His pinpoint centre was met by Francesco Graziani, and the Italian international headed past Parker.

Aggrieved Wrexham supporters reacted to Roma's goal by hurling fireworks onto the pitch, as a response to which the referee threatened to abandon the game.

The one bright spot in Wrexham's elimination was their gate receipts, which proved to be a Racecourse record.

~~~~~~
1985 – BANGOR CITY (Northern Premier League)
~~~~~~

Bangor City were beaten 1-5 on aggregate in the Welsh Cup final by the holders, Shrewsbury Town, but as the only Welsh side in the final they were assured of a return to Europe whatever the result. Bangor spent £25,000 to bring their ground up to UEFA standard, and hoped to recoup half that money from ground receipts alone.

Work was carried out on the concrete and steelwork at the Farrar Road end and corrugated iron sheeting removed from the St Paul's end. Perimeter fencing was erected around the pitch, the toilets were renovated and additional emergency exits provided.

Manager John Mahoney – the former Welsh international and member of Swansea City's 1981 Cup-Winners' Cup side – persuaded 37-year-old keeper Dai Davies to come out of retirement and solve a goalkeeping crisis. Davies had made four appearances for Wrexham in the 1978 and 1979 competitions and seven for Swansea in 1981 and 1982, but had been retired for fifteen months. He was to be one of only two players in the Northern Premier side with Football League experience. The other was Mark Palios, formerly of Tranmere Rovers. An official party of 50 joined dozens of Bangor City supporters making their way to Norway by boat and train.

Fredrikstad lifted their domestic cup with a 3-2 replay victory over Viking FK Stavanger. They had started the new season with six wins and a draw from their first seven games. Included in their team were two full internationals and one Under-21 international.

18 September 1985   *1st Round, 1st Leg*   *Fredrickstad Stadium*
Fredrikstad, Norway   *Attendance: 2,611*

FREDRIKSTAD (0) 1   **BANGOR CITY (0) 1**
Deunk 87   Williams E 60

FREDRIKSTAD: Olsen; Sorli, Ahlsen, Deunk, Englebretsen, Thomassen, Jensen, Hansen VB (Rafn), Mathisen, Kristoffersen, Hansen V.
BANGOR CITY: Davies; Cartwright, Lunn, Evans, Banks, Armor, Urquhart, Palios, Williams V (McGuire), Williams E, Powell.
Referee: Gudmundssen (Iceland)

Fredrikstad looked poor, even though the cold but clear conditions favoured them. Dai Davies, holder of 52 Welsh caps, had little to do in a scrappy game in which the visitors created most of the chances.

It was no surprise when, on the hour, Bangor gained the vital away goal with a diving header from Everton Williams. The referee issued cautions to Gerry Banks and Gary Evans as the visitors took no prisoners in their determination to retain their advantage. Bangor held the lead until the final moments, when Hans Deunk nodded in an ill-deserved equaliser.

---

2 October 1985   *1st Round, 1st Leg*   *Farrar Road*
Bangor   *Attendance: 2,750*

BANGOR CITY (0) 0   FREDRIKSTAD (0) 0

BANGOR CITY: Davies; Cartwright, Lunn, Evans, Banks, Armor, Urquhart, Palios, Williams V, Williams E, Powell (McGuire).
FREDRIKSTAD: Olsen; Sorli, Ahlsen, Deunk, Jensen, Thomassen, Englebretsen, Hansen V, Mathisen, Kristoffersen, Rafn.

(BANGOR won on away-goals rule)

The attacking play of Vivian Williams was reputed to have so impressed the Fredrikstad management that they were prepared to bid £10,000 for him there and then. Manager Mahoney dismissed the rumours as ridiculous, as Williams had only been on the pitch for an hour, and, in any case – according to Mahoney – he was the 'homely type' with little interest in travelling far from his Llanerchymedd home.

The Norwegians played with the wind and driving rain at their backs in the first half and peppered the Bangor goal with shots from distant parts, knowing they would be similarly disadvantaged in the second half. Twice, goal-bound efforts from Fredrikstad hit the woodwork, first an eighth-minute header from Deunk and – after half-time – a shot from Steinar Mathisen.

Bangor slowly got to grips with the game. Shots from Reg Maguire and Bruce Urquhart were blocked on the line, while the Fredrikstad keeper, Jan-Erik Olsen, saved at Everton Williams' feet.

In the closing stages the visitors gambled everything on attack, knowing they had to score. McGuire was presented with a golden chance in a rare breakaway, but mis-kicked from just six yards. Urquhart also went close after weaving his way through the visitors' defence.

When the final whistle came, Bangor had won through on the away-goals rule which – had it been in force in 1962 – would also have seen them triumph over Napoli. Mark Cartwright, the 19-year-old Bangor City defender, soon discovered that a footballer's life is not all fun and games. He was fired from his job for taking time off to make the trip to Norway.

---

23 October 1985   2nd Round, 1st Leg   *Farrar Road*
Bangor   *Attendance: 5,181*

BANGOR CITY (0) 0   **ATLETICO MADRID (2) 2**
                               Da Silva 5, Setien 25

BANGOR C: Davies; Cartwright, Lunn, Evans, Banks, Armor, Urquhart (Whelan), Palios, McMullen (Williams V), Williams E, Powell.
ATLETICO MADRID: Fillol (Mejias); Julio Prieto, Tomas, Arteche, Ruiz, Setien, Carbrera (Rubio), Quique, Da Silva, Marina, Landaburu.

The former World Club champions exhibited their technical superiority and greater speed in a blistering opening spell that all but sealed the tie. The Uruguayan, Jorge Da Silva, put the Spanish side ahead early on, and when Quique Setien added a second midway through the first half it seemed likely that the floodgates would open.

Surprisingly, Atletico Madrid seemed to sit back after that, and almost paid the price as Palios urged his team forward in a second-half resurgence that would have deserved a goal. The quicksilver Spanish forwards were rarely seen in the second period, but Bangor were unable to make their possession count.

---

6 November 1985   2nd Round, 2nd Leg   *Vicente Calderon*
Madrid, Spain   *Attendance: 8,000*

ATLETICO MADRID (1) 1   BANGOR CITY (0) 0
Landaburu 27

ATLETICO MADRID: Mejias; Tomas (Balbino), Arteche, Sergio, Clemente, Minguez, Landaburu, Marina, Quique (Rubio), Carbrera, Da Silva.
BANGOR CITY: Davies; Cartwright, Lunn, Evans, Banks, Armor, Urquhart (Whelan), Palios, Williams V (McGuire), Williams E, Powell.
                               (ATLETICO MADRID won 3-0 on aggregate)

Dai Davies was again the Bangor hero, saving a Da Silva penalty in the 38th minute after Les Armor had handled on the line. The North Walians' blanket defence frustrated the skilful home side and earned grudging applause from the appreciative crowd.

Bangor were beaten by a superb free-kick from Jesus Landaburu in the first half. For the rest of the match, a combination of zestful tackling, Davies' defiance and bruised woodwork prevented any further score. Having weathered the storm, Bangor went close themselves: Armor fired narrowly wide and Palios shaved the bar with a blistering drive from the edge of the area.

~~~~~~~~~~~~~~~~~~~~~~~~~~~~~~~~

1986 – WREXHAM (League Division 4)

~~~~~~~~~~~~~~~~~~~~~~~~~~~~~~~~

Wrexham won a quick return to Europe by defeating Kidderminster Harriers 2-1 in a replayed Welsh Cup final after a 1-1 draw. Wrexham began the season harbouring debts of around £400,000, and needed a good cup run to bring in much-needed revenue.

Under Dixie McNeil, now in his second season as manager, the Robins had made a reasonable start to the new campaign and lay tenth in Division Four. McNeil had chopped and changed his team, and only four players remained from Wrexham's last European match, against AS Roma, just two years previously.

FC Zurrieq – a team of part-timers in Malta who trained for just two hours each evening – were pulled out of the hat as Wrexham's first-round opponents.

17 September 1986   *1st Round, 1st Leg*   *Ta'Qali*
Valletta, Malta   *Attendance: 4,000*

FC ZURRIEQ (0) 0   **WREXHAM (1) 3**
                              Massey 14, Charles 65, Conroy 74

ZURRIEQ: Duca; Camilleri C, Camilleri A, Cutajar L, Schembri A, Brincat, Scicluna (Cutajar O), Falzon, Schembri B, Ferrugia, Micallef.
WREXHAM: Pearce; Salathiel, Cunnington, Williams, Cooke, Comstive, Massey, Horne (Preece), Steel (Buxton), Charles, Conroy.
Referee: C Dimitriadis (Greece)

A sun-baked pitch and blistering heat presented more of a challenge than did Zurrieq. Little was seen of the home team and it quickly became a question of how many goals Wrexham could score.

In the event, wasteful finishing, allied to the state of the pitch, meant that all Wrexham had to show for their first-half sweat was a Steve Massey goal. Steve Charles later made it two, and a 30-yard drive from Mike Conroy – who had signed from Blackpool in the close season – concluded the scoring.

---

1 October 1986   *1st Round, 2nd Leg*   *Racecourse*
Wrexham   *Attendance: 2,793*

WREXHAM (3) 4   **FC ZURRIEQ (0) 0**
Massey 10 pen, 40, Steel 35,
Horne 85

WREXHAM: Pearce; Salathiel, Cunnington (Wright D), Williams (Jones F), Cooke, Comstive, Conroy, Horne, Steel, Massey, Emson.
ZURRIEQ: Pace; Camilleri C, Camilleri A (Serafa), Navarro, Schembri A, Brincat, Bonnici, Micallef, Schembri B, Cutajar, Ferrugia (Camilleri P).
Referee: O Olsen (Iceland)

(WREXHAM won 7-0 on aggregate)

Wrexham needed a crowd of at least 4,000 to recoup the £9,000 outlay on the first leg. Not surprisingly, they were already looking beyond the second leg and hoping for a good second-round draw to alleviate mounting debt problems.

The Robins cruised through to the next round, as expected, in a totally one-sided game. The Maltese team only managed two half-hearted goal attempts in the entire match. The poor attendance was blamed on the quality of the opposition, live TV coverage of the second half, and a hike in admission charges – a consequence of which was a heavy loss of revenue over the two legs.

The Robins went ahead when Steve Massey scored from the spot after Barry Horne had been felled in the box. Despite continual pressure, the home side failed to make further inroads until Jim Steel drove in a cross from Massey.

It was Massey who claimed the third goal, when he collected a Horne centre, slalomed past two defenders, and planted the ball in the net. Wrexham's fourth goal did not materialise until the closing minutes. Horne's shot was saved by Pace in the Zurrieq goal, but the Wrexham player gave the keeper no chance when he swooped on the rebound.

---

22 October 1986   *2nd Round, 1st Leg*   *La Romareda*
Zaragoza, Spain   *Attendance: 25,000*

REAL ZARAGOZA (0) 0   WREXHAM (0) 0

REAL ZARAGOZA: Ruiz; Casuco, Cortez, Julia, Mejias, Guerra, Yanez, Senor, Sosa (Juan Carlos), Herrera, Ayneto (Pineda).
WREXHAM: Pearce; Salathiel, Cunnington, Williams, Cooke, Comstive, Horne, Charles, Massey (Buxton), Steel, Emson.
Referee: G Briquet (France)

The North Walians were drawn against Real Zaragoza in the second round and hoped to improve on Cardiff City's fortunes in the 1964-65 competition when the Bluebirds went down 2-3 on aggregate.

Zaragoza had finished third in their First Division, but won the Spanish Cup by beating Barcelona 1-0. This season they were fifth from bottom, but it was a slightly false position as they had played all the top sides.

A welcome by-product of the ban on English clubs imposed in the wake of the Heysel Stadium disaster was that Welsh and Scottish clubs received greater media coverage than usual.

Chris Pearce, the Newport-born goalkeeper, had been injured in the victory at Orient and was only able to perform light training on arrival in Zaragoza. The evergreen Dai Davies – now running a bookshop – was put on standby in case Pearce was ruled out.

Wrexham gave their hosts a scare, and Jim Steel was cautioned in the opening minutes for excessively robust play. The referee felt the need to warn manager Dixie McNeil to keep his players under wraps. Shaun Cunnington blocked a shot from Rueben Sosa, and Zaragoza's skipper, Juan Senor, grazed the upright.

The Spanish side were without regulars Francesco Pineda and Alfonso Fraile, yet still forced numerous corners. Wrexham, strong in the air, nevertheless coped well with the home attacks. Rafael Cortez hit the bar early in the second half as Zaragoza became ever more desperate, but it was the Welshmen who almost claimed the opener when a shot from Neil Salathiel struck the woodwork.

McNeil sent on Steve Buxton for Steve Massey. The Spanish coach, Luis Costa, countered by replacing the tiring Rueben Sosa with Juan Carlos, but the Robins defended valiantly to the end.

---

5 November 1986   *2nd Round, 2nd Leg*   *Racecourse*
Wrexham   *Attendance: 14,515*

WREXHAM (0) 2   **REAL ZARAGOZA (0) 2 aet**
Massey 102, Buxton 107   Yanez 98, 104

WREXHAM: Pearce; Salathiel, Cunnington, Williams, Cooke, Comstive, Massey, Horne, Steel, Charles, Emson (Buxton).
REAL ZARAGOZA: Cedrun; Casuco, Biesa, Julia, Fraile, Guerra, Ayneto (Yanez), Senor, Sosa, Herrera, Pineda (Justes).
Referee: U Erikson (Sweden)

(REAL ZARAGOZA won on away-goals rule)

The Zaragoza players were reported to be on a bonus of £15,000 per man to reach the quarter-finals. Wrexham would be happy enough with a large crowd to help recoup the loss incurred on the first leg. Jim Steel came through a late fitness test, but otherwise Dixie McNeil had no team worries.

Wrexham fell foul of the rule-book after a dramatic extra-time had seen four goals scored in nine minutes. But for a flying save from Spanish keeper Cedrun in the 117th minute, Steve Massey'a header might have settled the tie in the Robins' favour.

In their previous three matches in the competition Wrexham had not conceded a goal. That record was preserved at normal time and was only punctured eight minutes into extra-time when Senor sent substitute Patricio Yanez clear. The Chilean international raced into the area and shot wide of Pearce. Despite a despairing lunge, Cunnington could only help the ball over the line.

Four minutes later Wrexham were on level terms when Steve Massey added the finishing touch to a Barry Horne free-kick. The Robins, however, now needed to win on the night, or fall foul of the away-goals rule.

But it was Zaragoza who reclaimed the lead two minutes later when Ruben Sosa broke down the left and crossed to Yanez. Jim Steel had proved a handful for the visiting defence throughout, and though he was denied by Cedrun's save, substitute Steve Buxton nipped in to net the rebound. Wrexham almost clinched the winner with Massey's ill-fated header, but it was not to be.

Wrexham raked in more from that one match than from an entire season's revenue. Receipts were close to £50,000, and TV and advertising were expected to raise that figure to £60,000. That was £5,000 more than expected from a full season's gate money.

~~~~~~
1987 – MERTHYR TYDFIL (Beazer Homes League)
~~~~~~

The Beazer Homes League part-timers claimed their only excursion into Europe with a 1-0 Welsh Cup final replay win over Newport County. For many years, Merthyr had been acclaimed as the best non-league team in Wales, but not since automatic entry into Europe had been conferred upon the Welsh Cup winners had they – until now – managed to win it.

Atalanta of Bergamo in Italy were the Martyrs' opponents. The townspeople of Merthyr entered into the spirit of things by decking out the streets in Italian flags and dressing up shop windows in an Italian flavour. Backed by a £1,500 donation from the Welsh Development Agency and the Wales Tourist Board, Merthyr's Leisure Services staged a week of fun and frolics which included – among other items – a spaghetti-eating competition and a Fiat car show.

Chairman John Reddy recruited 84 members of the South Wales Police Band to provide pre-match entertainment. This was thought to be a clever ruse to avoid additional policing costs in the unlikely event of any trouble in the ground. Although Atalanta were a second division side, beaten in the Italian Cup final by champions

Napoli, they were rich enough to pay out huge sums for players. Oliviero Garlini arrived from Inter Milan for £500,000, and Claudio Prandelli was signed from Juventus for another hefty fee.

Eligio Nicolini, Atalanta's free-kick expert, failed a late fitness test and was named as a substitute. Atalanta's playmaker was Glenn Stromberg, the flaxen-haired Swedish international, who had played for IFK Gothenburg against Arsenal in the quarter-final of the Cup-Winners' Cup in 1979-80. Arsenal had gone on to reach the final, where they lost on penalties to Valencia. Merthyr included Kevin Rogers, who starred for Wrexham in the 1984 competition.

16 September 1987   *1st Round, 1st Leg*   *Penydarren Park*
Merthyr   *Attendance: 8,000*

MERTHYR TYDFIL (1) 2   **ATALANTA (1) 1**
Rogers 34, Williams Ceri 87   Progna 41

MERTHYR TYDFIL: Wager; Baird, Mullen, Evans, Tong, Rogers, French, Beattie, Williams Chris (Jones P), Webley, Williams Ceri.
ATALANTA: Piotti; Gentile, Pasciullo (Nicolini), Prandelli, Barcella, Progna, Stromberg, Icardi, Garlini, Fortunato, Incocciati (Cantarutti).
Referee: Gilson (Luxembourg)

Kevin Rogers was Merthyr's hero, setting the Martyrs on their way with a goal in the 34th minute. The referee had penalised the Atalanta keeper, Ottorini Piotti, for taking too many steps. David Tong touched the free-kick to Rogers, and his deflected shot looped into the net. Celebrations were cut short when Domenico Progna popped up to equalise. Stromberg was the architect, with a fine cross, and though Gary Wager initially kept the ball out, he could not deny Progna at the far post.

High balls pumped into Atalanta's penalty area caused constant trouble for the visitors, but when awarded a free-kick wide out on the left in the closing minutes Merthyr opted for a change of tactics. Ceri Williams drove the kick hard and low, and the ball was deflected into the net off Progna.

In a rousing finale, Chris Baird unleashed a powerful long-range drive, but Piotti palmed the ball around the post.

---

30 September 1987   *1st Round, 2nd Leg*   *Stadio Communale*
Bergamo, Italy   *Attendance: 14,000*

ATALANTA (2) 2   **MERTHYR TYDFIL (0) 0**
Garlini 16, Cantarutti 20

ATALANTA: Piotti; Prandelli, Gentile, Fortunato, Progna, Icardi, Stromberg, Nicolini, Cantarutti, Incocciati (Barcella), Garlini.
MERTHYR TYDFIL: Wager; Tong, Mullen, Evans, Baird, Rogers, French, Beattie (Hopkins), Williams Chris, Webley, Williams Ceri (Williams S).
Referee: Mintoff (Malta)

(ATALANTA won 3-2 on aggregate)

Around 300 Merthyr fans made the trip to Italy for the second leg. Coach parties stayed at Lake Lugano and Lake Como, making their way to Bergamo on the day of the match. The Italians had been so gratified by the reception their squad received in Merthyr, that various newspaper editorials came out in praise of Welsh hospitality. For fans unable to travel, giant screens were erected in Merthyr.

Nicolini was fit to take his place in the starting line-up, with the Italians reported to be on £2,000 per player to win the tie. Atalanta lost little time in going ahead on aggregate, though both goals were controversial. Gary Wager had already scrambled away Garlini's twelfth-minute shot, but Atalanta's summer signing from Inter Milan was not to be denied. Shortly afterwards, he nudged the ball in at the far post when Andrea Icardi's drive seemed to be going wide. Garlini looked offside, but the linesman did not think so.

In the twentieth minute, Garlini was again to the fore when he supplied a cross which was met by Aldo Cantarutti. His fierce header struck the underside of the bar and, according to the referee, crossed the line.

Wager's saves prevented the Italians extending their lead but, to their credit, Merthyr refused to crumble. Dave Webley twice went close, and Rogers forced Piotti to save his rasping free-kick.

~~~~~~~~~~~~~~~~~~~~~~~~~~~~~~~~~~~~~~
1988 – CARDIFF CITY (League Division 3)
~~~~~~~~~~~~~~~~~~~~~~~~~~~~~~~~~~~~~~

The Bluebirds defeated Wrexham 2-0 at the Vetch Field to win the Welsh Cup and so earn a twelfth season in Europe. It was however, eleven years since they had last appeared in the competition. City manager Frank Burrows had endured a wretched start to the new season, suffering three defeats in the opening eight days.

Cardiff were paired with Derry City in the First Round. Burrows watched Derry's 1-1 draw against Dundalk, the League of Ireland champions, who had beaten Derry in the Republic of Ireland Cup final. Derry were last in Europe in 1965, when playing in the Northern Ireland League. They played an away tie in Anderlecht, but boycotted the competition when the Irish FA decreed that their Brandywell Stadium was unsuitable for staging European football.

When the 'troubles' in the Province intensified, other clubs refused to play in Derry, and in 1972 the club was forced out of the Irish League. The club was in limbo for thirteen years before being accepted into the League of Ireland, in the Republic, and had subsequently risen from the ashes to play in Europe once more. Derry City thereby claimed to have represented two different countries in European competition. Cardiff City had played them in 1950 in a friendly and won 2-0.

In view of threats received, warning the club against going to the troubled area, the Cardiff management advised fans not to travel. Curiously, the director at Derry City was Terry Harkin, who had played for Cardiff against Standard Liege in 1965. Of those who had campaigned for Derry to be accommodated in the League of Ireland, Harkin was the only survivor still at the club.

Derry City's links with Wales went further, for their manager was Jimmy McLaughlin – who had appeared for Swansea Town back in 1966 against Slavia Sofia – and the player-coach was Jack Keay, a Wrexham player in the 1984 competition.

Cardiff had numerous injury problems to contend with, following a 0-4 defeat at Bolton in which Mark Kelly was dismissed.

7 September 1988   *1st Round, 1st Leg*   *Brandywell Stadium*
Derry, Northern Ireland   *Attendance: 10,500*

DERRY CITY (0) 0   **CARDIFF CITY (0) 0**

Derry City: Dalton; Vaudequin, Brady, Curran, Neville, Doolin, Hegarty (Carlyle), Larkin, Speak, Gauld, Healy (Keay).
Cardiff City: Wood, Bater, Stevenson, Boyle, Platnauer, Wimbleton (McDermott), Curtis, Walsh (Bartlett), Gilligan, Gummer, Kelly.

Brandywell Stadium was located in the heart of the Republican Bogside area, and such was the interest in the game that many would-be spectators viewed proceedings from vantage points outside the ground, including the cemetery just below the Creggan Estate.

Despite the unusual circumstances, Cardiff never lost concentration and they prevented the home side from building any worthwhile attacks. Terry Boyle and Nigel Stevenson commanded the heart of the Bluebirds' rearguard, and though Derry looked a useful outfit when they adopted their swift-passing game, they were reduced for long stretches to long-ball tactics.

Both Curtis and Stevenson had played in the Cup-Winners' Cup for Swansea City, as had striker Ian Walsh. The pacy Kevin Bartlett was brought on for Walsh, but City failed to prise open the Derry defence for that all-important away goal.

Jimmy Gilligan had three clear-cut chances to put the result beyond doubt, but failed on each occasion. A header from an Alan Curtis free-kick, and a run which ended with a shot over the bar, ought to have brought some reward for the striker, still seeking his first goal of the season.

Despite misgivings about the pre-match security, Cardiff's visit was an unqualified success and the locals made the Cardiff players and officials very welcome.

---

5 October 1988   *1st Round, 2nd Leg*   *Ninian Park*
Cardiff   *Attendance: 6,933*

CARDIFF CITY (1) 4   DERRY CITY (0) 0
McDermott 20, Gilligan 47, 64, 76

CARDIFF CITY: Wood; Bater (Perry), Wimbleton (Morgan), Stevenson, Boyle, Curtis, Platnauer, Bartlett, Gilligan, Kelly, McDermott.
DERRY CITY: Dalton; Keay, Brady, Curran, Neville, Doolin, Carlyle (Quigg), Larkin, Speak, Cunningham, Healy.

(CARDIFF CITY won 4-0 on aggregate)

City had Steve Lynex and Ian Rodgerson under treatment, and Ian Walsh had an appointment at Lilleshall Rehabilitation Centre in a bid to sort out a groin injury.

24-year-old Jimmy Gilligan stole the spotlight in the second leg with the first hat-trick of his career. City took control from the opening minutes and might have scored straight from the kick-off, but Kevin Bartlett shot tamely at Derry keeper Tim Dalton. Brian McDermott settled the nerves when he met an Alan Curtis cross to head over the stranded Dalton.

It was after the interval that Gilligan made his mark, seizing on a poor back-pass by Kevin Brady and threading the ball inside the near post. After McDermott and Bartlett had seen goal-bound shots blocked, Gilligan was on hand again to net from less than a yard out.

An injury to Paul Wimbleton saw him replaced by John Morgan, but City's rhythm was not disrupted. Gilligan completed his hat-trick in the final quarter, when he headed in a Phil Bater centre.

Jason Perry, an 18-year-old with only three full league appearances, replaced a tiring Bater for his first taste of European football. Jonathan Speake – the Derry striker who had been the League of Ireland's top goalscorer the previous season – was allowed only one chance, but George Wood palmed his drive over the bar.

---

26 October 1988   2nd Round, 1st Leg   *Ninian Park*
Cardiff   *Attendance 6,155*

CARDIFF CITY (1) 1   **AARHUS (1) 2**
Gilligan 41   Kristensen B 7, 73

CARDIFF CITY: Wood; Platnauer (Rodgerson), Bater, Wimbleton, Stevenson, Boyle, McDermott, Bartlett, Gilligan, Kelly, Lynex (Curtis).
AARHUS: Rasmussen; Wachmann, Kristensen B, Stampe, Rieper, Andersen, Morup (Donnerup), Beck, Kristensen K, Lundkvist, Mortensen.
Referee: R Philippi (Luxembourg)

Having been drawn against Aarhus of Denmark in the next round, City were grateful to be handed a dossier on the Danes by Terry Nicholson, whose Glenavon team had been beaten 2-7 on aggregate in Round One.

The Danish party arrived at Cardiff (Wales) Airport without their top scorer Frank Pingel, and with the news that their club coach, Allan Larsen, would shortly be quitting to take up a similar position with Esbjerg, City's first ever European opponents.

Larsen had paid Anderlecht a club record £90,000 to secure the services of Under-21 international Henrik Mortensen, who would spearhead their attack. The Danes were expected to put all their efforts into the tie, having nothing else to play for. They were already out of contention in their First Division and had been knocked out of their domestic cup.

Though Aarhus did not live up to their pre-match reputation, they were still too strong for a City side missing the guile of Alan Curtis, who was not fully fit.

For the first quarter, Cardiff hardly had a kick. The Danish side went ahead when Bjorn Kristensen took advantage of weak tackling to combine with Per Beck and chip neatly into the corner. George Wood was called into action several times as Aarhus pressed for a second goal.

Gradually, City found their bearings. Nigel Stevenson had a shot cleared off the line and Steve Lynex forced a good save from Danish international keeper Troels Rasmussen.

City equalised in controversial fashion just before the interval, when Jimmy Gilligan's head connected with Brian McDermott's cross. Despite the efforts of Rasmussen to claw the ball back, the referee and linesman consulted and adjudged it to have crossed the line. City now went all out for the winner, but left themselves vulnerable to a counter-attack, which landed midway through the second period. Kristensen was normally a defender, but had been pushed into a striking role following the injury to Pingel. Now he strode forward and beat Wood from an acute angle.

---

9 November 1988   *2nd Round, 2nd Leg*   *Aarhus Stadium*
Aarhus, Denmark   *Attendance: 3,700*

AARHUS (2) 4   **CARDIFF CITY (0) 0**
Pingel 15, Beck 25, 75, Stampe 83 pen

AARHUS: Rasmussen; Wachmann, Stampe, Andersen K, Reiper, Kristensen B, Christensen, Morup, Lundkvist, Mortensen, Pingel.
CARDIFF CITY: Wood; Rodgerson, Platnauer, Wimbleton, Abraham, Boyle, Curtis, Bartlett (Wheeler), Gilligan, Kelly, McDermott (Lynex).

(AARHUS won 6-1 on aggregate)

The Cardiff squad made an early start for Heathrow, but the flight was delayed, as a result of which a training session in Denmark was lost. Nigel Stevenson was left behind for treatment, having been injured in the 1-0 win over Gillingham. His place in the side went to Gareth Abraham.

Aarhus had suffered a surprise home defeat by lowly Vejle, but with Karsten Christensen and Frank Pingel fit, they would be at full strength for the second leg. Cardiff's hopes seemed to rest with the goalscoring of Jimmy Gilligan. Of his seven goals to date, four had come in the Cup-Winners' Cup.

City's faint hopes of overturning their first-leg deficit vanished in the opening 25 minutes, when the Danes raced into a 2-0 lead. The Bluebirds were put under the cosh from the start, and after George Wood saved a Claus Thomsen shot, the rebound was slammed in by Frank Pingel.

Before Cardiff could recover, Per Beck received a pass from Pingel and stroked in the second goal. Pingel then hit the crossbar and Wood saved from Beck as the Danes continued to dominate the play.

In the second period Cardiff came more into the game and Mark Kelly was just wide with a spectacular shot. Frank Burrows brought on Steve Lynex and Paul Wheeler as City looked for a consolation score, but it was the home side who found the net again, through Beck, to climax a sweeping Danish move.

The Welsh side's misery was complete in the final minutes when Terry Boyle rashly toppled an Aarhus player in the penalty area. John Stampe made no mistake from the spot. It was City's worst defeat in 24 years of European football and their players trudged off the pitch with their heads low.

~~~~~~
1989 – SWANSEA CITY (League Division 3)
~~~~~~

The Swans defeated Kidderminster Harriers 5-0 in the Welsh Cup final to earn a sixth tilt at the Cup-Winners' Cup. They were now managed by the former Welsh international Ian Evans, but had not enjoyed a bright start to the new season. They were seventh from bottom in Division Three with four points from four games.

Swansea's veteran player-coach Tommy Hutchison – approaching his 42nd birthday – was experiencing his first taste of European football. In contrast, the Swans' skipper was 20-year-old Andrew Melville, one of the youngest captains in the Football League. Terry Boyle was also in the Swansea team, having signed from Cardiff City, for whom he played in the 1988 Cup-Winners' Cup against Derry City and Aarhus.

The Olympic Stadium to the north of Athens was an ultra modern arena used for big games only. Panathinaikos, for example, normally played in their own smaller, 25,000 capacity stadium.

Swansea prepared at a luxury hotel in a quiet suburb not far from the stadium They trained in the evening, on account of the September daytime heat in the Greek capital.

13 September 1989   *1st Round, 1st Leg*   *Olympic Stadium*
Athens, Greece   *Attendance: 40,000*

PANATHINAIKOS (2) 3   **SWANSEA CITY (0) 2**
Vlachos 4, 53, Saravakos 39   Raynor 63, Salako 81

PANATHINAIKOS: Abadiocakis; Hatziathanasiou, Kolev, Kalitzakis, Kalantsis, Mavrides, Saravakos, Antoniou, Dimopoulos (Hristodoulou), Vlachos (Polak), Georgamlis.
SWANSEA CITY: Bracey; Hough, Coleman, Melville, Boyle, James (Davey), Cobb, D'Auria (Legg), Hutchison, Raynor, Salako.

The young Swans – with eight of the team 23 years old or under – were subjected to a torrid opening by the Greek Cup holders, who had no fewer than ten internationals in their squad. Panathinaikos forced four corners in as many minutes, and took the lead when Lee Bracey parried a shot to Vlachos, who swept the ball home.

Swansea did threaten on occasions, and Hutchison set up Paul Raynor, whose header went straight at the keeper. The Greeks went two up when Saravakos flighted the ball over Bracey from 30 yards.

The second period began as the first, and after Vlachos was left unmarked for an easy score, the Swans were in danger of being overwhelmed. Evans brought on Andrew Legg for David D'Auria, and the move paid dividends when Swansea netted a smartly taken goal. A Gary Cobb corner-kick was headed down by Chris Coleman, the keeper pushed the ball away, but Raynor dived full length to head it back into the net. The goal was celebrated with rapturous applause from the 150 die-hard Swansea supporters who had made the trip.

Though Robbie James had to go off injured – replaced by Simon Davey – the visitors still probed for another goal. It eventually came after a Hutchison corner had been helped on by Terry Boyle. John Salako – on loan from Crystal Palace – smashed the ball in from close range.

In the closing minutes Salako had a great chance of squaring the tie, but side-footed wide from a low cross.

---

27 September 1989   *1st Round, 2nd Leg*   *Vetch Field*
Swansea   *Attendance: 8,276*

SWANSEA CITY (1) 3   **PANATHINAIKOS (0) 3**
James 31 pen, Melville 46, 67   Dimopoulos 51,
     Saravakos 72 pen, 85

SWANSEA CITY: Bracey; Hough, Melville, Boyle, Coleman, James, Phillips, Legg (D'Auria), Hutchison, Raynor, Salako.
PANATHINAIKOS: Abadiocakis; Hatziathanasiou, Kubanos, Kalantsis, Kalitzakis, Mavrides, Saravakos, Polak (Antoniou), Dimopoulos, Kolev, Georgamlis.
Referee: H Lund-Sorensen (Denmark)
     (PANATHINAIKOS won 6-5 on aggregate)

Mark Harris, a 26-year-old centre-half, was signed from Crystal Palace to shore up a Swans' defence that had shipped six goals against Reading in Swansea's worst start for four years. Harris, however, was ineligible for the second leg.

John Salako's loan period had been extended, so he was available, but doubts hung over the fitness of Robbie James, who was still requiring treatment on the ankle injury that forced his early substitution in Athens. James was passed fit.

Panathinaikos coach Gunther Bengtsson had to do without Vangelis Vlachos – who had crocked a knee – for the visit to the Vetch. Also missing was John Samares.

Swansea's fate was sealed five minutes from time with a goal by Dimitris Saravakos, though at one stage – with the home team 2-0 up – a place in the next round looked on the cards for the Swans.

The Greeks showed little interest in attacking and it came as no surprise when the home side scored the opening goal. Paul Raynor was shoved off the ball while going for a David Hough cross and the referee pointed to the spot. The Panathinaikos players jostled the official, to no avail, and Robbie James hammered the spot-kick into the corner.

The second half began splendidly, when Andrew Melville scored after Andy Legg's throw-in caused confusion in the Greek defence. Panathinaikos struck back with a controversial goal that was to prove decisive. Kalantzis clearly handled as he controlled the ball, and when Lee Bracey deflected it away, the unmarked Dimopoulos had the simple task of tapping into an empty goal.

The Swans returned to the offensive, and when Salako swung over a deep cross, Raynor played the ball back to Melville, who struck his second goal with an angled drive.

With less than twenty minutes left, Terry Boyle pulled Saravakos down and Panathinaikos were awarded a penalty themselves. The scorer of the Greek side's first goal picked himself up and did the business from the spot.

The tie was heading for extra-time when Saravakos broke clear and made no mistake with a low shot. Tears for Swansea.

7

MAN UNITED AT THE RACECOURSE

~~~~~~~~~~~~~~~~~~~~~~~~~~~~~~
1990 – WREXHAM (League Division 4)
~~~~~~~~~~~~~~~~~~~~~~~~~~~~~~

The National Stadium in Cardiff was the setting for the 1990 Welsh Cup final, but it was an inauspicious occasion as Hereford United defeated Wrexham 2-1.

A new UEFA ruling was to have serious consequences for Welsh and English clubs in European competitions. The rule stated that a club could use only four 'foreign' players unless they were signed before 3 May 1988. As English players were counted as foreigners, in Welsh eyes, it meant fielding depleted teams. Player-manager Brian Flynn, for example, would have to make his first appearance of the season, and his first in Europe since he featured in the Leeds team knocked out of the UEFA Cup by Uni Craiova of Romania in 1979. Mike Williams had recovered from three knee operations in eighteen months to make the starting line-up, and Flynn juggled his resources to field his strongest possible side. Coincidentally, English clubs – with the exception of Liverpool – were allowed back for the first time since the 1985 Heysel disaster.

With only one win from their opening four games, Wrexham were already falling adrift at the nether reaches of Division Four. It would get even worse: they would eventually finish bottom of the Football League.

In their last league game before entertaining Lyngby – who were fifth from bottom of the Danish League – the Robins were thrashed 1-4 at Blackpool. One of the Seasiders' goals came from ex-Hereford United striker Phil Stant, on loan from Notts County.

Wrexham's tie was overshadowed by Manchester United's with Pecsi Munkas of Hungary on the same evening. Harlech Television had planned to broadcast United's match, but were barred from doing so after Wrexham's objection was endorsed by the FA of Wales. Wrexham rightly complained that the live TV coverage would adversely affect their gate.

19 September 1990   *1st Round, 1st Leg*   *Racecourse*
Wrexham   *Attendance: 3,417*

WREXHAM (0) 0   LYNGBY (0) 0

WREXHAM: Morris; Phillips, Beaumont, Owen, Williams M, Sertori, Flynn (Hunter), Cooper, Preece, Worthington, Bowden.
LYNGBY: Rindom; Kuhn H, Wieghorst, Gothenborg, Christiansen C, Larsen, Helt, Schaeffer, Christiansen F, Rode (Andersen), Kuhn A.

Three fine saves from understudy goalkeeper Mark Morris paved the way for a show of defiance by the Robins. Morris was born in Chester but had signed prior to May 1988. He played in place of regular Vince O'Keefe. Andy Thackeray and Sean Reck also missed out. The Danes' technical superiority could not overcome Wrexham, who boasted just one home defeat in eleven European games.

Lyngby, without key midfielder Peter Neilson, played patiently, with the strong running Morton Weighorst – later to play for Celtic – pushing up at every opportunity. Wrexham's first shot on target came from Graham Cooper after fourteen minutes, but his drive was gathered by Jan Rindom in the Danish goal. Gareth Owen, only eighteen, almost gave the Reds the lead when he chipped in from the right, but the keeper hurried back to collect under the bar.

The second half saw few chances, but Morris, playing his first senior game in ten months, reserved his best save until the death, when he turned Michael Gothenborg's shot over the bar.

Although HTV Wales blacked out the Manchester United tie, viewers in North, Mid and South Wales were able to watch that game on English channels. The sad consequence was that Wrexham recorded their second lowest attendance for a European match.

---

3 October 1990   *1st Round, 2nd Leg*   *Lyngby Stadion*
Copenhagen, Denmark   *Attendance: 1,548*

LYNGBY (0) 0   WREXHAM (1) 1
                                 Armstrong 12

LYNGBY: Rindom; Kuhn H, Wieghorst, Gothenborg, Christiansen C, Larsen, Helt, Rode (Clem), Christiansen F, Kirchoff (Rasmussen), Kuhn A.
WREXHAM: Morris; Phillips, Kennedy, Flynn, Williams M, Sertori, Owen, Cooper (Wright D), Armstrong, Worthington, Bowden.

(WREXHAM won 1-0 on aggregate)

A row over TV coverage overshadowed preparations for the second leg in Denmark. The FA of Wales blocked live coverage in South Wales of ties involving Manchester United and Aston Villa on the grounds that Wrexham's tie was not receiving equal TV exposure.

Brian Flynn named 36-year-old Alan Kennedy in the team. Kennedy had won two European Cup winners medals with Liverpool, and had also played for Newcastle in the 1977 UEFA Cup.

Teenage striker Chris Armstrong was Wrexham's hero with a first-half header that was enough to send the Robins through to the next round. Bowden had headed Brian Flynn's long pass across goal and Armstrong raced in to nod into the net.

Though the Robins were mostly on the back foot, they nearly grabbed a second goal when Armstrong's cross was met by Graham Cooper, and though the keeper parried his first attempt, he was helpless as Cooper miscued his second effort wide of a gaping goal.

---

23 October 1990   *2nd Round, 1st Leg*   *Old Trafford*
Manchester, England   *Attendance: 29,405*

MANCHESTER UNITED (2) 3   WREXHAM (0) 0
McClair 42, Bruce 44 pen, Pallister 59

MANCHESTER UNITED: Sealey; Blackmore, Martin, Bruce, Sharpe, Pallister, Webb, Ince (Beardsmore), McClair, Hughes, Wallace (Robins).
WREXHAM: Morris; Phillips, Kennedy, Reck, Williams (Hunter), Beaumont, Flynn, Owen, Armstrong, Cooper, Bowden.
Referee: A Navarrete (Spain)

Manchester United's game had, after all, been shown live in Wales, in defiance of a UEFA directive. Nevertheless, United were the plum draw that Wrexham chairman Pryce Griffiths hoped for in Round Two. For his part, Brian Flynn preferred an easier tie, the better to make progress. In the event, the chairman's wish was granted.

United and Arsenal had been involved in a brawl at Old Trafford. Both managers – Alex Ferguson and George Graham – were warned to take firm and appropriate action. Ferguson disciplined two of his players, while Arsenal fined Graham and five players.

Wrexham, 84 places below United in the Football League, had Mark Sertori and Darren Wright ruled out by injury. The Robins' hopes of staging a shock were shattered in a two-minute spell just before the interval. Neil Webb's cross was headed back across goal by Steve Bruce, and Brian McClair pounced. Ruabon-born Mark Hughes was then felled by Nigel Beaumont, and Bruce scored from the spot. Gary Pallister volleyed the third goal from eighteen yards.

The nearest Wrexham came to scoring in a one-sided second half was when a Webb back-pass almost caught Les Sealey in no-man's land. Young Lee Sharpe created many of United's scoring chances.

---

7 November 1990   *2nd Round, 2nd Leg*   *Racecourse*
Wrexham   *Attendance: 13,327*

WREXHAM (0) 0   **MANCHESTER UNITED (2) 2**
                                              Robins 31, Bruce 35

WREXHAM: Morris; Thackeray, Hardy, Hunter, Beaumont, Phillips, Flynn (Jones J), Owen, Armstrong (Jones K), Jones L, Cooper.
MANCHESTER UNITED: Sealey; Irwin, Blackmore, Bruce, Phelan, Pallister, Webb, Ince (Donaghy), McClair (Martin), Robins, Wallace.
Referee: K Milton (Denmark)
                    (MANCHESTER UNITED won 5-0 on aggregate)

Wrexham's warm-up for the second leg amounted to a dire 2-4 home defeat by Burnley. Brian Flynn had eleven players injured – including Alan Kennedy and Vince O'Keefe – and had to recall 35-year-old Joey Jones, who had not played since breaking an ankle in May. A combination of the long casualty list and UEFA's foreigner ruling meant that a starting place would go to Lee Jones, one of five YTS lads in the Wrexham squad.

On a brighter note, a five-figure match sponsorship by Guinness, plus TV fees, ancillaries, and a bumper crowd, would mean Wrexham's profit from the tie would exceed £50,000.

A neat flick by debutant Jones in the first few minutes set up Gareth Owen for a distant shot which flew wide. Chris Armstrong and Graham Cooper bustled up front against the experienced defensive partnership of Pallister and Bruce.

Paul Ince began the move that led to the opener with a teasing run across the front of the Wrexham defence. He squared to Mark Robins who slid the ball home. United wasted little time before claiming a second goal. Pallister powered a header goalwards, Mark Morris could only parry, and Steve Bruce bundled the ball in.

In the second period, a rare Welsh attack almost pulled a goal back when Andy Thackeray hit the post with Les Sealey beaten. Kevin Jones, a 16-year-old Manchester United fan, made his Wrexham debut when coming on as a late substitute for Armstrong.

Manchester United beat Barcelona 2-1 in the final in Rotterdam.

~~~~~~~~~~~~~~~~~~~~~~~~~~~~~~~~~~~~~

1991 – SWANSEA CITY (League Division 3)

~~~~~~~~~~~~~~~~~~~~~~~~~~~~~~~~~~~~~

In Swansea's first Welsh Cup final at the National Stadium they inflicted a second successive final defeat on Wrexham, 2-0. Swansea, however, were bottom of Division Three and given little chance against the millionaires of Monaco, who led the French First Division.

In view of the UEFA ruling, manager Frank Burrows included seven teenagers in the squad, five of whom had never played in a League match. Triallist striker Christian McClean was preferred to the transfer-listed Paul Raynor, who had played in both Panathinaikos ties. The other non-Welsh players were Mark Harris, skipper Terry Connor, and Steve Thornber. Connor had already agreed to join Bristol City in a £200,000 deal. Swansea's keeper was Mark Kendall who had been with Newport County in 1980 when they played in Europe for the only time. Unfortunately, Kendall had been signed too late to be eligible for County during that campaign.

Monaco included George Weah, Danish international and former Manchester United full-back John Sivebaek, and the Portuguese international Rui Barros. The former Monaco and Spurs hero, Glenn Hoddle, told Burrows what he could about the French team.

In seven European ties at the Vetch, Swansea had only lost twice, both of them single-goal defeats.

17 September 1991	*1st Round, 1st Leg*	*Vetch Field*
Swansea		*Attendance: 6,208*

SWANSEA CITY (0) 1 **MONACO (2) 2**
Legg 71 Passi 8 pen, Barros 27

SWANSEA CITY: Kendall; Jenkins, Thornber, Coughlin, Harris, Davies Mark, Davey, Davies Alan, McClean, Connor, Legg.
MONACO: Ettori; Sivebaek, Sonor, Petit, Mendy, Puel, Rui Barros (Gnako), Dib, Weah, Passi, Robert (Djorkaeff).
Referee: K Neilsen (Denmark)

Swansea's first-half efforts in front of Princes Rainier and Albert were undone by defensive lapses which gifted two goals to the French Cup holders. George Weah intercepted a misguided Steve Thornber back-pass, and although Mark Kendall denied the French League's leading scorer, the referee penalised the keeper for toppling Rui Barros as he chased the loose ball. Georges Passi, whose Cup final winning goal against Marseilles took Monaco into Europe, sent Kendall the wrong way from the spot.

Coached by Arsene Wenger, Monaco increased their lead after yet another defensive howler. Thornber was caught in possession and Rui Barros held off Mark Harris to finish with precision.

Monaco looked vulnerable to high balls into their area, but they resisted until twenty minutes from time when a poor back-pass by Claude Puel was seized upon by Andrew Legg, who beat the 36-year-old Monaco captain and keeper, Jean-Luc Ettori.

1 October 1991   1st Round, 2nd Leg   Stade Louis 11
Monte Carlo, Monaco   Attendance: 3,000

MONACO (5) 8   **SWANSEA CITY (0) 0**
Weah 6, 85, Fofana 18, Barros 30,
Passi 35, 89, Harris 39 (og),
Djorkaeff 75

Monaco: Ettori; Blondeau, Sonor, Petit, Mendy, Puel, Rui Barros
(Djorkaeff), Dib (Robert), Weah, Passi, Fofana.
Swansea City: Kendall; Jenkins, Thornber, Harris (Trick), Davies
Mark, Davies Alan, Coughlin, Legg, Gilligan, Raynor, Davey (Chapple).
                        (Monaco won 10-1 on aggregate)

Frank Burrows recalled Jimmy Gilligan – out for five months with
back trouble – for the second leg. He had bagged a hat-trick for
Cardiff against Derry City in 1988, and also netted Watford's first
goal in European competition when playing Kaiserslautern in 1983.
Swansea's new keeper, Roger Freestone, was ineligible, as was John
Ford, John Williams, and Derek Brazil – on loan from Old Trafford.
    A five-goal first-half collapse left Swansea in tatters, resulting in
the worst defeat of any Welsh side in Europe. First, Mark Kendall
cut out George Weah's header but allowed the ball to trickle over
the line. A misunderstanding between Steve Thornber and Simon
Davey let Marcel Dib cross from the right and Youssouf Fofana
scored from close in.
    Further disasters lay in store. Rui Barros hit a third, closely
followed by a goal from Passi. A bizarre own-goal by Mark Harris
completed the first-half avalanche. Substitute Youri Djorkaeff struck
number six with a well-taken goal, and Weah claimed his second –
and fourteenth of the season – with five minutes remaining.
Swansea's misery was completed in the final moments when Passi
struck goal number eight.
    Monaco reached the final of the Cup-Winners' Cup, where they
were beaten 0-2 by Werder Bremen of Germany.

~~~~~~
1992 – CARDIFF CITY (League Division 3: New Style)
~~~~~~

The Bluebirds thrashed Hednesford Town 5-0 at the National Stadium to win the Welsh Cup in front of a crowd of 10,300. It would
be City's thirteenth European campaign, but they would be without
Robbie James. It was realised only belatedly that he was on a one-
match suspension, having been cautioned twice in Swansea City's
1989 ties with Panathinaikos. Jason Perry had twisted a knee and

would also be missing for City. UEFA had reduced the number of permitted 'foreign' players from four to three, and Derek Brazil – an £85,000 signing from Manchester United who had been on loan at Swansea City – was named as one of them. City's five substitutes were all untried YTS youngsters, among them 16-year-old schoolboy Morgan Williams, selected as the reserve goalkeeper.

City were coached by Eddie May, who had played for Wrexham and Swansea during his long playing career, which included nine European matches for the North Walians. Under May, Cardiff had made a good start and were fifth in the new Division Three.

Cardiff City owner Rick Wright devised a number of innovations to promote the match, including allowing Austrian fans in free for the Ninian Park leg. This carried the proviso that City supporters would be given a similar privilege in Vienna. He also agreed to pay 10% of the first leg gate to the players, provided they went through to the next round.

Admira Wacker were coached by Siggi Held, who had played for West Germany in the 1966 World Cup final. Held had to do without top scorer, Ernst Ogris, who was suspended, but could call upon Swedish international Roger Ljung and Austrian cap Peter Artner.

15 September 1992	*1st Round, 1st Leg*	*Ninian Park*
Cardiff		*Attendance: 9,624*

CARDIFF CITY (0) 1   **ADMIRA WACKER (1) 1**
Pike 58   Abfalterer 44

CARDIFF CITY: Grew; Brazil, Baddeley, Abraham, Searle, Ramsey, Bird (Gorman), Griffith, Pike, Dale, Blake.
ADMIRA WACKER: Gruber F; Dotzl, Zingler, Gruber M, Messlender, Abfalterer, Gutlerderer (Bacher), Artner, Temm, Ljung, Marschall.
Referee: Jorge Monteiro Coroado (Portugal)

Without four regulars, Cardiff resorted to a sweeper defence hoping to catch the Austrians on the break. Goalkeeper Mark Grew pulled off some stunning saves, though he needed the help of Gareth Abraham after fifteen minutes when Michael Gruber exposed City's lack of a genuine right-back.

The Bluebirds had chances in the opening period, with Carl Dale and Tony Bird seeing shots saved by Admira keeper Franz Gruber. Chris Pike had an effort cleared of the line by Michael Gruber after the keeper flapped at a Damon Searle cross.

Grew saved from Gerard Messlender before half-time, but then City fell behind in sad circumstances. Gruber's cross deflected off Lee Baddeley into the path of Abfalterer, whose low shot ricocheted off Abraham and under Grew. The crowd fell silent, apart from a lone Wacker fan who celebrated wildly in the directors box.

City were back on level terms early in the second half. Searle's free-kick was met by Pike, who headed in. Cardiff sensed victory, and Dale and Searle went close before Cohen Griffith blazed over.

---

29 September 1992   *1st Round, 2nd Leg*   *Sudstadt*
Vienna, Austria   *Attendance: 4,700*

ADMIRA WACKER (0) 2   CARDIFF CITY (0) 0
Marschall 47, Abfalterer 89

ADMIRA WACKER: Gruber F; Dotzl, Muller (Zingler), Gruber M, Messlender, Abfalterer, Bacher, Artner, Temm, Ljung, Marschall.
CARDIFF CITY: Grew; James, Abraham (Bird), Searle, Brazil, Baddeley, Ramsey, Griffith, Pike, Dale, Blake.
Referee: L Spassov (Spain)

(ADMIRA WACKER won 3-1 on aggregate)

A twenty-strong City squad stayed overnight in a Gatwick hotel before flying to Vienna. Jason Perry had not recovered from injury but Robbie James was available after completing his suspension. Coach May was gratified that Guyanan-born Cohen Griffith was happy to be an honorary Welshman for the European campaign.

Messlender and Alois Dotzl passed fitness tests for Admira Wacker, but with first-choice Knapler still unfit Gruber continued in goal. Ernst Ogris was back after suspension to join the squad.

In the first period, City's enthusiasm was countered by dour defence by the Austrians. The tie came alive after the break when Derek Brazil mis-hit a clearance to Roger Ljung, whose shot reared up, struck Grew in the face, bobbed into the air and fell kindly for the German international Olaf Marschall, who headed in unopposed.

City worked tirelessly. Teenager Tony Bird came on in place of defender Abraham, but Pike and Dale were well shackled by the home defence. The only time the Austrian keeper was tested was from a powerful drive by Nathan Blake.

Wacker were swift on the break and put the result beyond doubt in the final minutes when Marschall set up Abfalterer for a tap-in.

~~~~~~~~~~~~~~~~~~~~~~~~~~~~~~~~

1993 – CARDIFF CITY (League Division 2)

~~~~~~~~~~~~~~~~~~~~~~~~~~~~~~~~

The Bluebirds made it two Welsh Cup victories in succession at the National Stadium by beating Rhyl 5-0, with Phil Stant claiming a hat-trick. That made it a season to remember, as Cardiff were also Division Three champions.

Kevin Ratcliffe had been signed by Rick Wright. Ratcliffe had skippered Everton to their 1985 Cup-Winners' Cup triumph over Rapid Vienna and his experience would prove invaluable. Stant had been in dispute with Wright after the Welsh Cup final, and was loaned out to Mansfield. Public outcry at the way in which a City favourite had been treated provoked a climb-down by Wright, and Stant returned to Ninian Park.

For the second time, City were drawn against Standard Liege. The Bluebirds had lost both legs back in 1965, and now the Belgians were even stronger. Yet their coach, Arie Haan – a former Dutch international and Anderlecht star – faced selection problems, with Patrick Vervoort injured and Dutchman Franz Van Rooy suspended by his club for missing training. Haan could only pick three of the four foreign players he regularly used.

The five-times Belgian cup winners were now playing their 121st European match, having reached the final of the Cup-Winners' Cup in 1982 when they lost to Barcelona. They were a seeded team, and had appeared in all three major European cup competitions.

15 September 1993   *1st Round, 1st Leg*   *Stade de Sclessin*
Liege, Belgium   *Attendance: 10,700*

STANDARD LIEGE (1) 5   **CARDIFF CITY (1) 2**
Bisconti 13, Wilmots 63, 84,   Bird 39, 62
Cruz 71 pen, Asselman 76

STANDARD LIEGE: Bodart; Smeets, Leonard, Bisconti, Cruz, Pister, Hellers, Asselman, Bettagno, Rychkov, Wilmots.
CARDIFF CITY: Kite; James, Searle, Baddeley, Perry, Ratcliffe, Bird, Richardson, Stant (Evans T), Griffith, Blake.
Referee: M Olafsson (Iceland)

Tony Bird scored twice, as Cardiff City rattled the Belgian giants before the tables turned. Bird's brace gave the Bluebirds a shock 2-1 lead early in the second half, but the Belgians retaliated and a late goal glut put the tie beyond the Welsh club. Standard had drawn first blood when the Russian, Sascha Rychkov, threaded a pass through for Roberto Bisconti to beat Phil Kite from just inside the area. Keeper Gilbert Bodart saved Nathan Blake's header before trouble flared after half an hour. Players squared up to each other after Marc Wilmots had been fouled off the ball, but Lee Baddeley was the only player cautioned. The Bluebirds then delighted their 1,500 travelling supporters when Bird dispossessed Andre Cruz and made no mistake from fifteen yards. Standard were stunned again in the second half, this time by Bird's far-post volley from a cross by Cohen Griffith.

This stung the home side into action. Wilmots dribbled through for a fine solo goal to equalise. Standard went 3-2 up when Blake felled Patrick Asselman and Cruz converted the spot-kick. Four minutes later a rampant Liege added the fourth when Asselman hit a superb cross-shot, and Wilmots completed the rout with a header.

---

28 September 1993   *1st Round, 2nd Leg*   *Ninian Park*
Cardiff   *Attendance: 6,096*

CARDIFF CITY (0) 1   **STANDARD LIEGE (2) 3**
James 59   Wilmots 14, Lashaf 36, Bisconti 50

CARDIFF CITY: Williams S; James, Searle, Perry, Baddeley, Ratcliffe, Bird (Wigg), Millar (Bartley), Stant, Thompson, Griffith.
STANDARD LIEGE: Bodart (Munaron); Bisconti, Leonard, Vervoort, Cruz, Pister, Hellers, Asselman, Lashaf, Van Rooy, Wilmots.
Referee: G Cesari (Italy)

(STANDARD LIEGE won 8-3 on aggregate)

City had lost form and gone eight matches since their last victory. They were not helped by an injury to Nathan Blake. In goal, Eddie May selected 18-year-old Rhayader-born keeper Steve Williams in place of the experienced Phil Kite. This left May with an extra place for a foreign player, which he gave to Gary Thompson.

The classy Belgians shattered Cardiff with two first-half goals. Williams failed to cut out Van Rooy's corner-kick and Marc Wilmots was unmarked to power in a header. City responded immediately, and Lee Baddeley's header from Damon Searle's cross was turned over the top by Bodart.

The Welsh defence cracked again when Baddeley's skewed clearance flew goalwards. Although Williams saved, the Moroccan Mohamed Lashaf bundled in the loose ball. Liege extended their lead early in the second period when Wilmots freed Bisconti.

City's disappointment was marred by crowd trouble at the start of the second half. Munaron, who had just replaced Bodart in goal, was pelted with coins as he took up position at the Grangetown end. Midfielder Robbie James restored City some self-respect with a thunderous 25-yard drive that flew past substitute keeper Munaron. It was to be the last goal ever scored in European competition by a Welsh club playing in the Football League.

8

THE LEAGUE OF WALES TAKES OVER

~~~~~~~~~~~~~~~~~~~~~~~~~~~~~~~

1994 – BARRY TOWN (League of Wales)

~~~~~~~~~~~~~~~~~~~~~~~~~~~~~~~

Barry Town's sensational 2-1 Welsh Cup final victory over Cardiff City at the National Stadium earned the newly dubbed 'Dragons' a place in Europe. But the Welsh League Division One champions were depleted during the summer with several experienced players leaving. These included player-coach Andy Beattie – a member of the Merthyr Tydfil team that played Atalanta in 1987 – and Paul Wimbleton, who was in Cardiff City's 1988 Cup-Winners' Cup side. But the newly installed League of Wales outfit still had players with European experience to call on, including 40-year-old Alan Curtis, now about to play in Europe for his *fifth* different British club.

Zalgiris Vilnius had ranked among the USSR's stronger teams. But when Lithuania regained her independence following the disintegration of the Soviet empire, UEFA initially suspended her teams. This resulted in her best players fleeing abroad, which effectively disqualified them from Lithuania's national team.

Barry changed their training schedule for the ties, using the excellent facilities at RAF St Athan. As Jenner Park needed upgrading to UEFA standard, the home leg was staged at Ninian Park.

10 August 1994   *Preliminary Round, 1st Leg*   *Ninian Park*
Cardiff   *Attendance: 1,914*

BARRY TOWN (0) 0   **ZALGIRIS VILNIUS (0) 1**
Vencevicius 77

BARRY TOWN: Livingstone; Griffiths, Williams, Boyle, Davies (Leask), Ellis, Giles P, D'Auria, Wright (Mitchell), Jones, Scott.
ZALGIRIS: Spetyla; Suliauskas, Maciulevicius, Baltusnikas, Stonkus, Novikovas, Karvelis (Vencevicius), Tereskinas, Jankauskas, Preiksaitis, Poderis.
Referee: Roy Helgar Olsen (Norway)

The Dragons opened with a three-man midfield, but found it hard to make headway against the tall Lithuanians, who flooded the central area. Barry still created several chances, with Phil Williams forcing a save from Vilnius keeper Spetyla, and David D'Auria having a shot blocked before sending a header just wide. It was to prove a short but eventful match for D'Auria, who had been in the Swansea side that played Panathinaikos in 1989. Midway through the second half he was sent off for a second booking.

With skipper Mark Davies having already been substituted by Garfield Leask, Barry's problems increased. Glen Livingstone made several fine stops, and new player-coach Terry Boyle – playing for his third Welsh club in Europe in only six years – cleared off the line from Eimantas Poderis.

Darius Maciulevicius, on the left – and Poderis, were Zalgiris's best players, with Poderis involved in the only goal. It was scored by sub Donatas Vencevicius, who pounced when Williams failed to clear. It was Zalgiris's first goal in Europe in their fifth match.

---

25 August 1994   *Preliminary Round, 2nd Leg*   *Zalgiris Stadium*
Vilnius, Lithuania   *Attendance: 2,900*

ZALGIRIS VILNIUS (2) 6   **BARRY TOWN (0) 0**
Karvelis 18, 50, Baltusnikas 40,
Poderis 47, Maciulevicius 68,
Jankauskas 89

ZALGIRIS: Spetyla (Koncevicius); Novikovas, Maciulevicius, Baltus-nikas, Stonkus, Vencevicius, Suliauskas, Tereskinas, Preiksaitis (Urbonas), Karvelis (Jankauskas), Poderis.
BARRY TOWN: Livingstone; Curtis, Griffiths, Boyle, Leask, Ellis, Giles P, Sanderson, Jones, Mitchell, Threlfall (Scott).

(ZALGIRIS won 7-0 on aggregate)

Mark Davies was still out, following his first-leg injury, while David D'Auria had left the club to rekindle his Football League career with Scarborough. Veteran Alan Curtis took his place in a side that showed five changes. He would play as a stopgap right-back, with Ashley Griffiths switching to left-back to cover the absence of Phil Williams, who failed a late fitness test. The party flew to Copenhagen, and then on by Aeroflot to the Baltic state.

Any hopes that Barry entertained were dashed when Maciulevicius exposed the Barry defence and set up Karvelis, who side-footed into the net. Zalgiris doubled their lead when Livingstone pushed out a shot to the feet of Baltusnikas.

Barry were in disarray, and within two minutes of the change-round Poderis swept the ball in from twelve yards, after Terry Boyle had fluffed a clearance. Then came a second goal from Karvelis, exploiting an outnumbered Barry defence. Maciulevicius hit a fifth midway through the second period, and in the final minute Barry's humiliation was complete when substitute Jankauskas ran 30 yards before scoring.

Though Paul Giles buzzed down both flanks and fired in a couple of shots, Barry's front runners had been generally isolated. It was a bitter defeat, and had far-reaching consequences for the club.

~~~~~~~~~~~~~~~~~~~~~~~~~~~~~~~~~

1995 – WREXHAM (League Division 2)

~~~~~~~~~~~~~~~~~~~~~~~~~~~~~~~~~

The Robins' win over Cardiff City at the National Stadium enabled them to lift the Welsh Cup for a record 23rd – and final – time. The FA of Wales decreed that clubs playing in English leagues would in future be barred from the Welsh Cup. Wrexham's appearance in the European Cup-Winners' Cup would be their last. Thenceforth, they, Cardiff City and Swansea City would be denied entry.

Wrexham manager Brian Flynn faced the usual selection problems, with injuries being aggravated by UEFA's three-foreigner rule. Matters were exacerbated by each of his three new signings – Peter Ward, Kevin Russell and Craig Skinner – falling into the 'foreigner' category and missing out. The Robins were also without leading scorer Gary Bennett, transferred to Tranmere Rovers during the summer for £300,000.

The Robins undertook a successful pre-season tour of Ireland which culminated in a 3-1 victory over Irish Cup winners Linfield at Windsor Park.

As for Petrolul Ploiesti, they hailed from Romania's oil region and were a young side with limited European experience. Their only capped players were Stefan Preda in goal, and full-back Daniel Chirita, who was an Under-21 international.

10 August 1995   *Preliminary Round, 1st Leg*   *Racecourse*
Wrexham   *Attendance: 4,308*

WREXHAM (0) 0   **PETROLUL PLOIESTI (0) 0**

WREXHAM: Marriott; Brace, Hardy, Phillips, Hunter, Jones B, Futcher, Owen, Connolly, Watkin, Durkan.
PETROLUL: Preda; Chirita, Leanu, Balaceanu, Grigore, Rachita, Pirlog (Bastina), Abaluta, Zafiris (Andreicut), Zmoleanu, Toader (Cadar).

Playing in Romania's national colours of yellow and blue, Petrolul played a more patient game than Wrexham, and in Daniel Zafiris and Adrian Toader they were well served by willing front-runners. Zafiris pounced on a poor back-pass from Barry Jones, but the onrushing Andy Marriott snuffed out the danger. The Robins came close in the eighteenth minute, when an error by Chirita caused consternation in the visitors' goalmouth. Preda had to scramble the ball off the Ploiesti goal-line.

Debutant Stephen Futcher – nephew of the former Luton Town twins – did not look out of place in the side. In the second half he created Wrexham's best chance of the match when Karl Connolly rounded three players but over-ran the ball. It was cleared straight to Gareth Owen, whose chip-shot sailed over the crossbar. At the death Keiron Durkan drove just wide with the keeper beaten.

---

24 August 1995   *Preliminary Round, 2nd Leg*   *Petrolul*
Ploiesti, Romania   *Attendance: 10,000*

PETROLUL PLOIESTI (0) 1   WREXHAM (0) 0
Pirlog 59

PETROLUL: Preda; Chirita, Leanu, Balaceanu, Grigore, Rachita, Pirlog, Abaluta, Zafiris (Toader), Zmoleanu (Bastina), Andreicut (Balasam).
WREXHAM: Marriott; Thomas, Hardy, Phillips, Hunter, Jones B, Futcher (Barnes), Owen, Connolly, Watkin, Cross.

(PETROLUL PLOIESTI won 1-0 on aggregate)

Wrexham's three new signings were again absent when the twenty-strong squad flew to Ploiesti. Brian Flynn again preferred Barry Jones, Alan Hunter and Karl Connolly as the three permitted foreign players. The game was dour, with both sides defensively minded. Wrexham rarely looked capable of unlocking the Romanian back line, and their only chance came midway through the first period when Karl Connolly went close. Ploiesti stepped up a gear after half-time and were rewarded when Mihail Pirlog notched the only goal. It was a sad way to bring the curtain down on Welsh clubs in the Football League participating in the Cup-Winners' Cup.

1996 – LLANSANTFFRAID (League of Wales)

The first Welsh Cup to be contested without Wales' three Football league clubs was won by Llansantffraid, who defeated the League of Wales champions, Barry Town, on penalties after a 3-3 draw.

The 'Saints' were already assured of a place in the Cup-Winners' Cup before the final, as Barry Town would contest the UEFA Cup.

Llansantffraid is a small village near Oswestry with a population of only 950. The club's annual wage bill was around £30,000, and they finished the season twelfth, a massive 45pts behind champions Barry. With a seating capacity of just 120 in a stand tucked away by the local community centre, there was no way a European tie could be staged at the Recreation Ground. It was decided to switch the home leg to Wrexham, which would widen interest in the match.

Saints' opponents, Ruch Chorzow, had five internationals in their squad. Their coach, Jerzy Wyrobek, had claimed three Polish titles in thirteen years at the club.

8 August 1996   *Qualifying Round, 1st Leg*   *Racecourse*
Wrexham   *Attendance: 1,558*

LLANSANTFFRAID (0) 1   **RUCH CHORZOW (1) 1**
Gesior 83 (og)   Gesior 3

LLANSANTFFRAID: Mulliner; Whelan J, Curtiss, Brown, Jones Arwel, Thomas, Jones Adrian, Evans, Morgan (Davies), Edwards (Whelan C), Abercrombie.
RUCH CHORZOW: Kolodziejczyk; Fornalak, Pieniazek, Bak M, Jaworski, Gesior, Bak A, Mosor, Rowicki (Wawrzyciek), Srutwa (Mizia), Grzesik.
Referee: E Olafsson (Iceland)

The Saints' £30-per-week collection of part-time footballers held the Polish cup winners to a creditable draw after withstanding intense pressure for most of the game. When Polish international Dariusz Gesior headed in after just three minutes it might have opened the floodgates, but the home defence held firm and denied the Poles further clear-cut chances. With time running out, Llansantffraid equalised in fortuitous fashion. Gesior, scorer of the opening goal, deflected a shot from Aneurin Thomas past his own keeper.

---

22 August 1996   *Qualifying Round, 2nd Leg*   *Ruch Stadion*
Chorzow, Poland   *Attendance: 6,700*

RUCH CHORZOW (1) 5   **LLANSANTFFRAID (0) 0**
Bak A 1, 57, Jones Arwel 48 (og),
Bak M 64, 65

RUCH CHORZOW: Lech; Gasior, Bak A, Mosor, Gaca (Rowicki), Gesior, Srutwa, Grzesik, Bak M (Wawrzyciek), Pieniazek, Mizia (Zaba).
LLANSANTFFRAID: Mulliner; Jones Arwel, Brown (Davies), Thomas, Whelan J (Whelan C), Curtiss, Jones Adrian, Abercrombie, Edwards, Morgan (Jones G), Evans.

Referee: S Gionw (Croatia)

(RUCH CHORZOW won 6-1 on aggregate)

The cost of the trip to Chorzow for the second leg was around £10,000, but by exploiting their marketing potential the Saints raised enough money from the first leg to cover their costs. They also staged social events in the village and secured sponsorship deals with local companies.

The team flew out from Manchester Airport to Zurich, with a second flight taking them to Chorzow. For the return flight they travelled by coach to Warsaw and flew back from there.

The Saints' slim hopes were dashed within the first minute, when the Polish First Division side caught the visitors cold. Tadeusz Bak accepted an easy opportunity.

Andy Edwards had the chance of a swift response, but the keeper saved at his feet. Andy Mulliner was the busier goalkeeper, and he made several fine saves to keep the Saints in contention, but a four-goal burst in seventeen second-half minutes shattered the Welshmen. Arwel Jones started the rot, slicing the ball into his own net. Three more goals came in quick succession. With the Poles attacking at will, Bak netted his second before Miroslav Bak found the target twice in a minute.

Andy Edwards was given the opportunity of a late consolation score for the visitors, but his penalty-kick was easily saved.

~~~~~~~~~~~~~~~~~~~~~~~~~~~~~~~~~~~~

1997 – CWMBRAN TOWN (League of Wales)

~~~~~~~~~~~~~~~~~~~~~~~~~~~~~~~~~~~~

FC National Bucuresti were Cwmbran's opponents for their second tilt at European competition – the Crows had been League of Wales trail-blazers in the 1993 European Champions Cup.

Neither side were national cup holders. Both had been beaten by their respective champions – Barry Town winning 2-1 at Ninian Park, and Steau Bucharest claiming the Romanian cup with a 4-2 win. Sponsored by the National Bank of Romania, FC National were highly rated and were ranked 52nd in FIFA's world listings.

No sooner were the Romanian side booked into their hotel in Llanyrafon than their club doctor and coach headed for the kitchens to make an inspection. They detailed the food portions to be given to each player and requested that no ice be given to anyone. They also brought all their own water with them.

Their coach, Florian Halagian, was angry that a Cwmbran match video was not made available until the morning of the game, making it difficult for him to plan tactics. Their top player was the £1.5

million rated Radu Niculescu, who had attracted the attention of Spanish and Dutch clubs. For their part, Cwmbran officials were irritated by the lack of TV coverage for such a prestigious event. It meant that lucrative advertising contracts went begging, and left the club with a huge deficit over the two legs.

The Cwmbran side included Jimmy Blackie, who had played for the club in the Champions Cup against Cork City. Having also appeared in the Inter Toto Cup for Ton Pentre, he became the first player to appear in three European competitions for Welsh clubs. Goalkeeper Pat O'Hagan and Wayne Goodridge were also survivors from the 1993 Cwmbran team.

14 August 1997   *Preliminary Round, 1st Leg*   *Cwmbran Stadium*
Cwmbran   *Attendance: 800*

CWMBRAN TOWN (0) 2   **NATIONAL BUCURESTI (1) 5**
Parfitt 76 pen, Townsend 83   Vasc 32, Niculescu 47, 61, Lita 78, 80

CWMBRAN TOWN: O'Hagan (Speare); Carter (Powell), Jones, Gibbins, Parfitt, Blackie, Moore, Dyer (Johnson), Watkins, James, Townsend.
NAT BUCURESTI: Stefanescu; Ciubotariu, Sburlea, Necula, Marin (Lita), Carabas, Petre, Vasc, Duna, Niculescu, Pigulea.
Referee: S Shmolik (Belarus)

Cwmbran were left facing an early exit from the cup after the Romanians romped to an impressive victory. The first half had given little hint of what was to follow, as the Crows matched the visitors in most departments.

The only goal in the opening period came out of the blue, when Cristian Vasc picked up a loose ball 40 yards out and fired a shot that flew past Pat O'Hagan.

O'Hagan suffered an injury towards the end of the half, and was replaced by Jimmy Speare after the interval. Speare's first job was to pick the ball out of the net after Radu Niculescu hammered in a Marin Duna cross. Niculescu was then gifted a second goal, when lack of communication between Speare and veteran player-coach Roger Gibbins allowed him a free shot at an empty goal.

Cwmbran were given hope when the referee awarded a penalty. Adrian Pigulea was adjudged to have fouled a Town player in the area and Mark Parfitt slotted home the spot-kick.

This reverse stung the Romanians into action, and within four minutes substitute Nicolae Lita had bagged two further goals. Cwmbran, however, had the last word when Richard Townsend beat the scrambling Paul Stefanescu with an angled shot.

28 August 1997   *Preliminary Round, 2nd Leg*   *Cotroeni Stadium*
Bucharest, Romania   *Attendance: 1,552*

FC NATIONAL BUCURESTI (5) 7   CWMBRAN TOWN (0) 0
Niculescu 15, Pigulea 21, 41, 75,
Albeanu 30, 39, Savu 47

NAT BUCURESTI: Stefanescu; Petre (Lita), Ciubotariu, Sburlea (Vochin), Necula, Marin, Pigulea, Vasc, Carabas, Niculescu, Albeanu (Savu).
CWMBRAN TOWN: Speare; Blackie, Gibbins (James), Parfitt, Jones, Moore, Powell, Goodridge, Dyer, Walker (Davies), Townsend (Watkins).
Referee: R Philippi (Luxembourg)

(NATIONAL BUCURESTI won 12-2 on aggregate)

The Cwmbran management decided against cutting back their itinerary for the second leg, despite the heavy losses likely to be borne after the poor attendance at home. The club anticipated a deficit of around £12,000 after completion of both ties.

The squad members were besieged by the media on their arrival at Bucharest Airport. The team bus was given a police escort and raced through the city at such speed that many players were grateful to arrive at their headquarters in one piece.

Manager Tony Willcox plumped for a more defensive formation, with Wayne Goodridge and John Powell replacing Philip James and Chris Watkins. Wing-back Paul Walker also came into the team for Richard Carter, who was unwell. The game was scheduled to take place at the newly built Cotroeni Stadium.

Cwmbran were outplayed by the classy Romanians, and when the interval was reached with the scoreboard already reading 0-5, a double-figure thrashing looked a distinct possibility. Niculescu had begun the deluge when he nodded in a Cristian Albeanu centre. This was closely followed by the first of Adrian Pigulea's hat-trick.

The Romanians were by this time storming forward at will, and on the half-hour the overworked Jimmy Speare had to retrieve an Albeanu shot from the back of the net. There was still time before the interval for second goals for Albeanu and Pigulea. When substitute Marian Savu netted within two minutes of the turnaround, Cwmbran heads might have dropped. To their credit, they fought back as the home side slackened. But in the final quarter, the Welsh side were unable to prevent the impressive Pigulea completing his hat-trick.

When Mattie Davies – Cwmbran's leading scorer the previous season – was brought on, he hit the bar with a shot on the turn. Adam Moore was presented with a chance by Simon Dyer but could not get in a shot.

1998 – BANGOR CITY (League of Wales)

Bangor's latest season of European football came from a Welsh Cup final win over Connahs Quay Nomads. The game had ended 1-1, but Bangor held their nerve to win on penalties. That success had ushered in many changes. Manager Graeme Sharp and his assistant John Hulse left the club, along with many of the cup-winning side.

John King, formerly manager at Altrincham, was brought in to replace Sharp and his first job was to replace the 60-goal twin strike force of Marc Lloyd-Williams and Ken McKenna. This he did by signing two Under-21 caps – Sammy Ayorinde of Nigeria, and Paul Roberts, who had been released by Wrexham. Other recruits came from clubs around the north-west of England.

Pre-season friendly results were encouraging, with a 1-1 draw against top Greek side Aris Salonika followed by a 3-0 victory over Marine from the Unibond League.

Bangor's opponents – Haka – were based 120 miles north of Helsinki. They had won the Finnish Cup ten times and claimed the championship on five occasions. Leading their front line was 18-year-old Marlon Harewood, on loan from Nottingham Forest. Haka's coach was Keith Armstrong, a Geordie who had played for Newport County during a short spell on loan from Sunderland.

13 August 1998   *Qualifying Round, 1st Leg*   *Farrar Road*
Bangor   *Attendance: 1,425*

BANGOR CITY (0) 0   **HAKA (1) 2**
                              Niemi 40, Salli 60

BANGOR C: Williams L; Williams G, Fox, Allen, McLoughlin, Horner, Hilditch, Taylor (Langley P), Ayorinde, Sharratt, McGoona (Wenham).
FC HAKA: Vilnrotter; Karjalainen, Salli, Rasanen, Makela, Ivanov (Okkenen), Harewood (Torkkell), Popovitch, Ylonen, Niemi (Ruttanen), Heikkinen.
Referee: G Yakubovski (Belarus)

Harewood gave Bangor a fright by rifling an angled shot into the side-netting in the first minute, but Ayorinde responded by forcing a fine save from the Finnish keeper. Bangor conceded a goal just before the break, Jari Niemi being unmarked to score from fifteen yards. The tie drifted away from Bangor on the hour, when a badly cleared corner was fired back from the edge of the box by Janne Salli. The Finns then proceeded to show their class, stroking the

ball about, but the keen-tackling Bangor rearguard restricted the
visitors to long-range efforts for the remainder of the match.

---

27 August 1998   *Qualifying Round, 2nd Leg*   *Tehtaan Kenta*
Valkeakoski, Finland   *Attendance: 2,451*

FC HAKA (1) 1   **BANGOR CITY (0) 0**
Ruttanen 28

BANGOR C: Williams L; Mooney (Gibney), Fox, Allen, Lloyd,
Horner, Hilditch, Taylor, Ayorinde, Sharratt, Langley P.
FC HAKA: Vilnrotter; Karjalainen, Salli, Rasanen, Makela, Ivanov,
Ruttanen (Torkkell), Popovitch, Ylonen, Niemi (Rantala), Heikkinen
(Okkenen).
Referee: S Braga (Latvia)

(HAKA won 3-0 on aggregate)

Bangor's plans for the second leg were upset by the shock decision
of Wales Under-21 striker Paul Roberts to move to Porthmadog as
player-coach. Although eligible to play for both the Cymric Alliance
side and Bangor, Roberts declined, and so left the League of Wales
club short of strikers. Bangor were dealt further blows when Mike
McLoughlin and Gareth Williams suffered injuries in a morning
training session and had to be ruled out.

A stout defensive performance restored much of Bangor City's
pride as they rode their luck in the face of almost constant Haka
attacks. Janne Salli struck a post early on before Bangor came close
– Jamie Taylor forcing the Finnish keeper to push his shot around
the post. Neil Horner then had a close-range header blocked on the
line by Harri Ylonen, following a Darren Hilditch corner. But it was
the home side who scored first when Jukka Ruttanen touched home
Oleg Ivanov's corner-kick at the far post. City's offside trap foiled
several threats as the Finns gradually took command, though the
hosts missed clear chances to add to their lead.

Hilditch sent Samuel Ayorinde through to net after 69 minutes,
but the effort was ruled offside. At the final whistle, Haka manager
Keith Armstrong paid tribute to the fighting qualities of John King's
Bangor side. It was to be King's first and last tilt at European glory,
as he departed from the club less than three weeks later.

The news that UEFA intended scrapping the Cup-Winners' Cup
at the end of the 1998-99 season would, if realised, mean that
Bangor City had brought the curtain down on 37 years of Welsh
participation in that competition.

9

THE EUROPEAN CHAMPIONS CUP

~~~~~~

1993 – CWMBRAN TOWN (League of Wales)

~~~~~~

It was with surprise and delight that – one year after the inception of the League of Wales – the Welsh FA announced that the champions were eligible for the European Champions Cup. There had been much debate on the pros and cons of such a league in the Principality, and it is to the credit of the FA of Wales that European recognition arrived sooner than expected. Wales would now have two teams in Europe, as they would still be represented in the Cup-Winners' Cup.

The inaugural champions, Cwmbran Town, finished the season with only three defeats. They had joined the Welsh League in 1960, moving to the impressive facilities of the Cwmbran Stadium in 1975. As recently as 1981 Cwmbran had finished sixteenth in Division Two, but they rose swiftly through the ranks to reach their present elevated status. Team manager Tony Willcox had formerly been in charge of rivals Barry Town, having two seasons with the Seasiders before joining the Crows.

As for Cork City – Cwmbran's first opponents – they had enjoyed a meteoric rise since being formed in 1984 under the stewardship of former Chelsea and England star Bobby Tambling. Cork had subsequently represented the Republic in the Cup-Winners' Cup (v Moscow Torpedo, losing 0-6 on aggregate), and in the UEFA Cup (drawing 1-1 at home with Bayern Munich before losing away 0-2). Cork were now managed by Damien Richardson, who had played for Shamrock Rovers against Cardiff City at Ninian Park in 1967. He was formerly with Gillingham.

18 August 1993   *Preliminary Round, 1st Leg*   *Cwmbran Stadium*
Cwmbran   *Attendance: 8,000*

CWMBRAN TOWN (3) 3   **CORK CITY (0) 2**
King 3 pen, Ford 25, 27   Caulfield 62, Buckley 76

CWMBRAN TOWN: O'Hagan; Burrows, King, Dicks (McNeil), Blackie, Copeman, Parselle (Payne), Goodridge, Powell, Wharton, Ford.

CORK CITY: Harrington; Daly, Napier, O'Donoghue, Hague, Roche, Barry (Buckley), Hyde, Glynn (Caulfield), Gaynor, Morley.
Referee: G Thor Orasson (Iceland)

Cwmbran made a winning debut in the European Cup, but had to hang onto a 3-2 lead, having scored three first-half goals. The Crows had the best possible start, a penalty in the third minute after Francis Ford – the League's top scorer in its inaugural season – had been brought down by Dave Barry. Left-back Simon King made history when he thundered the ball into the roof of the net for the first goal by a Welsh club in the Champions Cup.

Ford himself then struck twice in the space of two minutes. The Irish defence could not clear a corner-kick and he slotted home from close range. Shortly afterwards, he unleashed a spectacular angled drive. Cwmbran's dream start had turned into raptures.

Cork manager Richardson made a couple of inspired substitutions. New York-born John Caulfield had only been on the pitch four minutes when he reduced the arrears. Anthony Buckley, the other sub, who had joined Cork from Peterborough, completed the transformation with Cork's second goal – from a Caulfield cross.

---

1 September 1993   Preliminary Round, 2nd Leg   Bishopstown
Cork, Republic of Ireland   Attendance: 5,000

CORK CITY (0) 2   **CWMBRAN TOWN (1) 1**
Morley 76, Glynn 85   McNeil 8

CORK CITY: Harrington; Daly, Hague, O'Donoghue, Napier, Buckley, Roche (Glynn), Hyde (Murphy), Gaynor, Morley, Caulfield.
CWMBRAN TOWN: O'Hagan; Burrows, Blackie, Copeman, King, Payne, McNeil, Goodridge, Dicks (Vaughan), Wharton (Clissold), Ford.
(CORK CITY won on away-goals rule)

Cwmbran were still smarting for having allowed a three-goal lead to be pegged back. They were not helped in the second leg when Norman Parselle failed a fitness test: the former Newport County player was replaced by veteran Phil McNeil. The Welsh team opened strongly, going ahead when Francis Ford's back-heel wrong-footed the Cork defence to present the chance to McNeil. Early in the second half Cwmbran might have gone further ahead, but McNeil's blockbuster was smothered at the second attempt by Cork goalkeeper Phil Harrington. Born in Bangor, North Wales, Harrington was a Welsh Youth and Under-21 cap who had signed from Rhyl in 1988.

With less than fifteen minutes remaining and the Crows leading 4-2 overall, prospects looked bright for the Welsh champions, but the Irish team clawed back a goal through Pat Morley. Morley had been voted Irish soccer writers Personality of the Year for 1993, and was the previous season's leading scorer in the League of Ireland, establishing a new club record of twenty goals.

Tragedy befell Cwmbran in the closing minutes, when yet again a substitute came on to make a telling contribution. Johnny Glynn snatched the winner to put Cork through on away goals.

~~~~~~~~~~~~~~~~~~~~~~~~~~~~~~~~~~~
1997 – BARRY TOWN (League of Wales)
~~~~~~~~~~~~~~~~~~~~~~~~~~~~~~~

Having performed so well in the previous season's UEFA Cup, Barry Town's hopes of having a say in the Champions Cup were dented when they were drawn to play Dynamo Kiev – Soviet champions thirteen times and Ukrainian champions for five successive seasons. Since independence from the Soviet Union, Dynamo Kiev had dominated the Ukraine national team: eight of their players started Ukraine's World Cup home qualifier with Germany, which ended 0-0. The Ukraine had also faced Northern Ireland in a recent international, in which no fewer than nine Dynamo players turned out. Barry Town's player-coach, Gary Barnett, enlisted the help of Gerry Armstrong – Northern Ireland's assistant manager – for any tips. But a cloud hung over Dynamo Kiev. Two years previously they had been barred from European competition for alleged match-fixing in a Champions League tie with Panathinaikos. A three-year suspended sentence hung over the club.

The first leg with Barry was scheduled for the smaller 20,000 capacity Dynamo Stadium, rather than Kiev's alternative venue, the 100,000 capacity Republica Stadium.

Barry had lost all their pre-season friendlies, so the party left for Kiev – only 60 miles south of Chernobyl – in sombre mood.

23 July 1997   *Preliminary Round, 1st Leg*   *Dynamo Stadium*
Kiev, Ukraine   *Attendance: 15,000*

DYNAMO KIEV (1) 2   **BARRY TOWN (0) 0**
Rebrov 20, Maksymov 83

DYNAMO KIEV: Shovkovsky; Holovko, Vaschuk, Dmytrulin, Kalitvintsev, Rebrov, Husyn, Khatskevych (Mykhailenko), Shkapenko (Maksymov), Radchenko, Belkevitch.
BARRY TOWN: Ovendale; Evans T, York, Lloyd, Knott, Loss, Johnson, Huggins, Ryan, Bird, Evans C (O'Gorman).

The Stadium was almost three-quarters full, in stark contrast to Kiev's previous home match, which had been watched by a crowd of only 4,000. Eight Barry fans made the long trip to the Ukrainian capital. Once play began the Dragons put the onus on caution, quite unlike the attack-minded philosophy which had carried all before them in Wales.

Dynamo were denied until their busy striker, Sergei Rebrov, gave them a deserved lead on twenty minutes. Barry maintained their discipline, and with the aid of stout defending dispelled fears of a Ukrainian goal avalanche. It was not until the final minutes that Mark Ovendale was beaten for the second time, when Ukrainian international Yuri Maksymov was on target.

---

30 July 1997   *Preliminary Round, 2nd Leg*   *Jenner Park*
Barry   *Attendance: 2,500*

BARRY TOWN (0) 0   **DYNAMO KIEV (0) 4**
                             Belkevitch 53, Maksymov 67, 78,
                             Vashchuk 80

BARRY TOWN: Ovendale; Evans T, Lloyd, York, Jones, Barnett (Evans C), Ryan, Huggins (Johnson), Bird, Pike (Loss), O'Gorman.
DYNAMO KIEV: Shovkovsky; Holovko, Luzhny, Vashchuk, Kalitvintsev, Husyn, Khatskevych (Radchenko), Shkapenko (Maksymov), Belkevitch (Mykhailenko), Dmytrulin, Rebrov.
Referee: G Thor Orrason (Iceland)

(DYNAMO KIEV won 6-0 on aggregate)

The Barry players were given a few days off to recover from the tiring journey to the former Soviet state. Gary Barnett and Richard Jones were available for selection for the second leg after suspension, with Barnett having also recovered from knee surgery.

The Ukrainians made some unexpected requests in the Barry dressing rooms prior to kick-off. They asked for four kilos of dry ice, boiling water, and bottles of sparkling mineral water. At least they had the grace, via a spokesman, to praise the condition of the Jenner Park pitch.

This time the Dragons matched their star-studded opponents blow by blow for the opening 37 minutes, until Darren Ryan was sent off for flinging the ball at Dynamo's Dmytrulin. By coincidence, referee Orrason had also been in charge of Cwmbran Town's Champions Cup home tie with Cork City.

Barry's ten men held out until half-time, when Chris Pike made way for Colin Loss. The aim was to pack the midfield and prevent the Ukrainians exploiting their extra man. The plan failed, however, and Kiev broke through for Belkevitch to net the opening goal.

Unlike the first leg, Barry could not keep the ball-playing Dynamo at bay, and Yuri Maksymov hit the target twice before their accomplished sweeper, Vashchuk, completed the scoring.

Tony Bird, who had scored goals in both the Cup-Winners' Cup and the UEFA Cup, missed out on the chance to become the first player to score in three different European competitions while playing for Welsh clubs. Along with Dave O'Gorman, he was transferred shortly afterwards to Swansea City, ending any further hopes of participating in Europe in the near future.

~~~~~~~~~~~~~~~~~~~~~~~~~~~~~

1998 – BARRY TOWN (League of Wales)

~~~~~~~~~~~~~~~~~~~~~~~~~~~~~

The draw was cruel to Barry, who were paired for the second successive season with six times Ukrainian champions, Dynamo Kiev. It was a daunting challenge for the Dragons: Dynamo had reached last season's quarter-finals. But at least Barry would not have to face Yuri Maksymov, scorer of three goals against them. His clever play had earned a big-money move to Werder Bremen in the Bundesliga.

Barry player-coach Gary Barnett had rung the changes in the close season and brought in seven new players. A 30-strong party left Gatwick for the long and tiring trip to the Ukrainian capital.

20 July 1998   *Preliminary Round, 1st Leg*   *Dynamo Stadium*
Kiev, Ukraine   *Attendance: 15,500*

DYNAMO KIEV (4) 8   **BARRY TOWN (0) 0**
Rebrov 9, 16, 37,82,
Shevchenko 33, 59,
Gerassimenko 48, Belkevitch 65

DYNAMO KIEV: Shovkovsky; Holovko, Vaschuk, Dmytrulin, Kaladze, Kalitvintsev (Gerassimenko), Kossovsky (Venhlinskyi), Shevchenko, Rebrov, Husyn (Belkevitch), Khatskevych.
BARRY TOWN: Nurse; Lloyd, Jones, York, Barrow, Barnett, Carter, Williams (Evans C), Dempsey, Thorpe, Evans T.
Ref: A Giorgiou (Cyprus)

Barry's worst fears were realised when they were taught a soccer lesson by the Ukrainians. Sergei Rebrov hit a first-half hat-trick and then completed the rout with eight minutes to go as the Dragons equalled the worst result by any Welsh side in Europe. They managed just three attempts on goal and were completely over-run.

Andrei Shevchenko, much admired by Italian and Spanish clubs, made it 4-0 by half-time and netted a second after the interval.

---

29 July 1998   *Preliminary Round, 2nd Leg*   *Jenner Park*
Barry   *Attendance: 1,250*

BARRY TOWN (1) 1   **DYNMAO KIEV (1) 2**
Williams 30   Mykhailenko 11, Venhlinskyi 50

BARRY TOWN: Mountain; Evans T, Lloyd, Jones, York, Barrow, Barnett, Carter, Evans C, Williams, Dempsey.
DYNAMO KIEV: Kernozenko; Luzhnyi, Khatskevych, Kaladze, Vaschuk, Shevchenko (Gerassimenko), Federov, Mykhailenko, Konovalov (Rebrov), Belkevitch (Kossovsky), Venhlinskyi.
Ref: B Pregja (Albania)

(DYNAMO KIEV won 9-0 on aggregate)

After such a drubbing, the return leg at Jenner Park became an exercise in damage limitation. For Barry Town to restore pride and respectability to Welsh football, they needed a committed display against a team whose recent scalps included Barcelona – beaten 0-4 in Spain and 0-3 in Kiev in the previous season's competition.

Barnett selected Pat Mountain in goal in place of former Millwall keeper David Nurse, while up front Craig Evans, hero of the victories over Dinaburg and Vasutas Budapest in the 1996 UEFA Cup, started the match.

The visitors seemed content with their first-leg performance and barely went through the motions during the opening half. But they still found time to make the aggregate score 9-0, when Dmytro Mykhailenko capitalised on Shevchenko's through ball to beat Mountain with a crisp shot. Danny Carter was prominent for the Dragons and his diagonal run gave Barnett a shooting chance which flew straight at the keeper.

Barry spurned another opportunity when Eifion Williams, top marksman in the League of Wales the previous season, missed with a close-range header. But on the half-hour Williams brought the Barry fans to their feet, nodding in Carter's measured cross.

Kiev brought on Rebrov for the second half and his introduction quickly paid dividends. Shevchenko was again the provider, with Oleg Venhlinskyi chipping the advancing keeper. Barry were not done, however, and Viacheslav Kernozenko in the Kiev goal was applauded for a spectacular save from Carter's header. Williams had a late chance to strike an equaliser, but shot wide.

10

THE UEFA CUP

~~~~~~~~~~~~~~~~~~~~~~~~~~~~~~~

1994 – BANGOR CITY (League of Wales)

~~~~~~~~~~~~~~~~~~~~~~~~~~~~~~~

In 1994-95 Welsh representation in Europe was raised to three clubs, when Wales were awarded a second UEFA Cup place – to put alongside their Cup-Winners' Cup slot. Sadly, the League of Wales champions, Bangor City, were denied their rightful place in the Champions Cup and were shunted into the UEFA Cup. This downgrading was softened by a £125,000 sweetener from UEFA.

Bangor's 29-year-old player-manager was Nigel Adkins – a former Tranmere and Wigan goalkeeper who left League football in 1993 to study for a degree in physiotherapy at Salford University. In Bangor's championship winning season he conceded only ten goals in nineteen home games.

Adkins faced selection headaches. With eight English players in the regular Bangor line-up, he would be forced to include a number of untried youngsters in order to conform to UEFA's 'three foreigner' ruling. Bangor's task was made even harder by their lack of competitive football prior to the first leg. Two survivors of the Bangor team of 1962 – skipper Ken Birch and full-back Iorys Griffiths – attended the Farrar Road match. Akranes had six Icelandic internationals in their squad, plus three rugged Yugoslavs.

9 August 1994 *Preliminary Round, 1st Leg* *Farrar Road*
Bangor *Attendance: 3,426*

BANGOR CITY (0) 1 **IA AKRANES (1) 2**
Mottram 53 Reynisson 42, Jonsson 47

BANGOR C: Adkins; Jones, Middleton, Evans, Rutter, Humphreys, Wiggins, Barnett, Mottram, Lloyd-Williams (McClennan), Noble.
AKRANES: Thordarssen T; Adolfsson, Miljhovic, Hervasson, Haraldsson S, Haraldsson P, Jonsson, Thordarssen S, Ingolfsson, Reynisson (Thordarssen O), Bibercic (Petursson).

The Icelandic team immediately settled into a five-man midfield, with Yugoslav Mihaljic Bibercic prominent. Lee Noble's pace down the left flank suddenly began to open up the Akranes defence, and one 40-yard run was halted only by a crude tackle from Zoran Miljhovich, which rightly brought him a booking. A well-worked corner, flicked on by Harry Wiggins, was nodded over the top by Frank Mottram, and shortly afterwards Olafur Adolfsson became the second visitor cautioned.

Mark Rutter's stinging free-kick was tipped away by Tordur Thordarssen, but it was the Icelanders who scored first, just before the interval, when Karl-Steinn Reynisson beat keeper Adkins at the near post.

Straight after the turnaround Akranes increased their lead with a goal from Siggi Jonsson, formerly of Sheffield Wednesday and Arsenal. Bangor refused to wilt, and Chirk-born striker Mottram finally got on the scoresheet with a strong header from Humphreys' centre. Akranes steadied after this reverse, and denied Bangor opportunities of levelling the tie.

---

24 August 1994   *Preliminary Round, 2nd Leg*   *Akranesvollur*
Akranes, Iceland   *Attendance: 1,200*

IA AKRANES (2) 2   **BANGOR CITY (0) 0**
Ingolfsson 8, Thordarssen O 21

IA AKRANES: Thordarssen T; Hognason, Miljhovic, Hervasson, Haraldsson S (Thordarssen S), Haraldsson P, Jonsson, Thordarssen O, Ingolfsson, Gislason, Bibercic (Petursson).
BANGOR CITY: Adkins; Jones, Middleton, Evans, Rutter, Humphreys (Hughes), Wiggins, Barnett, Mottram, Lloyd-Williams (Barry), Noble.
                                        (AKRANES won 4-1 on aggregate)

The Bangor squad flew out on a charter flight from Manchester to Reykjavik, whereupon Akranes supplied a coach to transfer the party for their two-hour journey to Akranes.

Handicapped by having to leave out some of their League regulars, Bangor were also left cursing after just three minutes when a shot by Steve Humphreys curled inches over the bar. Two goals gave the classy Icelanders an unassailable advantage, and the North Wales side had no one to match the skill of Siggi Jonsson.

Akranes made no mistake with their first strike, when Haraldur Ingolfsson cut inside unchallenged and shot from fifteen yards past Adkins at his near post. Bangor's makeshift defence was caught napping again when Olafur Thordarssen picked his spot for the second goal. To add to Bangor's dismay, Lee Noble was dismissed for a second yellow-card offence. Adkins made a brilliant save from

Thordarssen in the final minutes of the game, but was beaten by a Jonsson shot that struck the crossbar and rebounded into play.

~~~~~~~~~~~~~~~~~~~~~~~~~~~~~~~~~

1994 – INTER CARDIFF (League of Wales)

~~~~~~~~~~~~~~~~~~~~~~~~~~~~~~~~~

Inter Cardiff finished as runners-up to Bangor City in the League of Wales and received £43,000 from UEFA for the privilege of joining the Welsh champions in the UEFA Cup. All British sides playing in Europe at this time suffered to a greater or lesser extent from the foreigner rule, Welsh clubs particularly. Added to which, Inter Cardiff were hampered by injuries to key players. Young midfielder John Morgan, for example, had fractured a foot.

Inter Cardiff had no ground facilities of their own, sharing Ninian Park for a short period, before basing themselves at Penydarren Park, Merthyr. The Inter manager, Lyn Jones, had masterminded Merthyr Tydfil's first-leg victory over Atalanta. In goal he could call on the experienced George Wood, the former Cardiff City and Scotland keeper. Wood had played in the Bluebirds' 1988 Cup-Winners' Cup team against Derry City and Aarhus. Jones also recruited Mickey Thomas to bolster the midfield. The former Welsh international, and man of many clubs, had only recently been released from serving a spell at Her Majesty's pleasure, but he had been able to keep fit during his incarceration.

An unkind draw paired Inter Cardiff with Katowice, an experienced Polish side making their 25th sortie in European competition and currently lying third in their domestic league.

9 August 1994   *Preliminary Round, 1st Leg*   *Penydarren Park*
Merthyr   *Attendance: 1,015*

INTER CARDIFF (0) 0   **KATOWICE (0) 2**
Sermak 84, 89

INTER CARDIFF: Wood; Knight, John, O'Brien, Batchelor, Lewis, Thomas, Jones L, Beattie, Evans P (Williams C), Taylor (Burrows).
KATOWICE: Jojko; Wegrzyn, Swierczewski, Maciejewski, Strojek, Widuch, Sermak, Borawski, Wolny, Janoszka (Walczak), Kucz (Nikodem).

The experienced Thomas – veteran of ten of Wrexham's opening twelve European encounters – buzzed in midfield alongside Andy Beattie, who had captained Merthyr Tydfil against Atalanta. Lyndon Jones and Dudley Lewis were two others with Football League experience, Lewis having played in the Swansea side in both 1982 and 1983 Cup-Winners' Cup-ties.

Inter were put under intense pressure from the opening whistle, and Wood kept Katowice at bay with a string of tremendous saves. The Cardiff side defended stoutly, and even found time to mount an isolated raid on the Polish goal when Willie Batchelor almost found the net. Yet another former Merthyr player, 39-year-old Chris Williams, entered the fray as a late substitute.

Two superb strikes from Andrej Sermak finally overcame the home resistance. With just six minutes left, he drove in a 30-yard angled shot, and when the Welshmen pushed forward for an equaliser, he repeated the dose after being put through by Strojek.

---

23 August 1994   *Preliminary Round, 2nd Leg*   *Municipal Stadium*
Katowice, Poland   *Attendance: 4,500*

KATOWICE (3) 6   **INTER CARDIFF (0) 0**
Walczak 25, 83, Maciejewski 33, 44 pen,
Jojko 75 pen, Wolny 89

KATOWICE: Jojko; Maciejewski, Borawski, Wegrzyn, Nikodem (Szala), Wolny, Kucz (Szczygiel), Strojek, Walczak, Swierczewski, Sermak.
INTER CARDIFF: Wood (Jones W); Knight, Jones V, Batchelor, O'Brien, Lewis, Burrows, Jones L, Beattie, Hunter, Taylor (Fisher).
Referee: J Bulent (Turkey)

(KATOWICE won 8-0 on aggregate)

Inter had been forced to play five debutants in the first leg, including the League of Wales' top scorer the previous season, Dave Taylor – who had been signed from Porthmadog. Still more changes were forced on Lyn Jones for the second leg, with the absence of Mickey Thomas being a particular blow. Vaughan Jones and Paul Hunter were brought in as Inter attempted to recover from the two-goal deficit.

The experienced Polish professionals were just too good for the part-timers, though it was midway through the opening period before they added to their first-leg score. Wood was again prominent with a string of fine saves, Andy Beattie worked tirelessly in midfield, and, up front, Dave Taylor and Paul Hunter pressed the home defence when the few attacking opportunities arose.

Katowice struck their first, and best, goal when Walczak seized onto a defence-splitting pass from Borawski. The second goal arrived from a free-kick by Maciejewski, awarded after Neil O'Brien had been cautioned for bringing down Wolny.

Worse was to follow when Dudley Lewis tripped Wolny in the area and dead-ball expert Maciejewski slotted home the spot-kick.

Wood's heroics denied the Poles until the final quarter, when Huw Knight held back Wolny. Up strode home keeper Jojko to ram in the second penalty. Walczak and Wolny completed the debacle.

~~~~~~~~~~~~~~~~~~~~~~~~~~~~~~~~
1995 – BANGOR CITY (League of Wales)
~~~~~~~~~~~~~~~~~~~~~~~~~~~~~~

Bangor retained their League of Wales championship but were given a tough draw when they were paired with the Polish League runners-up, Widzew Lodz. It seemed that the Poles had been around for ever, and they had beaten Liverpool, Manchester United and Manchester City in previous competitions. Their squad contained three Polish internationals, but top striker Grzegorz Mielcarski had recently been sold to FC Porto for £600,000.

Bangor player-manager Nigel Adkins named an eighteen-man squad, including Kevin Langley, the former Everton player signed from Witton Albion. Jimmy Carberry – who missed out the previous season because of the three-foreigner rule – was also in the squad, together with Mark Deegan, the former Holywell Town goalkeeper. Deegan had left Oxford United in the summer and would replace Adkins in goal.

The Polish side's most recent European excursion in the UEFA Cup, in 1993, had ended in a 0-9 thrashing by Eintracht Frankfurt of Germany, but coach Fransiasek Smuda helped them to the Polish runners-up spot behind Legia Warsaw, and after two games of the current season they headed the table.

8 August 1995   *Preliminary Round, 1st Leg*   *Farrar Road*
Bangor   *Attendance: 1,623*

BANGOR CITY (0) 0   **WIDZEW LODZ (2) 4**
                               Czerwiec 25, 42, Koniarek 51, 89

BANGOR C: Deegan; Jones K, Carberry (Jones A), Langley, Rutter, Humphreys (Parry D), Wiggins, Parry J (Barry), Mottram, Colville, Evans.
WIDZEW LODZ: Wosniak; Szymkowiak, Kapinski, Bogusz, Bajor (Bogus), Miaszkiewicz, Wyciszkiewicz (Podolski), Szarpak, Koniarek, Czerwiec (Michalczuk), Siadaczka.

The technically gifted Poles played with pace and power that denied the home side many attacking opportunities, other than in the eleventh minute when Bogusz's clearance fell to Frank Mottram. The Bangor striker lifted his shot over the bar.

Ryzard Czerwiec claimed the opening goal when he seized on a rebound to drive the ball past Deegan from an acute angle. Just before the interval, a teasing cross by Siadaczka found Czerwiec, who slammed in a second goal with a shot to Deegan's right.

With club captain Dave Barnett falling victim to the foreigner rule, it was left to Kevin Langley – later to become Bangor City manager – to raise hopes with a rising shot that struck the crossbar. Szymkowiak raced down the right and crossed to Marek Koniarek, who volleyed past Deegan. Koniarek added to Bangor's woes with a close-range header in the dying seconds.

---

22 August 1995   *Preliminary Round, 2nd Leg*   *Lodz Stadium*
Lodz, Poland   *Attendance: 4,371*

WIDZEW LODZ (0) 1   **BANGOR CITY (0) 0**
Pikuta 84

WIDZEW LODZ: Muchinski; Szymkowiak, Kapinski (Bogus), Bogusz, Bajor, Miaszkiewicz, Wyciszkiewicz (Podolski), Szarpak (Pikuta), Koniarek, Czerwiec (Michalczuk), Siadaczka.
BANGOR CITY: Innes; Jones K, Jones A, Langley, Rutter, Parry D, Wiggins, Barnett, Mottram, Parry J (Evans), Noble.

(WIDZEW LODZ won 5-0 on aggregate)

Although the second leg appeared to be a foregone conclusion, the Bangor squad flew from Manchester to Warsaw, via Amsterdam, in good spirits, having beaten Rhyl 3-0 in their first match of the new season. They stayed at the Holiday Inn in the Polish capital, enjoying a coach tour of the city before travelling the 75 miles to the textile area of Lodz. The problem of too many English players was compounded when goalkeeper Mark Deegan left Bangor for Barrow of the Unibond League. Adkins, in consequence, would have to be one of the permitted foreigners in the squad.

The Welshmen put the accent on defence in an attempt to avoid a rout, and were far from disgraced in front of a partisan crowd. The Bangor players stuck to the task and denied the Poles a sight of goal until late in the game, when superior fitness began to tell. Bogdan Pikuta finally ended Bangor's spirited resistance.

~~~~~~~~~~~~~~~~~~~~~~~~~~~~~~

1995 – AFAN LIDO (League of Wales)

~~~~~~~~~~~~~~~~~~~~~~~~~~~~~~

With two UEFA Cup places available, Afan Lido qualified for Europe by finishing runners-up in the League of Wales. They were managed by Nigel Rees, who made his name by providing the cross for Brian Clark's goal in Cardiff City's epic win over Real Madrid.

As their own facilities were considered by UEFA to be sub-standard, the Lido were obliged to play their home leg at Talbot Athletic Ground, the home of Aberavon Rugby Football Club.

8 August 1995   *Preliminary Round, 1st Leg*   *Talbot Athletic Ground*
Aberavon   *Attendance: 2,117*

AFAN LIDO (1) 1   **RAF RIGA (1) 2**
Moore 29   Karashauskas 21, Bogdans 69

AFAN LIDO: Thomas; Duggan (Jones D), Preece, Cook, Rickard, Glover, Moore, Evans, Radford, Bartley, Patton (Jones N).
RAF RIGA: Olienk; Ivanov, Erglis, Zakrishevski, Dolgopoulos, Gilis, Zuyevs, Karashauskas, Sergeyev, Savalnieks, Bogdans.
Referee: K Fisker (Denmark)

Lido's chances of making progress to the next round were boosted after only fifteen minutes when the Riga defender Vasili Ivanov, was sent off for deliberate handball.

But Lido failed to capitalise on their numerical superiority, and it was the Latvians who scored first when a long ball caught the home defence napping. A blatant handball was missed by the referee, and Yuri Karashauskas slotted the ball beyond Brian Thomas.

Still Lido had chances to level, and new signing Adam Moore equalised with a powerful header from David Evans' cross. The extra man proved to be of little benefit to Lido and they fell behind again following a quick break out by RAF Riga. Following a swift interchange of passes, Valeri Bogdans was left with an easy tap-in.

Afan Lido dominated the closing stages, but were denied an equaliser when David Evans hit the upright.

---

22 August 1995   *Preliminary Round, 2nd Leg*   *National Stadium*
Riga, Latvia   *Attendance: 2,800*

RAF RIGA (0) 0   **AFAN LIDO (0) 0**

RAF RIGA: Olienk; Mastyanica, Erglis, Zakrishevski, Dolgopoulos, Gilis, Zuyevs, Karashauskas, Sergeyev, Savalnieks, Bogdans.
AFAN LIDO: Thomas; Glover, Evans (Preece), Webber, Rickard, Jones N (Evans P), Radford, Moore, Duggan, Bartley (Jones D), Patton.

(RAF RIGA won 2-1 on aggregate)

The Afan Lido squad flew from Gatwick to Riga, training on the morning of the match. Nigel Rees was satisfied with the first-leg performance and did not want to make unnecessary changes.

The Latvians started strongly and had several near misses as the Welsh side acclimatised. Although the home team generally held the upper hand, Afan Lido took control in the second period, and Andrew Rickard and Andrew Webber screwed goal-attempts wide. Webber had been on holiday and missed the first leg. He needed a late fitness test before being included in the return.

It was a poor game, with Lido not good enough to repair the damage inflicted at home. In fact, what happened after the match featured more prominently than what happened in it. The trouble erupted within hours of the final whistle, in a nightclub, of all places. Kevin Bartley – a playing substitute for Cardiff City against Standard Liege in 1993 – had to have his broken jaw wired, and six other players needed treatment for an assortment of head wounds and cuts after being attacked by a local gang.

Welsh soccer bosses initially planned to protest to UEFA about the attack. The FA of Wales pointed out that no club could be held responsible for what happened outside the ground. The wisdom of entering that particular establishment was questioned when it was discovered that the previous week two people had been shot there.

~~~~~~~~~~~~~~~~~~~~~~~~~~~~~~
1996 – NEWTOWN (League of Wales)
~~~~~~~~~~~~~~~~~~~~~~~~~~~~~~

The League of Wales runners-up, Newtown, were drawn against the Latvian league champions Skonto Riga. It was Skonto's fourth successive title, won by 27 points over second-placed Dinaburg. Skonto players comprised half the current Latvian national side.

Newtown manager Brian Coyne called up his old Scottish connections for insight into the Latvians, who had knocked out Aberdeen two seasons previously. Dons manager Roy Aitken, who had been at Parkhead with Coyne, gave him the low-down. Coyne's assistant, Jake King, happened to be the two-goal star of Wrexham's 1984 triumph over FC Porto.

Newtown unveiled their new 400-seater stand at the opening leg. This enabled them to play the tie at Latham Park. Newtown were the first League of Wales club to transfer *two* players to Football League sides: they received £60,000 for selling Andy Cooke to Burnley and Gareth Hanmer to West Bromwich Albion.

17 July 1996	*Preliminary Round, 1st Leg*	*Latham Park*
Newtown		*Attendance: 2,012*

NEWTOWN (0) 1   **SKONTO RIGA (1) 4**
Brown 89   Astafyev 37, 71, Lobanyov 79, 85

Newtown: Barton; Evans J (Thomas), Evans M, Reynolds, Wilding, Pike, Williams, Roberts, Holmans (Wickham), Brown, Pryce.
Skonto Riga: Laizans; Pindeyev (Pakhar), Astafyev, Zemlinsky (Ivanov K), Shevlyakov, Stepanov, Ivanov V, Blagonadezhdin, Jelisejev, Babicev, Shtolcers (Lobanyov).
Referee: J Brito Arceo (Spain)

The Latvian side, brimming with internationals, looked far too good in the opening stages for the League of Wales outfit, who for long periods struggled even to get out of their own half. Vitaly Astafyev was outstanding for the visitors, but despite Skonto's dominance, it took a mistake by Newtown keeper Michael Barton – allowing a weak shot from Astafyev to slither under his body – to give them an interval lead.

Resolute defence by Newtown denied the Latvian side any further score until midway through the second half, when Astafyev notched his second goal. Despite peppering the home goal, Skonto did not score a third until they introduced substitute Valentin Lobanyov, who netted twice in six minutes. The home supporters were rewarded at the end when Romilly Brown claimed a goal for Newtown in injury-time.

---

24 July 1996   *Preliminary Round, 2nd Leg*   *National Stadium*
Riga, Latvia   *Attendance: 3,500*

SKONTO RIGA (1) 3   **NEWTOWN (0) 0**
Astafyev 43, Konstantin 65,
Jelisejev 85

Skonto Riga: Laizans; Ivanov K (Stepanov), Astafyev, Zemlinsky, Shevlyakov, Jelisejev, Ivanov V, Blagonadezhdin (Pakhar), Pindeyev, Babicev (Lobanyov), Shtolcers.
Newtown: Barton; Evans J, Wilding, Evans M, Reynolds, Thomas (Pike), Roberts, Pryce, Brown, Williams, Robinson.
Referee: M Milevski (Poland)

(Skonto Riga won 7-1 on aggregate)

For the away leg in Latvia, Newtown enjoyed the unexpected backing of a small posse of Barry Town supporters. They had travelled to watch their side play Dinaburg in Daugavpils, then undertaken a three-hour journey to the Latvian capital Riga, to lend their cheers to Newtown's cause.

Once again, Skonto's team of nine Latvian and one Russian international proved too strong for the Mid Wales part-timers.

Skonto's top-rated player, Astafyev – who was being monitored by Inter Milan – scored his third goal of the tie just before the interval. In the second period, further goals from Konstantin Ivanov and Aleksandr Jelisejev eased the home side through to the next round, where they faced Malmo of Sweden.

Newtown's supporters, accompanied by the 33 Barry fans who had come to cheer, then set off on their 40 hour, 2,000 mile coach journey back to Wales, travelling through nine countries.

~~~~~~~~~~~~~~~~~~~~~~~~~~~~~~~~~~~~

1996 – BARRY TOWN (League of Wales)

~~~~~~~~~~~~~~~~~~~~~~~~~~~~~~~~~~~~

The Dragons were the only full-time professional club in the League of Wales. They had set a high standard since returning to the Welsh football scene and cleaning up all the trophies, including the Welsh Cup in 1994.

With the experience gained from their Cup-Winners' Cup defeat by Zalgiris Vilnius, Barry became the second Welsh club – after Bangor City – to play in two different European competitions. Only Richard Jones, the former Hereford United and Newport County player, remained of the side that lost 0-7 on aggregate to the Lithuanian side.

The UEFA Cup home leg – against yet another Baltic team, Dinaburg of Latvia – marked the opening of the new 2,000-seater stand at Jenner Park. Player-coach Gary Barnett could select from a full squad, with the exception of the former Cardiff City player Cohen Griffith, while recent signing from Merthyr Tydfil, Andrew York, was only due back from holiday 24 hours before kick-off, but he made the team.

Dinaburg, playing in Europe for the first time, included their most recent signing – Latvian international Sergei Tarasov.

18 July 1996   *Preliminary Round, 1st Leg*   *Jenner Park*
Barry   *Attendance: 2,500*

BARRY TOWN (0) 0   **DINABURG (0) 0**

BARRY TOWN: Ovendale; Evans T, Lloyd, French, York, Norman, Barnett, Loss (Ryan), Bird, Jones, Evans C (Pike)
D'BURG: Diguliev; Glazov, Zizilev (Smirnov), Isakov, Pogodin, Burlakov, Fedotov, Shmikov, Karashauskas, Baushev (Zhavoronkov), Tarasov.
Referee: J Pratas (Portugal)

The runners-up in the Latvian League began brightly, but without seriously threatening the home goal. Tarasov missed one chance with a poor header, and Karashauskas wasted another opportunity in the first half.

In front of a capacity crowd, Barry gradually warmed to their task, and after the break the midfield trio of Barnett, Jones, and Colin Loss began to take a grip. In the 55th minute Tony Bird's pace left the Dinaburg defence flatfooted as he raced onto Terry Evans' pass. Bird went down under a challenge by Dinaburg keeper Sergei Diguliev, for which the referee awarded a penalty. Bird took responsibility, but sent his kick whistling past the post.

Chris Pike, another former Cardiff City player with European experience, was thrown into the fray, but the visitors held out. No goals, but three cautions for Barry – Bird, York and Terry Evans – along with a number of Dinaburg players.

---

23 July 1996   *Preliminary Round, 2nd Leg*   *Tseltnieks Stadium*
Daugavpils, Latvia   *Attendance: 2,250*

DINABURG (0) 1   **BARRY TOWN (1) 2**
Tarasov 60   Pike 35, Evans C 85

D'BURG: Diguliev; Glazov, Beraya, Isakov, Pogodin (Smirnov) (Zizilev), Burlakov, Fedotov, Shmikov, Karashauskas, Baushev (Zhavoronkov), Tarasov.
BARRY TOWN: Ovendale; Evans T, Lloyd, French, York, Norman, Barnett, Loss, Bird, Jones, Pike (Evans C).
Referee: S Dougall (Scotland)

(BARRY TOWN won 2-1 on aggregate)

A handful of ardent Barry supporters made the long trip to Latvia's second city, Daugavpils, confident that the League of Wales side would prevail. Barry made one change to their starting eleven, with Chris Pike replacing Craig Evans up front as partner to Tony Bird.

Barry fully deserved this outstanding victory – the first in Europe by a League of Wales side – as they defended superbly and posed a constant threat in attack. Chris Pike struck Barry's first European goal in the 35th minute, sending the few Welsh supporters in the sparse crowd wild. Pike's goal also made him the first player with a Welsh club to score goals in two different European competitions. Buttressed by their away goal – which meant Dinaburg needed to score two – Barry continued to tackle hard, but fairly, and kept the home side on the back foot until the dangerous Tarasov equalised on the hour.

Dinaburg pressed for the second goal they required, and Mark Ovendale had to pull off several crucial saves from the technically sound Latvians. Barry brought on Craig Evans for the tiring Pike, and with time running out he struck the winner.

The Scottish referee booked seven players, including Colin Loss, Richard Jones, Ian French – and more significantly – Tony Bird.

---

6 August 1996   *Qualifying Round, 1st Leg*   *Fay Utcai*
Budapest, Hungary   *Attendance: 3,500*

VASUTAS BUDAPEST (2) 3   BARRY TOWN (1) 1
Bukszegi 5, Egressy 42,   Evans T 14
Farkas 67 pen

VASUTAS: Vegh; Bondarenko, Djurasobic, Molnar, Farkas, Eros, Bukszegi (Csordas), Stanici, Egressy, Horvath, Fuzi (Javor).
BARRY TOWN: Ovendale; Evans T, Lloyd (Ryan), French, York, Norman, Barnett, Loss, Jones, Evans C (O'Gorman), Pike (Mountain).
Referee: A Marcel (Portugal)

When the draw for the next stage was held, in Geneva, Barry Town came out of the hat with the Hungarian side, Vasutas Budapest. It was a tough draw, but Barry were thankful to have avoided Moscow Dynamo, who were also in their section.

The Welsh party stayed in a Budapest hotel overlooking the Danube. Barry were forced to make at least one change: Tony Bird's two cautions against Dinaburg in the previous round had earned him a one-match suspension.

The Hungarians – coached by the former international manager, Giorgy Mezny – took an early lead when Ian French's slip let in the Romanian, Constantin Stanici, who set up the unmarked Zoltan Bukszegi. Barry were not in arrears for long. Terry Evans sent over an awkward cross which home keeper Zoltan Vegh helped into his own net.

The Dragons now had the bit between their teeth, and Colin Loss and Craig Evans both went close. Vasutas failed to threaten until Vegh's towering clearance was misjudged by Dave Norman. Gabor Egressy took advantage, slipping round the back to beat Mark Ovendale with a perfect lob.

In the second half, Ovendale saved from Stanici and substitute Javor as Barry were hard-pressed to keep the Magyars out. The home side took a 3-1 lead when Norman needlessly fouled Janos Horvath in the area, and skipper Josef Farkas drilled home the spot-kick.

Barry were now in disarray, and they were plunged into further trouble when Ovendale handled a shot from Javor outside his area and was sent off. Substitute keeper Pat Mountain took over in goal and pulled off a good save from Egressy in injury-time.

---

20 August 1996   *Qualifying Round, 2nd Leg*   *Jenner Park*
Barry   *Attendance: 2,500*

BARRY TOWN (1) 3   **VASUTAS BUDAPEST (0) 1**
Pike 45 pen, O'Gorman 46,   Egressy 63
Evans C 78

BARRY TOWN: Mountain; Johnson, Lloyd, French, York, O'Gorman (Evans C), Barnett (Misbah), Huggins, Ryan (Griffith), Pike, Bird.
VASUTAS: Vegh; Komlosi (Bognar), Molnar, Eros, Bukszegi, Stanici, Egressy, Horvath (Csordas), Fuzi, Pomper (Farkas), Feher.
Referee: A Georgiou (Cyprus)

(BARRY TOWN won on penalties)

Barry were severely hampered for the return leg, with Ovendale out and Jones and Loss suspended after receiving two cautions. Terry Evans would also miss the tie through injury, but Tony Bird would return after completing his one-match suspension. Also included in the team was Dean Huggins, the first League of Wales player ever to have been selected for the Wales Under-21 side.

Barry attacked from the whistle, determined to claw back the deficit. Gary Barnett's ploy of using two wide players – Dave O'Gorman and Darren Ryan – paid off, as their pace and accurate crossing caused trouble in the Vasutas defence. Tony Bird also proved to be a handful, setting up an early chance for Chris Pike. Constantin Stanici carried the visitors' only threat, putting a half-chance wide in a rare Hungarian breakaway.

On the stroke of half-time the Dragons took the lead when Pike stroked in a penalty awarded after Bird had been impeded by Adam Komlosi. Immediately after the interval, Barry sensationally doubled the score when O'Gorman's shot flew over Vegh's head.

The visitors raised the tempo, and though Mountain saved from Karoly Eros and Jorge Bognar, the keeper was helpless when Bukszegi's shot cannoned off French to present the Hungarian Olympic squad member Egressy with a simple far-post header.

Needing to score to force extra-time, Barry brought on Cohen Griffith and Craig Evans. The substitutions were rewarded when Evans raced onto a Pike flick to fire home.

With the scores level on aggregate and each side having one away goal, extra-time was required. It was a cagey 30 minutes, with both sides determined to protect their goal rather than score one at the other end. Mind you, it might have been different had an early Egressy strike not been disallowed for offside.

The match had to be decided on a penalty shoot-out. Stanici and Pike were both on target, as were Bird, Farkas, and Gary Lloyd, before Mountain produced a splendid save by tipping Bukszegi's kick onto the crossbar. Craig Evans fired the winning penalty.

---

10 September 1996   1st Round, 1st Leg   *Pittodrie*
Aberdeen, Scotland   *Attendance: 13,500*

ABERDEEN (1) 3   **BARRY TOWN (1) 1**
Windass 7, Glass 58, Young 65   Jones 9

ABERDEEN: Walker; McKimmie, Tzvetanov, Young (Rowson), Grant, Inglis, Miller (Woodthorpe), Dodds (Shearer), Windass, Kiriakov, Glass.
BARRY TOWN: Ovendale; Johnson, Lloyd, French, York, Barnett, Loss, Bird, Jones, Pike, Ryan.
Referee: A Snoddy (Northern Ireland)

The South Wales club was besieged by the Scottish media after the first-round draw paired the Dragons with Aberdeen. The squad flew to the Granite City the day before the match and trained on the Pittodrie pitch that evening. Over 200 fans journeyed north, grateful that it was not another arduous trip to the likes of Latvia and Hungary.

Barry's Euro earnings had soared. They were set to bank around £40,000 for each round, not to mention the £100,000 compensation owed from UEFA for being national champions excluded from the Champions Cup.

Aberdeen had defeated Zalgiris Vilnius – conquerors of Barry in the 1994 Cup-Winners' Cup – to reach this stage. The Dons had been in prolific scoring form of late, with thirteen goals in their last three games. Their supporters were anticipating another goal-glut to rival their 10-0 victory over IFK Reykjavik in their very first European match, back in 1967.

When Dean Windass, the former Hull striker, chipped the ball over Mark Ovendale with only seven minutes played, a repeat of that scoreline looked on the cards. But Barry bounced back immediately with what the Aberdeen skipper Stewart McKimmie later described as a wonder goal. It was scored by Barry midfielder Richard Jones, who hit an awkward bouncing ball from twenty yards that screamed into the net for what might prove to be a priceless away goal. For Jones it was sweet revenge: he was the only survivor of Barry's team that had been humbled by Vilnius.

Barry held out until almost the hour mark, when a disputed goal allowed Aberdeen to restore their lead. Ovendale was impeded by Billy Dodds, and the ball ran to Stephen Glass – later transferred to Newcastle – who struck it into the net past Phil Johnson.

Aberdeen's two Bulgarian internationals, Tzanko Tsvetanov and Ilian Kiriakov, now began to exert their influence. Tsvetanov floated over a centre for 17-year-old Darren Young to cap a fine display with the third goal. For all their efforts, Aberdeen could not add a fourth, and the Dragons were applauded from the field at the end.

---

24 September 1996   *1st Round, 2nd Leg*   *Jenner Park*
Barry   *Attendance: 6,000*

BARRY TOWN (1) 3   **ABERDEEN (2) 3**
O'Gorman 4, Ryan 71 pen,   Dodds 15, 25, Rowson 84
Bird 83

BARRY TOWN: Ovendale; Johnson, Lloyd, French, York, Barnett, Jones, Bird, Ryan (Huggins), Pike (Griffith), O'Gorman (Evans C).
ABERDEEN: Walker; McKimmie, Irvine, Young, Tsvetanov, Woodthorpe, Rowson, Grant, Kiriakov (Shearer), Dodds, Windass.
Referee: L Michel (Czech Republic)

(ABERDEEN won 6-4 on aggregate)

Temporary seating was installed behind both goals at Jenner Park in readiness for the second leg. Aberdeen would be without Stephen Glass, Joe Miller and Paul Bernard, all injured, and their bubble appeared to have burst: they had lost their last two matches.

The game began in a downpour. After Barry skipper Ian French had cleared a Billy Dodds shot off the line, the home side scored the early goal they coveted. Swift inter-passing between Tony Bird and Chris Pike opened up a chance for Dave O'Gorman. The wingman had missed the first leg at Pittodrie, but now he swooped on a rebound from the keeper and fired into the net.

The packed crowd were silenced by a Dodds double inside ten minutes, both goals stemming from defensive mistakes. First, Dodds equalised on the night when he ran through unchallenged to meet Dean Windass's header and shoot past Mark Ovendale. He then made it 2-1 when he scored from a Windass pass – though he appeared to be offside. The Dragons roared back. Gary Barnett went close with two strikes and O'Gorman's shot was well saved by Nicky Walker in the Aberdeen goal.

Chris Pike's calf injury meant a second-half switch, with Cohen Griffith replacing his former Cardiff City colleague. The introduction of Griffith posed problems for the Scots, and skipper Stewart McKimmie was given a torrid time. Richard Jones almost duplicated his Pittodrie goal with an effort that rebounded from the underside of the crossbar.

Barry's pressure finally paid off when Bird was fouled in the area and Darren Ryan tucked away the spot-kick. Indeed, Barry were so much on top in the second half it was not until the final quarter that Ovendale was brought into action, saving from Ilian Kiriakov.

The Dragons took a deserved lead on the night when Walker fumbled Ryan's shot and Bird seized on the rebound. The Welsh team were now on the brink of an historic victory, but Aberdeen broke out and David Rowson drove in a late equaliser at the far post. Barry finished the match with ten men after Jones suffered concussion in a clash with Brian Irvine.

Hot showers were ruled out as a dressing room pump had broken. But this failed to dampen spirits. Barry Town were estimated to have profited to the tune of £400,000 from their UEFA Cup participation. Aberdeen went out to Brondby in the next round.

~~~~~~

1997 – INTER CABLETEL (League of Wales)

~~~~~~

The Cardiff based side earned the plum draw of the preliminary stages when they were paired with the mighty Celtic. First thoughts were to play the home leg at the Cardiff Athletic Stadium, Inter's home ground, but when the size of Celtic's travelling support was taken into consideration it was decided to move over the road and play the match at Ninian Park.

Manager George Wood and the club nutritionist put Inter's players on a strict diet regime, comprising skimmed milk, fish, pasta and chicken, all washed down with still water. Eggs, chips and mayonnaise were banned as Inter prepared for the biggest game in their history.

Inter were taken to a secret hideaway for two days to escape the huge media attention that the match had generated. New Celtic coach Wim Jansen – who had played in two World Cup finals for Holland, in 1974 and 1978, and had helped Feyenoord lift the European Cup in 1970 – was hoping for a winning start in Europe. On a short Irish tour undertaken to improve match fitness, Celtic had suffered an embarrassing loss to Derry City. Keeping the Celtic bench warm was their new £1.5 million signing from Hibernian, Darren Jackson, but there was no place for want-away foreign stars Paolo di Canio or Jorge Cadette.

23 July 1997   *Preliminary Round, 1st Leg*   *Ninian Park*
Cardiff   *Attendance: 6,980*

INTER CABLETEL (0) 0   **CELTIC (2) 3**
                                  Thom 6 pen, Johnson 45
                                  Weighorst 81

INTER CABLETEL: Ellacott; Hewitt, Rickard, David, Philpott, Davies, Wharton, Burrows (Jenkins), Haig (Wile), Gibson (Murray), Williams.
CELTIC: Marshall; Boyd, McKinlay, McNamara, Stubbs, Thom, Johnson (Jackson), Donnelly, Hannah, Weighorst, Gray.
Referee: A Ibanez (Spain)

The League of Wales side made a disastrous start when Wayne Hewitt brought down Jackie McNamara, and German international Andreas Thom netted from the spot.

Ninian Park was awash with green and white, and the Celtic supporters were in carnival mood as they anticipated their favourites romping to an easy victory. Inter held out until the stroke of half-time, when Tommy Johnson, the former Aston Villa striker, crashed in the second from a centre by Tosh McKinlay.

The overworked Marty Ellacott, a member of Ton Pentre's Inter Toto Cup team, was not beaten again until Jansen brought on new signing Darren Jackson. The former Hibs player pepped up the Celtic front line, and it was not long before Danish international Morten Weighorst headed in the third. This was not the first time Weighorst had faced Welsh opposition. He had been in the Lyngby team beaten by Wrexham in the 1990 Cup-Winners' Cup. Wieghorst also made his mark in the 1998 World Cup finals when he was sent off only three minutes after being brought on as a substitute for Denmark against South Africa.

---

29 July 1997   *Preliminary Round, 2nd Leg*   *Parkhead*
Glasgow, Scotland   *Attendance: 41,537*

CELTIC (3) 5   **INTER CABLETEL (0) 0**
Thom 19 pen, Jackson 42,
Johnson 44, Hannah 63, Hay 86

CELTIC: Marshall; Boyd, McKinlay, McNamara, Stubbs, Hannah (McBride), Donnelly, Gray (Annoni), Jackson, Johnson (Hay), Thom.
INTER CABLETEL: Ellacott; Hewitt, Rickard, David, Philpott, Davies, Wharton, Burrows (Jenkins), Haig, Gibson (Murray), Williams (Richards).
Referee: Micallef (Malta)

(CELTIC won 8-0 on aggregate)

The Inter party travelled to Scotland two days prior to the second leg and trained in Lanark. Celtic preferred to stay at Seamill, on the Ayrshire coast, their traditional base before important matches. Alan Stubbs and Andreas Thom overcame injury worries and were included in the Celtic team.

The Scots took the lead in the same manner as in the first leg, when Andreas Thom stroked in a penalty. It was awarded after Richard David felled Simon Donnelly in the area. Thereafter the part-timers kept the Bhoys at bay until the interval approached, when sloppy defending gifted Celtic headers from Darren Jackson and Tommy Johnson.

Inter never flagged, and Marty Ellacott made a string of fine saves before being beaten by a fierce shot from David Hannah. Chris Hay completed the scoring in front of the largest crowd ever to watch a match involving a League of Wales side.

Presentation boxes containing Celtic's own brand of whisky were awaiting each player in the dressing room at the end of the match. Everyone in the Welsh party also received a replica Celtic jersey in a fine show of hospitality by the Scottish giants.

~~~~~~~~~~~~~~~~~~~~~~~~~~~~~~

1998 – NEWTOWN (League of Wales)

~~~~~~~~~~~~~~~~~~~~~~~~~~~~~~

Newtown enlisted the help of diet and fitness experts as they prepared for their second UEFA Cup campaign. Extra temporary seating was installed at their Latham Park ground to comply with UEFA's ruling that 80% of spectators must be seated for European matches. Together with the 450 extra seats installed in a brand new £250,000 stadium complex – that incorporated new changing rooms – seating capacity was raised to 1,800.

The Robins' first opponents – Wisla Krakow of Poland – were a top-quality side with six full Polish internationals plus a Nigerian Under-21 cap. Wisla had been saved from bankruptcy eighteen months previously, due to the intervention of a cable TV company, Tele-Fonika, which was reputed to have invested £12 million in the club.

Newtown were without the previous season's leading scorer, Kevin Morrison, who had an ankle injury and whose target was to get fit in time for the second leg.

22 July 1998   *Preliminary Round, 1st Leg*   *Latham Park*
Newtown   *Attendance: 1,200*

NEWTOWN (0) 0   **WISLA KRAKOW (0) 0**

NEWTOWN: Barton; Thomas M (Line), Evans G, Reynolds, Thomas A, Roberts, Evans M, Wickham, Williams, Yates, Ruscoe.
WISLA KRAKOW: Sarnat; Kaluzny, Bogdan, Wegrzyn, Pater (Nowak), Kaliciak, Czerweic, Kulawik, Sunday, Zajac, Nicinski (Dubicki).
Referee: S Prolic (Bosnia-Herzegovina)

The Mid Wales outfit produced a tremendous battling performance to stifle a side that had finished third in the Polish League and who were now competing in Europe for the sixth time. Wisla camped in Newtown's half for much of the game but the home side always looked capable of hitting back on the break.

Jonathan Williams burst onto Justin Wickham's pass and forced a hurried save from Wisla keeper Artur Sarnat. Wisla's experience told as they forced numerous corners, but with skipper Colin Reynolds and Aneurin Thomas pillars of strength at the heart of the Newtown defence, goalkeeper Michael Barton was rarely troubled.

---

29 July 1998   *Preliminary Round, 2nd Leg*   *Wisla Stadion*
Krakow, Poland   *Attendance: 10,000*

WISLA KRAKOW (2) 7   **NEWTOWN (0) 0**
Kulawik 28, 46, Sunday 35,
Kaliciak 49, Nicinski 54,
Pater 62, Wegrzyn 66.

WISLA KRAKOW: Sarnat; Zajac, Wegrzyn, Matyja, Dubicki, Pater, Kulawik (Piszczek), Czerwiec, Sunday, Nicinski (Skrzinski), Kaliciak.
NEWTOWN: Barton, Line, Evans G, Reynolds, Thomas A, Roberts, Wickham (Clifford), Williams, Yates (Commerford), Evans M, Ruscoe (Davies).
Referee: I Baskakov (Russia)

(WISLA KRAKOW won 7-0 on aggregate)

A Newtown party of 60, including club officials and Latham Park staff, left Heathrow for Warsaw two days before the date of the second leg. The journey would be completed by a three-hour coach trip to Krakow. Kevin Morrison had not recovered from his ankle injury and would miss out.

Newtown fought bravely and held out for almost half an hour before the Wisla skipper, Tomasz Kulawik, put the Polish side in front. Shortly afterwards, Nigerian Under-21 cap Ibrahim Sunday unleashed an unstoppable shot to virtually seal the tie.

The Robins wilted in the second period and the Poles ran in five goals in a twenty-minute spell shortly after the resumption. The League of Wales side rarely managed to reach their opponents half, and all they had to show for their efforts was a feeble shot from the right foot of Jonathan Williams.

Not even the introduction of their new recruit – the former Bristol Rovers and Welshpool striker, Steve Clifford – made any impact. It was an embarrassing result, given Newtown's fine showing in the first leg.

11

THE INTER TOTO CUP

~~~~~~~~~~~~~~~~~~~~~~~~~~~~~~~~~

1995 – TON PENTRE (League of Wales)

~~~~~~~~~~~~~~~~~~~~~~~~~~~~~~~~~

Ton's reward for finishing third in the 1994-95 League of Wales season was a place in the first Inter Toto Cup. This new-fangled competition was constructed as a close-season feeder to the UEFA Cup, places being on offer to those clubs which survived the group stage, then semi-finals and finals. For smaller clubs, the Inter Toto Cup offered certain attractions – even though the summer fixture schedule effectively did away with the close season. For bigger clubs, it presented an unwelcome extension to an already congested fixture list. English participants – Tottenham, Wimbledon and Sheffield Wednesday – fielded teams of unknowns, for which the clubs, and the FA, were reprimanded and threatened with sanctions.

Groups consisted of five teams, each to play the others once only. Ton's first opponents were Heerenveen, who had finished sixth in the Dutch First Division and been the only team to score three goals against Ajax. Ynys Park was declared unacceptable for the staging of a European tie, so the home legs were played at Cardiff Rugby Club.

1 July 1995	*Match 1*	*Cardiff Arms Park*
Cardiff		

TON PENTRE (0) 0   **HEERENVEEN (3) 7**
Hansma 10, 24, Regtop 15, 82
Tammar 56, 75, Tomasson 78

TON PENTRE: Ellacott; Davies (Hedditch), Clements, Blackie, Gibson, Thomas, Richards, Evans, Davey, Haig, Gullett (Watkins).
HEERENVEEN: L'Ami; Doesburg, Pastoor, Hansma, Sier, Roclotsen, Hellinga (Tammar), De Visser, Tomasson, Regtop, Wouden.
Referee: S Lodge (England)

Brett Davey joined Paul Evans up front. Davey had appeared at Cardiff RFC on numerous occasions whilst playing rugby union for Maesteg and Bridgend. Evans had previous European experience to call upon, as had Jimmy Blackie, who been in Cwmbran Town's 1993 side.

Presently lying ninth in their league, Heerenveen were a skilful side, but Ton made chances in the opening minutes and skipper Paul Clements was denied by a point-blank save from L'Ami. It was not long, however, before the visitors' cultured football brought them a three-goal lead, though even then Ton refused to hide behind a blanket defence. The late goal blitz was inevitable, given the chasing that the Bulldogs had been subjected to, and it was a relief when the end came. The Welsh side sportingly formed a guard of honour to applaud the Dutch players off the field.

---

8 July 1995   *Match 2*   *Bekescsaba Stadion*
Bekescsaba, Hungary

BEKESCSABAI ELORE (4) 4   TON PENTRE (0) 0
Szarvas 26, 40, Kulcsar 35, 36

TON PENTRE: Ellacott; Wile (Davey), Davies, Blackie, Gibson, Clements, Richards, Evans, Watkins, Haig, Gullett.
BEKESCSABAI ELORE: Baji; Szenti, Usmaev, Balog, Czipo, Dobi (Geczi), Szarvas, Csato (Nagy), Kulcsar, Kasik, Mracsko.
Referee: P Ianinski (Bulgaria)

The Ton Pentre squad flew from Heathrow to Budapest, spending two nights in the Hungarian capital before travelling the 90 miles to the venue on match day. They returned to Wales the following day.

The inexperienced Welsh side learnt more lessons the hard way, and were effectively beaten in the first 45 minutes. Once again they created some early chances, with Richard Haig and Paul Evans off target, but after Marty Ellacott had twice saved well the Hungarian team broke through to race into a commanding lead. First, Ellacott let a Szarvas corner slip through his hands, and nine minutes later Alexandru Kulcsar grabbed the second. Ton then lost possession at the restart, and Kulcsar raced through for his second goal inside a minute. Szarvas claimed number four. Brian Gullett switched to sweeper for the second half, helping to shore up Ton's defence.

---

13 July 1995   *Match 3*   *Cardiff Arms Park*
Cardiff

TON PENTRE (0) 0   UNIAO LEIRA (2) 3
                                     Pinto 10, 31, Manuel 86

TON PENTRE: Ellacott; Blackie, Clements, Hedditch, Davey (Gibson), Thomas, Richards (Wile), Davies (Evans), Watkins, Haig, Gullett.
UNIAO LEIRA: Ferreira; Bilro, Paulito, Abel (Joao Manuel), Crespo, Paulo Duarte, Tahar, Germino, Pinto, Reinaldo, Fua (Mario Artur).
Referee: H Barr (Northern Ireland)

Next up for the Bulldogs were the Portuguese side, Uniao Leira, who had finished their domestic season in sixth place. By this stage in the competition Ton needed financial support from the FA of Wales, and they benefited from an undisclosed loan, to be repaid over a specified period.

The Portuguese were faster on the ball and technically superior to the honest endeavour provided by the League of Wales side. Richard Haig probed tirelessly up front, and Paul Clements enjoyed a stirring battle with Bilro down the left flank. Ton's best chance of opening their scoring account fell to Mark Davies, but he failed to control a misdirected back-pass from Paulito. A shot by Brett Davey was the only Ton effort to cause Uniao alarm, but Ferreira kept it out. Ton keeper Marty Ellacott was constantly on his toes and pulled off outstanding saves to deny Moroccan midfielder Tahar.

Pinto struck twice in the first half, and the final goal came from Manuel as the Bulldogs tired in the closing minutes.

---

22 July 1995   *Match 4*   *Naestved Stadion*
Naestved, Denmark

NAESTVED (1) 2   **TON PENTRE (0) 0**
Jacobsen 34, 72

NAESTVED: Fallentin; Christensen S (Neilsen N), Neilsen T, Bank, Neilsen A, Houggard, Petersen (Spur-Mortensen), Juel (Jensen), Jacobsen, Mathiesen, Christensen A.
TON PENTRE: Ellacott; Blackie, Davies, Clements, Gibson (James), Thomas, Richards (Wile), Evans, Watkins, Gullett (Davey), Haig.
Referee: B Bergmann (Iceland)

Ton Pentre flew out to Copenhagen the day before their match with Naestved. The stadium, 40 miles from the Danish capital, was reached by coach, and the Welsh party were taken back to Copenhagen after the match. They returned home on the Sunday.

Brian Gibson and Paul Evans were restored, having come off the bench during the previous match. The Bulldogs were desperate to score before the tournament ended, and Gibson forced the home keeper to tip a shot onto the bar. Evans then rounded Claus Fallentin and prodded the ball goalwards, only to see defender Nicolas Juel hack the ball clear. Richard Haig was felled in full flight, but Ton could not take advantage of the free-kick.

The Rhondda side were beaten by two goals from Lars Jacobsen, the second of which looked offside. Juel also missed a sitter, heading over from point-blank range. Despite all their efforts, Ton Pentre were unable to score the goal they craved.

Participation in the Inter Toto Cup would have serious repercussions for Ton Pentre. The costs were so great that it strained the finances of the club to such an extent that they withdrew from the League of Wales at the close of season 1996-97. Their subsequent admittance to the Welsh League will give them the opportunity of rebuilding, and possibly returning once more to their position as one of the leading clubs in Welsh football.

	GROUP 4	P	W	D	L	F	A	Pts
1	Heerenveen	4	3	0	1	13	2	9
2	Uniao Leira	4	2	2	0	7	3	8
3	Naestved	4	1	2	1	7	6	5
4	Bekescabai	4	1	2	1	9	9	5
5	Ton Pentre	4	0	0	4	0	16	0

1996 – CONWY UNITED (League of Wales)

The second season of the Inter Toto Cup was shorn of English and Scottish representation, though the value of the competition could be seen in the progress of Bordeaux, who had seized one of the UEFA Cup places on offer and stormed all the way to the final.

Conwy United began training for their European matches in May, but found their preparations hampered by being unable to organise friendlies in the close season. They even hired an astroturf surface in Ellesmere Port for squad training, as their own pitch at the Morfa Ground was being re-seeded.

Conwy's 'home' matches in the Inter Toto Cup would take place at the Racecourse, Wrexham. It was hoped that sufficient gate money would be taken at the first match to help pay the travelling expenses to Poland and Denmark. Manager John Hulse enlisted the help of Wales goalkeeper Neville Southall for his team preparations.

29 June 1996   *Match 1*   *Racecourse*
Wrexham

CONWY UNITED (0) 0   **SC CHARLEROI (0) 0**

CONWY U: Bamford; Cross, Mullen, McAuley (Jones MA), Edwards, Barnett, Brookman, Doran, Camden (Taylor S), McKenna, Noble.
CHARLEROI: Begasse; Suray, Mairy, Teklak (Brncic), Wuillot, Rasquin, Omelianovitch (Remy), Balog, Fiers, Mommens, Bukran (Silvagni).
Referee: A Snoddy (Northern Ireland)

Ken McKenna almost began the match sensationally when he burst clear from the kick-off. Belgian keeper Julien Begasse rushed out to deny him. Blessed with Belgian, Hungarian and Ukrainian internationals in their side, Charleroi began to dominate proceedings, forcing the Conwy rearguard to defend stoutly.

Raymond Mommens, a veteran Belgian international, oozed class in midfield. He set up Oliver Suray, who hit a fierce shot against a post. Conwy keeper Ian Bamford saved from Filip Fiers, and again from Suray, as the visitors looked likely to breach the dam. In the second half the Belgians had two players cautioned as their frustrations boiled over, and they introduced three substitutes in their search for the elusive goal.

It was the home side who went nearest to scoring, but Begasse saved Chris Camden's snap shot. McKenna sent a header inches over the bar from a Hugh McAuley corner, and in the last minute his goal-bound shot was blocked by the keeper.

---

8 July 1996   *Match 2*   *Zaglebie Stadion*
Lubin, Poland

ZAGLEBIE LUBIN (0) 3   **CONWY UNITED (0) 0**
Grzybowski 53, 75, Gorski 86

CONWY U: Bamford; Cross, Mullen, McAuley (Jones M), Edwards, Barnett (Taylor C), Brookman, Doran, Camden (Taylor S), McKenna, Noble.
ZAGLEBIE: Dreszer; Lewandowski, Nalepka, Przerywacz, Bubnowicz, Szczypkowski, Grzybowski, Krzyzanowski, Gorski, Jasinski, Piekarski.
Referee: S Tivold (Slovenia)

After the well-deserved result against Charleroi, Conwy were forced to go cap-in-hand to the FA of Wales for a £20,000 loan. The money was needed to cover the cost of the trip to Poland to play Zaglebie Lubin, and also to finance their final match – against the Danish side Silkeborg.

After paying for the use of the Racecourse, as well as police and stewarding costs, the club had only £3,000 in the kitty, nowhere near the £11,000 needed for the Polish trip, never mind the Danish one. The FA of Wales agreed to the loan, which would be deducted from the prize money due to the club for taking part.

The party flew from Manchester to Berlin with a change of plane in Frankfurt. From Berlin they needed a five-hour coach journey to western Poland, arriving at Lubin seventeen hours after setting off. The return journey required a change of planes at Dusseldorf.

Zaglebie Lubin had finished mid-table in the Polish League, but little else was known about them, other than that they had been Polish champions in 1991 and had four players named in a recent Poland squad.

In the first half Conwy packed men behind the ball and forced the Polish side to shoot from outside the area. With a little luck, Conwy might have scored – Ken McKenna's overhead kick flew wide and Hugh McAuley's free-kick was saved at the foot of the post by Miroslaw Dreszer. The effects of the tortuous journey finally began to tell, however, and Conwy went into arrears when Zbigniew Grzybowski deflected a shot past a stranded Ian Bamford. The same player headed a second goal, helped by poor marking from the Conwy defence.

Lee Noble, who had played in the UEFA Cup for Bangor City, had a shot blocked following a promising Conwy attack, and McKenna went close again. But it was the home side who completed the scoring through Wojciech Gorski's header. The Welsh team had a chance to pull a goal back when they won a free-kick on the edge of the area, but Ian Doran's shot was pushed away.

---

13 July 1996　　　　　　　*Match 3*　　　　　　　*Racecourse*
Wrexham

CONWY UNITED (1) 1　　　　**SV MARCO POLO RIED (0) 2**
McAuley 4　　　　　　　　　　Oerlemans 67, Stanislavgevic 81

CONWY UNITED: Bamford; Cross, Edwards, McAuley, Taylor C, Barnett (Young), Wiggins, Brookman (Doran), Camden (Taylor S), McKenna, Mullen.
SV MARCO POLO REID: Unger; Steininger, Kramer, Angerschmidt (Bogl), Schutterle, Kiesenthofer (Drechsel), Klinge, Stanislavgevic, Mraz, Oerlemans, Waldhur.
Referee: Jorn West Larsen (Denmark)

Though losing to the Austrian side, Conwy had the consolation of scoring the first ever goal by a League of Wales side in the Inter Toto Cup. This followed four blank games by Ton Pentre and two from Conwy, amounting to more than nine hours of football.

Their goal came early. Hugh McAuley profited from a defensive blunder by the Ried skipper Leopold Kiesenthofer and drove the ball in from twelve yards. With Mark Edwards and Harry Wiggins – the former Bangor City player – in outstanding form at the back, Conwy continued to threaten and McAuley shot over when he might have done better.

In the second half, the Austrian side laid siege to the Conwy goal and Ian Bamford was forced to save from Marcel Oerlemans and Michael Angerschmidt. Bamford also pushed a long-range shot from Dirk Klinge onto the crossbar, but could do little to prevent a looping shot from Oerlemans finding the net, following a corner from substitute Herwig Drechsel. It was the outstanding Oerlemans who set up the winner by threading a pass to Goran Stanislavgevic.

---

20 July 1996   *Match 4*   *Silkeborg Stadion*
Silkeborg, Denmark

SILKEBORG (2) 4   **CONWY UNITED (0) 0**
Fernandez 11, 86, Duus 28,
Roell 85

SILKEBORG: Kjaer; Meluang, Hansen, Zivkovic, Duus, Risom, Mueldrup, Thygesen (Pedersen B), Reese (Roell), Jokovic (Pedersen H), Fernandez.
CONWY U: Bamford; Cross, Edwards, McAuley (Young), Taylor C, Barnett, Wiggins, Brookman, Camden (Doran), Taylor S, Mullen.

The final match in the series was in Denmark against a Silkeborg side which boasted a useful European record. They were coached by the former Danish international striker Preben Elkjaer, who had scored 38 goals in 69 appearances for Denmark. A win for Silkeborg would enable them to top the group.

The Conwy squad flew from Manchester to Copenhagen, where they changed planes to continue on to Aarhus. From there it was a one-hour coach journey to Silkeborg.

The slick and skilful Danes threatened to over-run Conwy in the opening period. The Welsh team fell behind after two defenders collided trying to clear the ball, leaving Heine Fernandez all on his own. Conwy's defence was again at fault for the second goal, when Christian Duus scored after being given room to run unchallenged into the area.

Conwy regrouped after the interval to give a better account of themselves, forcing their first corner-kick after 50 minutes. Mark Edwards had a shot saved, after good work by Paul Mullen, and with substitute Ian Doran fitting in well in midfield, Conwy looked a totally different proposition.

With a few minutes remaining, substitute Tomas Roell beat Chris Taylor to head in the Danish team's third goal, and within 60 seconds, a misjudged back-pass from Steve Cross was intercepted by Fernandez. Those two late goals soured a creditable performance by the League of Wales side.

The Inter Toto experience cost Conwy United dearly, leaving them with a deficit of £13,500. In retrospect, they should have played their home ties at the Morfa Ground where gates could have been higher than was the case at Wrexham. The switch also meant extra cash being needed for policing, stewarding, transport and hire of the stadium. The £30,000 payout by UEFA for participation in the tournament was reduced after costs to just £1,300.

	GROUP 4	P	W	D	L	F	A	Pts
1	Silkeborg	4	3	1	0	11	2	10
2	Zaglebie	4	2	2	0	5	1	8
3	Charleroi	4	1	2	1	5	5	5
4	Ried	4	1	0	3	4	9	3
5	Conwy	4	0	1	3	1	9	1

1997 – EBBW VALE (League of Wales)

The Gwent side claimed third place in the League of Wales after edging out Caernarfon Town on goal-difference. Their immediate aim was to be the first Welsh side to record a victory in the competition, and also the first to make a profit over the four group games. To this end they would be helped by playing their home games at Eugene Cross Park.

The Cowboys were able to call on the experience of three players who had already sampled European football. Lyndon Jones – the former Cardiff City and Newport County full back – had played for Inter Cardiff in the 1994 UEFA Cup; Paul Giles had been in the Barry Town side beaten in the 1994 Cup-Winners' Cup, and David Webley led the line for Merthyr Tydfil against Atalanta in the 1987 Cup-Winners' Cup.

Manager John Lewis masterminded the Vale preparations, calling the players in three weeks before the opening game. Some idea of his misgivings can be seen from his instruction to his groundsman to narrow the pitch by four yards on either side – eight yards in total – thereby giving his players more chance of closing down the technically superior visitors in midfield.

29 June 1997   Match 1   *Eugene Cross Park*
Ebbw Vale

EBBW VALE (0) 0   CASINO GRAZ (0) 0

EBBW VALE: Williams D; Price, John, Thomas, Wigley, Giles, Williams S, Jones L (Evans A), Chiverton, Perry (Graham), Webley (Tyler).
CASINO GRAZ: Almer, Schranz, Vukovic, Dieter, Temm, Dietrich, Muzek, Strafner, Hartmann, Sabitzer, Radovic.
Referee: H Barr (Northern Ireland)

There were few goalmouth chances in the opening exchanges. The neat inter-passing of the Austrian team was countered by stiff resistance from the home side. The Cowboys relied on breakaways to relieve the pressure, and, after Lee Price's long throw-in was not cleared, David Webley flashed in a header which was saved by Franz Almer. Graz quickly responded, and when Zeljko Vukovic found space in the box, his attempted chip was easily foiled by former Cardiff City goalkeeper, David Williams.

After the break, Klaus Dietrich fired in a 25-yarder that was deflected onto an upright with Williams beaten. The visitors almost snatched the winner in the final minute, when Williams tipped a header from Dietrich over the bar.

The performance from the League of Wales side was praised by Graz coach Klaus Augenthaler, the former German international.

---

6 July 1997   Match 2   *Valekr Golaca*
Zagreb, Croatia

HRVATSKI DRAGOVOLJAC (2) 4   EBBW VALE (0) 0
Musa 14, Dolonga 24,
Katulic 67, 89

HRVATSKI DRAG: Simunic; Bosnjak, Dolonga, Musa, Kulesevic, Skopljanac, Sitar (Bazina), Katulic, Juric, Vukoja (Tolic), Miletic (Susac).
EBBW VALE: Williams; Wigley, Thomas, John, Hughes (Jones L), Williams S (Mayer), Graham, Needs(Edwards), Giles, Perry, Tyler.
Referee: R Beck (Liechtenstein)

Ebbw Vale's second game required a trip to Croatia, a country torn apart by war in recent memory. Only formed in 1982, Hrvatski Dragovoljac did not have a ground of their own, yet still finished third in Croatia's Division One.

The Ebbw Vale party booked into a five-star hotel in Zagreb, taking their own water and glucose tablets to combat the heat. Lee

Price twisted his ankle on tramlines outside the hotel and ruled himself out of the match. The Vale side was further disrupted when two players absconded from training on the morning of the match and were severely reprimanded.

The Croatians forced Vale onto the defensive from the whistle. David Williams was frequently called into action as the home side searched for their first goal in the competition. It came when skipper Ray John's mistake enabled Dragan Vukoja to set up Musa, who fired past Williams. Vale's defence was opened up again ten minutes later, when swift passing around the penalty area left Dolonga with an easy tap-in at the far post.

In the second half Dragovoljac continued to bemuse the Welsh team with their own brand of incisive football. Manager John Lewis brought on Lyndon Jones in an attempt to stem the tide, but the Croats would not be denied and a defence-splitting pass from substitute Tolic found an unmarked Katulic, who side-footed past Williams. Dogged defence kept the rampant home side out until the final minute, when Katulic scored his second goal.

---

13 July 1997   *Match 3*   *Eugene Cross Park*
Ebbw Vale

EBBW VALE (0) 1   **SC BASTIA (2) 2**
Tyler 54   Siljak 12, 32

EBBW VALE: Williams D; Wigley, Thomas (Dowd), John, Graham, Williams S, Chiverton, Evans A, Tyler (Webley), Mayer, Giles.
BASTIA: Durand; Perez, Deguerville, Moreau, Swierczewski, Carnadini, Faye, Jurietti, Saumah, Gohel (Jestrovic), Siljak.
Referee: T McCurry (Scotland)

Next up for Vale were group leaders SC Bastia, an accomplished side who had finished seventh in the French First Division, just six points behind second-placed Paris St Germain. Included in Bastia's squad were internationals from Poland, Slovenia, and Guinea. Vale manager Lewis had second thoughts about the two players he had disciplined for missing training, and reinstated them.

Vale's hopes of further progress in this competition were quickly dashed by the Corsican side, but they had the consolation of netting only the second goal by any Welsh club in the Inter Toto Cup. By then, however, Slovenian international Erwin Siljak had opened up a two-goal lead for Bastia. The first stemmed from a mistake by Russell Wigley – who was slow to clear after Mamadou Faye's shot had come back off a post – and the second was headed in from a

Patrick Deguerville cross. Veteran Simon Tyler netted the Ebbw Vale goal when he blasted in from close range after Mike Mayer had headed on a Paul Giles centre.

Tyler was substituted following a nasty clash of heads and David Webley entered the fray, but Vale were unable to grab the equaliser.

---

20 July 1997   *Match 4*   *Silkeborg Stadion*
Silkeborg, Denmark

SILKEBORG (2) 6   **EBBW VALE (0) 1**
Fernandez 5, Jokovic 30, 73,   Webley 70
Thygesen 69, 71 pen, 90

SILKEBORG: Kjaer; Bruun, Hansen, Zivkovic, Duus, Sonksen (Suika), Knudsen, Sorensen, Thygesen, Jokovic, Fernandez (Neilsen).
EBBW VALE: Williams D; Wigley, Mayer, Dowd, John, Williams S, Graham, Chiverton, Giles, Tyler (Webley), Needs.

Vale's final group match was in Denmark against Silkeborg, the 4-0 victors over Conwy United the previous season. John Lewis had limited scope for changes, though he preferred Brendan Dowd at the heart of the defence in place of Barry Thomas. Simon Tyler had recovered from his head injury to resume up front.

Now managed by Sepp Piontek, Silkeborg were playing in Europe for the sixth season. The Danes were quick and comfortable on the ball, and with only two players under 6ft tall they made their superior strength and fitness tell on the wide pitch.

Silkeborg never relaxed, consigning the Cowboys to last place in their group. Four goals in four minutes, including one for Vale and a penalty for Silkeborg, signalled the end of Vale's resistance. Jesper Thygesen completed his hat-trick in the final minute.

	GROUP 2	P	W	D	L	F	A	Pts
1	Bastia	4	3	0	1	5	3	9
2	Graz	4	2	1	1	5	4	7
3	Silkeborg	4	2	0	2	11	4	6
4	Dragovoljac	4	2	0	2	7	7	6
5	Ebbw Vale	4	0	1	3	2	12	1

~~~~~~~~~~~~~~~~~~~~~~~~~~~~~~

1998 – EBBW VALE (League of Wales)

~~~~~~~~~~~~~~~~~~~~~~~~~~~~~~

Much to the relief of the League of Wales clubs, the much-maligned Inter Toto Cup was given a complete revamp in 1998. Out went the four-match group qualification, which had incurred heavy travelling expenses. In its place came a straight knock-out on a two-leg basis. The three previous Welsh representatives had all struggled to break even in their European quests; now it was Ebbw Vale again who flew the flag. They had finished the League season strongly to claim third place and so qualified for a second successive season in the competition. Sadly, the Cowboys were still reeling from the financial after-effects of the previous year's globe-trotting.

The FA of Wales confirmed Ebbw Vale's entry only three weeks before the first match, and then only after receiving certain financial guarantees.

Andy Mulliner – who had played for Llansantffraid against Ruch Chorzow in the Cup-Winners' Cup – was signed on loan, along with Merthyr Tydfil's Ian Mitchell, Colin Loss and Cohen Griffith. It was Griffith's third club and his third European competition, having previously turned out for Cardiff City in the Cup-Winners' Cup and Barry Town in the UEFA Cup.

20 June 1998	*1st Leg*	*Eugene Cross Park*
Ebbw Vale		

EBBW VALE (1) 1   **KONGSVINGER (2) 6**
Perry 18   Evensen 20, Ernstsson 35, Berg 56,
      Solberg 72, Dybendahl 80, Alm 84

EBBW VALE: Mulliner, Price, Needs, Chiverton, Morgan, Lima, Giles, Williams, Mitchell (Evans Alun), Perry (Griffith), Evans Andy (Loss).
KONGSVINGER: Langnes, Hoiland, Bergman, Johnson, Ahmed, Hadnes, Alm (Gullerud), Dybendahl, Berg, Evensen (Hansen), Ernstsson (Solberg).
Referee: C Kapitanis (Cyprus)

Ebbw Vale FC needed use of their pitch when it was booked for the local cricket club. When the cricketers refused to switch their home fixture away from Eugene Cross Park, the League of Wales arranged for the home leg to be staged at Merthyr Tydfil's Penydarren Park. Only then was it discovered that Merthyr's ground lacked the necessary safety certificate. When Vale explained their predicament to the Council owners of Eugene Cross Park, it was agreed that the European game should take precedence, and the cricketers were forced to re-arrange their match.

The Cowboys' dream of becoming the first League of Wales side to win an Inter Toto match was hit for six by the classy Norwegians. Vale matched their opponents in the opening minutes, and when Justin Perry opened the scoring, realising that dream seemed on the cards. Within two minutes, however, Vidar Evensen strode through the middle to equalise, and by half-time Ludwig Ernstsson had put the Scandinavian team ahead. A flurry of goals – three in twelve minutes – put the tie beyond Vale. In a clean game, devoid of malicious tackles, the referee still found time to dismiss Ebbw Vale's Mark Williams and the visitors' Pal Hadnes, both for seemingly innocuous offences.

---

28 June 1998   *2nd Leg*   *Gjemselund*
Kongsvinger, Norway

KONGSVINGER (0) 3   EBBW VALE (0) 0
Ernstsson 68, 79, Dybendahl 74

KONGSVINGER: Langnes; Berstad, Hansen, Bergman, Ahmed, Gullerud, Alm (Stormoen), Berg (Dybnedahl), Solberg (Evensen), Ernstsson, Johnson.
EBBW VALE: Thomas N, Price, Needs, Morgan (Brown), Thomas B, Lima, Giles, Wigg, Evans Alun, Perry (Durham), Loss.
Referee: O Timofeyev (Estonia).
(KONGSVINGER won 9-1 on aggregate)

Ebbw Vale's financial troubles were not over. The travel company that organised the trip to Norway refused to release tickets until an invoice dating back to the previous season had been settled. The FA of Wales stepped in to pay it, agreeing to deduct the amount from Vale's appearance money when it was received from UEFA.

In an incident-packed encounter, two players were sent off and Kongsvinger missed two penalties. Vale comfortably held their hosts at bay during the first half but were left a man short after the 54th minute, when Barry Thomas was dismissed for handball in the area. Though Neil Thomas pushed away Abdul Karim Ahmed's consequent penalty, the Norwegian side made full use of their extra man to net three times.

Langnes became the second player to receive his marching orders. It was a black day for him: he had missed the Norwegians' first penalty in the opening half.

It was to be the last competitive match played by Ebbw Vale. A ballot of League of Wales clubs voted to deny them entry to the 1998-99 season on the grounds of 'conduct detrimental to the league'. Ebbw Vale decided not to appeal against the decision, and in consequence folded.

EUROPEAN CUP-WINNERS' CUP

16.10.1961	SWANSEA T 2 Motor Jena 2
18.10.1961	Motor Jena 5 SWANSEA T 1
05.09.1962	BANGOR C 2 Napoli 0
27.09.1962	Napoli 3 BANGOR C 1
10.10.1962	BANGOR C 1 Napoli 2
15.09.1963	Sliema Wands 0 BOROUGH U 0
03.10.1963	BOROUGH U 2 Sliema Wands 0
11.12.1963	BOROUGH U 0 Slovan B'slava 1
15.12.1963	Slovan B'slava 3 BOROUGH U 0
09.09.1964	Esbjerg 0 CARDIFF C 0
13.10.1964	CARDIFF C 1 Esbjerg 0
15.12.1964	Sporting Lisbon 1 CARDIFF C 2
23.12.1964	CARDIFF C 0 Sporting Lisbon 0
20.01.1965	Real Zaragoza 2 CARDIFF C 2
03.02.1965	CARDIFF C 0 Real Zaragoza 1
08.09.1965	CARDIFF C 1 Standard Liege 2
20.10.1965	Standard Liege 1 CARDIFF C 0
21.09.1966	SWANSEA T 1 Slavia Sofia 1
05.10.1966	Slavia Sofia 4 SWANSEA T 0
20.09.1967	Shamrock Rovers 1 CARDIFF C 1
04.10.1967	CARDIFF C 2 Shamrock Rovers 0
15.11.1967	NAC Breda 1 CARDIFF C 1
29.11.1967	CARDIFF C 4 NAC Breda 1
06.03.1968	CARDIFF C 1 Moscow Torpedo 0
19.03.1968	Moscow Torpedo 1 CARDIFF C 0
03.04.1968	CARDIFF C 1 Moscow Torpedo 0
24.04.1968	SV Hamburg 1 CARDIFF C 1
01.05.1968	CARDIFF C 2 SV Hamburg 3
18.09.1968	CARDIFF C 2 FC Porto 2
02.10.1968	FC Porto 2 CARDIFF C 1
17.09.1969	Mjoendalen 1 CARDIFF C 7
01.10.1969	CARDIFF C 5 Mjoendalen 1
12.11.1969	Goztepe Izmir 3 CARDIFF C 0
26.11.1969	CARDIFF C 1 Goztepe Izmir 0
16.09.1970	CARDIFF C 8 PO Larnaca 0
30.09.1970	PO Larnaca 0 CARDIFF C 0
21.10.1970	CARDIFF C 5 FC Nantes 1
04.11.1970	FC Nantes 1 CARDIFF C 2
10.03.1971	CARDIFF C 1 Real Madrid 0
24.03.1971	Real Madrid 2 CARDIFF C 0
15.09.1971	Dynamo Berlin 1 CARDIFF C 1
29.09.1971	CARDIFF C 1 Dynamo Berlin 1
13.09.1972	FC Zurich 1 WREXHAM 1
27.09.1972	WREXHAM 2 FC Zurich 1
25.10.1972	WREXHAM 3 Hajduk Split 1
08.11.1972	Hajduk Split 2 WREXHAM 0
19.09.1973	CARDIFF C 0 Sporting Lisbon 0
03.10.1973	Sporting Lisbon 2 CARDIFF C 1
18.09.1974	Ferencvaros 2 CARDIFF C 0
02.10.1974	CARDIFF C 0 Ferencvaros 4
17.09.1975	WREXHAM 2 Djurgardens 1
01.10.1974	Djurgardens 1 WREXHAM 1
22.10.1975	WREXHAM 2 Stal Rzeszow 0
05.11.1975	Stal Rzeszow 1 WREXHAM 1
03.03.1976	Anderlecht 1 WREXHAM 0
17.03.1976	WREXHAM 1 Anderlecht 1
04.08.1976	CARDIFF C 1 Servette 0
11.08.1976	Servette 2 CARDIFF C 1
15.09.1976	CARDIFF C 1 Dynamo Tbilisi 0
29.09.1976	Dynamo Tbilisi 3 CARDIFF C 0
14.09.1977	CARDIFF C 0 Austria Memphis 0
28.09.1977	Austria Memphis 1 CARDIFF C 0
13.09.1978	NK Rijeka 3 WREXHAM 0
27.09.1978	WREXHAM 2 NK Rijeka 0
19.09.1979	WREXHAM 3 FC Magdeburg 2
03.10.1979	FC Magdeburg 5 WREXHAM 2
16.09.1980	NEWPORT CO 4 Crusaders 0
01.10.1980	Crusaders 0 NEWPORT CO 0
22.10.1980	Haugar 0 NEWPORT CO 0
04.11.1980	NEWPORT CO 6 Haugar 0
04.03.1981	Carl Zeiss Jena 2 NEWPORT CO 2
18.03.1981	NEWPORT CO 0 Carl Zeiss Jena 1
16.09.1981	SWANSEA C 0 Loko Leipzig 1
30.09.1981	Loko Leipzig 2 SWANSEA C 1
17.08.1982	SWANSEA C 3 Sporting Braga 0
25.08.1982	Sporting Braga 1 SWANSEA C 0
15.09.1982	SWANSEA C 12 Sliema Wands 0
29.09.1982	Sliema Wands 0 SWANSEA C 5
20.10.1982	SWANSEA C 0 Paris St Germain 1
03.11.1982	Paris St Germain 2 SWANSEA C 0
24.08.1983	SWANSEA C 1 FC Magdeburg 1
31.08.1983	FC Magdeburg 1 SWANSEA C 0
19.08.1984	WREXHAM 1 FC Porto 0
03.10.1984	FC Porto 4 WREXHAM 3
24.10.1984	AS Roma 2 WREXHAM 0
07.11.1984	WREXHAM 0 AS Roma 1
18.09.1985	Fredrikstad 1 BANGOR C 1
02.10.1985	BANGOR C 0 Fredrikstad 0
23.10.1985	BANGOR C 0 Atletico Madrid 2
06.11.1985	Atletico Madrid 1 BANGOR C 0
17.09.1986	FC Zurrieq 0 WREXHAM 3
01.10.1986	WREXHAM 4 FC Zurrieq 0
22.10.1986	Real Zaragoza 0 WREXHAM 0
05.11.1986	WREXHAM 2 Real Zaragoza 2
16.09.1987	MERTHYR TYDFIL 2 Atalanta 1
30.09.1987	Atalanta 2 MERTHYR TYDFIL 0
07.09.1988	Derry City 0 CARDIFF C 0
05.10.1988	CARDIFF C 4 Derry City 0
26.10.1988	CARDIFF C 1 Aarhus 2
09.11.1988	Aarhus 4 CARDIFF C 0
13.09.1989	Panathinaikos 3 SWANSEA C 2
27.09.1989	SWANSEA C 3 Panathinaikos 3
19.09.1990	WREXHAM 0 Lyngby BK 0
03.10.1990	Lyngby BK 0 WREXHAM 1
23.10.1990	Manchester U 3 WREXHAM 0
07.11.1990	WREXHAM 0 Manchester U 2
17.09.1991	SWANSEA C 1 Monaco 2
01.10.1991	Monaco 8 SWANSEA C 0
15.09.1992	CARDIFF C 1 Admira Wacker 1
29.09.1992	Admira Wacker 2 CARDIFF C 0
15.09.1993	Standard Liege 5 CARDIFF C 2
28.09.1993	CARDIFF C 1 Standard Liege 3
11.08.1994	BARRY T 0 Zalgiris Vilnius 1
25.08.1994	Zalgiris Vilnius 6 BARRY T 0
10.08.1995	WREXHAM 0 Petrolul Ploiesti 0
24.08.1995	Petrolul Ploiesti 1 WREXHAM 0
08.08.1996	LLANS'FRAID 1 Ruch Chorzow 1
22.08.1996	Ruch Chorzow 5 LLANS'FRAID 0
14.08.1997	CWMBRAN T 2 Nat Bucuresti 5
28.08.1997	Nat Bucuresti 7 CWMBRAN T 0
13.08.1998	BANGOR C 0 Haka 2
27.08.1998	Haka 1 BANGOR C 0

EUROPEAN CHAMPIONS CUP

18.09.1993	CWMBRAN T 3 Cork City 2	
01.09.1993	Cork City 2 CWMBRAN T 1	
23.07.1997	Dynamo Kiev 2 BARRY T 0	

30.07.1997	BARRY T 0 Dynamo Kiev 4
20.07.1998	Dynamo Kiev 8 BARRY T 0
29.07.1998	BARRY T 1 Dynamo Kiev 2

UEFA CUP

09.08.1994	BANGOR C 1 IA Akranes 2
24.08.1994	IA Akranes 2 BANGOR C 0
09.08.1994	INTER CARDIFF 0 Katowice 2
23.08.1994	Katowice 6 INTER CARDIFF 0
08.08.1995	AFAN LIDO 1 RAF Riga 2
22.08.1995	RAF Riga 0 AFAN LIDO 0
08.08.1995	BANGOR C 0 Widzew Lodz 4
22.08.1995	Widzew Lodz 1 BANGOR C 0
18.07.1996	BARRY T 0 Dinaburg 0
24.07.1996	Dinaburg 1 BARRY T 2

06.08.1996	Vasutas Budapest 3 BARRY T 1
21.08.1996	BARRY T 3 Vasutas Budapest 1
10.09.1996	Aberdeen 3 BARRY T 1
24.09.1996	BARRY T 3 Aberdeen 3
17.07.1996	NEWTOWN 1 Skonto Riga 4
24.07.1996	Skonto Riga 3 NEWTOWN 0
23.07.1997	INTER CABLETEL 0 Celtic 3
29.07.1997	Celtic 5 INTER CABLETEL 0
22.07.1998	NEWTOWN 0 Wisla Krakow 0
29.07.1998	Wisla Krakow 7 NEWTOWN 0

INTER TOTO CUP

01.07.1995	TON PENTRE 0 Heerenveen 7
08.07.1995	Bekes' Elore 4 TON PENTRE 0
15.07.1995	TON PENTRE 0 Uniao Leira 4
22.07.1995	Naestved 2 TON PENTRE 0
29.06.1996	CONWY U 0 RSC Charleroi 0
08.07.1996	Zaglebie Lubin 3 CONWY U 0
13.07.1996	CONWY U 1 Marco Polo Ried 2

20.07.1996	Silkeborg 4 CONWY U 0
29.06.1997	EBBW VALE 0 Casino Graz 0
06.07.1997	Hrvatski Drag'ac 4 EBBW VALE 0
13.07.1997	EBBW VALE 1 SC Bastia 2
20.07.1997	Silkeborg 6 EBBW VALE 1
20.06.1998	EBBW VALE 1 Kongsvinger 6
28.06.1998	Kongsvinger 3 EBBW VALE 0

Red Dragon penalties

Cup-Winners' Cup
16.10.1961	M Nurse (Swansea v Motor Jena)
05.09.1962	K Birch (Bangor C v Napoli)
04.10.1967	R Brown (Cardiff v Shamrock R)
18.09.1968	R Bird (Cardiff v FC Porto)
27.09.1989	R James (Swansea v Panathinaikos)

14.08.1997	M Parfitt (Cwmbran v Nat Bucuresti)

Champions Cup
18.08.1993	S King (Cwmbran T v Cork City)

UEFA Cup
20.08.1996	C Pike (Barry v Vasutas Budapest)
24.09.1996	D Ryan (Barry v Aberdeen)

Red Dragon dismissals

Cup-Winners' Cup
16.10.1961	C Webster (Swansea v Motor Jena)
02.10.1968	G Coldrick (Cardiff C v FC Porto)
08.11.1972	M Evans (Wrexham v Hajduk Split)
13.09.1978	J Roberts (Wrexham v NK Rijeka)
30.09.1981	A Curtis (Swansea v Loko Leipzig)
10.08.1994	D D'Auria (Barry v Zalgiris Vilnius)

UEFA Cup
24.08.1994	L Noble (Bangor C v IA Akranes)
06.08.1996	M Ovendale (Barry v Vasutas B'pest)

Champions Cup
30.07.1997	D Ryan (Barry v Dynamo Kiev)

Inter Toto Cup
20.06.1998	M Williams (E Vale v Kongsvinger)
28.06.1998	B Thomas (E Vale v Kongsvinger)

Red Dragon hat-tricks

Cup-Winners' Cup
01.10.1969	S Allan (Cardiff v Mjoendalen)

15.09.1982	I Walsh (Swansea v Sliema Wands)
05.10.1988	J Gilligan (Cardiff v Derry C)

Red Dragon own-goals

AGAINST
Cup-Winners' Cup
25.08.1982	C Marustik (Swansea v Sp Braga)
01.10.1991	M Harris (Swansea v Monaco)
22.08.1996	A Jones (Llans'fraid v R Chorzow)

FOR
Cup-Winners' Cup
25.10.1972	Musinic (Hadjuk Split v Wrexham)
17.08.1982	Cordoso (Sp Braga v Swansea)
08.08.1996	Gesior (R Chorzow v Llans'fraid)

SUBSCRIBERS

NAME	FAVOURITE PLAYER	NAME	FAVOURITE PLAYER
Phil Pots Bridle	Brian Harris	James Hughes	Brian Clark
Terry Brown	John Toshack	Paula Jenkins	
Graham T Bucknell	Peter King	Martin Jacques	
Cardiff Hibernian AFC	John Toshack	Cec Jones	
Cyril Cazanave	John Toshack	Graham Jones	Ronnie Bird
Sarah-Jane Cazanave	Roberto Baggio	Gregg Jones	Mark Hughes
Yvan Cebenka	Michel Platini	Reg Jones	John Toshack
M Clements		Rhea Jones	Brian Clark
Robert Cole	John Charles	Ross Jones	Ryan Giggs
David Collins	Ceri Williams	John Kennedy	John Charles
Robert Collins	David Webley	John Lee	Brian Clark
Jo Connolly	Jeremy Charles	S Mitchell	Ronnie Bird
James Darke	Brian Clark	Phil Morris	Robbie James
Kevin Darke	Derek Tapscott	John Nash	John Charles
D M Davies	Tony Evans	Simon Nash	Brian Harris
Robert W'm Dowling	Kevin Richards	Yvonne Nash	Adrian Alston
John H Dyer	John Charles	Stephen Parrott	Gareth Davies
A C Edwards		David Phillips	Brian Clark
Tim Evans	Alan Hansen	Tony Prangley	Don Murray
Iain Francis	Kenny Dalglish	Andrew Pratt	Marco van Basten
Terry Godwin	Zinedine Zidane	Ian Pratt	Johann Cruyff
Michael Gouge	Don Murray	Geraint Pritchard	Ian Gibson
Colin Grandin	Peter King	Tony Rees	
Jason Grandin	Rob Rensenkbrink	Simon Rimmer	Kenny Dalglish
Sarah Grandin	Mark Hughes	Simon Roberts	Ryan Giggs
Yvonne Grandin	Brian Clark	David Rogers	
Iorys Griffiths		A J Smith	Brian Clark
Steve Gurner	Ian Gibson	A J Smith	Derek Tapscott
Kenny Hibbitt		Timothy Watts	Mark Hughes
Dave Hollins	Kevin Keegan	Tony Webb	Alan Shearer
		Westgate Sports Agency	